A Resource Guide for Secondary School Teaching

A
Resource Guide for Secondary School Teaching

Planning for Competence

Eugene C. Kim
Richard D. Kellough

4 *th edition*

California State University, Sacramento

Macmillan Publishing Company
NEW YORK

Collier Macmillan Publishers
LONDON

Macmillan Publishing Company
866 Third Avenue, New York, New York 10022

Collier Macmillan Canada, Inc.

ISBN 0-02-363850-8

Printing: 1 2 3 4 5 6 7 8   Year: 7 8 9 0 1 2 3 4 5 6

We Are One

Truth, love, peace, and beauty,
We have sought apart
*   but will find within, as our*
Moods—explored, shared,
*   questioned, and accepted—*
Together become one and all

*   Through life my friends*
*   We can travel together,*
*   for we now know*
*   each could go it alone.*

*   To assimilate our efforts into one,*
*   While growing in accepting,*
*   and trusting, and sharing the*
*   individuality of the other,*
*   Is truly to enjoy God's greatest gift—*
*   Feeling—knowing love and compassion.*

*   Through life my friends*
*   We are together,*
*   for we must know*
*   we are one.*

—R. D. Kellough

Preface

Recent research findings coupled with the educational reform movement of the 1980s have prompted us to make major changes in this edition of our resource guide. However, we continue in our desire to provide a practical and succinct guide useful to people who are

- students in a secondary methods course in teacher education.
- students who are in a field component of teacher education.
- practicing teachers who wish to continue the development of their teaching competencies.

We believe that learning should be active, pleasant, fun, and productive. Thus, we have attempted to prepare this resource guide in an enthusiastic, cognitive-humanistic way that is helpful to teachers and teacher candidates. Let us further explain what we believe and how we have incorporated those beliefs into this fourth edition of our resource guide.

We believe teaching competency can be learned. As in medicine, where there are skills and knowledge to be learned and developed before the student physician is licensed to practice with "live" patients; as in law, where there are knowledge and skills to be learned and developed before the law student is licensed to practice a "real" legal case; so it is in teacher education: *there are knowledge and skills to be learned and developed before the teacher candidate is licensed to practice the art and skills of teaching with active, responsive learners.* We would never consider allowing a person "off the street" to treat our own child's illness or to defend us in a legal case; the professional education of teachers is no less important. Receiving professional education in how to teach is absolutely necessary and certain aspects of that education must precede any interaction with alert, lively young people, if we are to become truly competent and professional.

We believe there are developmental elements involved in becoming a competent professional secondary-school teacher. This resource guide continues to be organized around four developmental elements: *what, why, how, and how well.* The teacher needs to know what is to be taught, and why; Parts I and II of this resource guide are devoted to these elements. For this fourth edition, Part I was updated and rewritten; we hope you find Chapter 3 on teaching styles informative and well-balanced, and Chapter 4 on competencies current and useful. The subject of competencies is revisited several times in the book, reflecting our interest in helping the teacher develop his/her specific teaching competencies. Part II on planning has been reordered into a more practical sequence with the addition of relevant material in each chapter. Chapter 8 on preparing instructional plans, a popular chapter in previous editions, has been revised to focus the reader's attention on specific teacher behaviors appropriate for consideration during lesson and unit planning.

We believe that the *how* component of professional teacher education is essential to becoming a competent teacher. This element is reflected in a major portion of this resource guide, but particularly in Parts III and IV. It is very difficult to anticipate the twenty-first century, particularly to predict what specifically the young people of today will really need to know when they are in the work force in that century. We do believe that they will always need to know how to learn, how to read, and how to reason and to think critically. We believe that secondary-school students need skills in acquiring knowledge, in processing information, and in learning experiences that will utilize their fullest potentiality for thinking; they need skills that foster effective communication and productive, cooperative behaviors. We want students to feel good about themselves, about others, and about their schools. For reaching these goals we believe the best teaching strategies are those that incorporate careful planning, honesty, trusting, sharing, risking, communicating, and cooperating. We hope that the world of the twenty-first century consists of nations of peoples who are cooperating, communicating, and utilizing fully the creative capacities of each and every individual. Our resource guide is dedicated to that hope. Part III of our resource guide has been reordered with updated content beginning with a description of enabling behaviors in Chapter 10. Chapter 11 on specific teaching strategies was rewritten with a new inclusion of content about delivery and access modes, and a balanced description of inquiry and discovery strategies.

Part IV has been revised to include a balanced description of approaches to classroom management in Chapter 15 with practical guidelines to the teacher. Part V focuses attention on the fourth and final element, the element of how well the teacher and students are doing. We have included useful information about written teacher comments, conferencing with parents, and we have in this edition increased our emphasis on practice and feedback for the student teacher or the practicing teacher in the continued development of their competencies.

As with previous editions, Part VI continues to be a guide for the practice teaching component of teacher education and provides suggestions for finding that first teaching job. Part VI has also been rewritten, and in a way we hope you will find interesting and enjoyable to read.

We continue to respond to the many reviewers and users of this resource guide and have made changes as a result of that feedback. We have increased the number of exercises by 50 percent. Most of the exercises are new in this edition, as are many of the questions for class discussion at the end of each chapter. The references at the end of chapters (or Parts) have been completely updated. Pages of the text continue to be perforated for easy tear-out for class use. The index and table of contents have been expanded for better cross reference and aid to the reader. This fourth edition is really a new book; we hope you find it useful now and during your professional career. Let us know as we appreciate your feedback.

Finally, we continue to appreciate the help we get from people—former students who forgave us our trespasses; teachers and colleagues who continue to share their ideas and successes and have permitted us to include their names in this book; authors and publishers who graciously granted their permissions to reprint materials; and manuscript reviewers that have helped us improve this resource guide, although we assume full responsibility for any of its shortcomings.

Reviewers who provided valued in-depth suggestions and for which we are deeply grateful are Robert Green of Clemson University, J. Vernon Hoyle of the University of North Carolina at Charlotte, Edward S. Jenkins of SUNY-Buffalo, and Alan R. Miller of Fort Hays State University.

Special thanks are extended to Mary Jane Pearson, who provided helpful information pertaining to children with special needs (Chapters 1 and 9), to Arthur Costa, who continues to help us with the section on enabling behaviors (Chapter 10), and to Patricia Roberts, coauthor of *A Resource Guide for Elementary School Teaching* (Macmillan, 1985) and in which some of the materials were first published, and who has helped in more ways than she will ever know.

We express our continued admiration and appreciation to the competent people at Macmillan, especially to our editor Lynne Greenberg, and to our former editor Lloyd Chilton.

To our families, we thank you for allowing us the alone time to write. Indeed, we are indebted to and grateful for all the people in our lives, now and in the past, who have interacted with us and reinforced that which we have always known: teaching is the most rewarding profession we know.

E.C.K.
R.D.K.

Contents

Part I *Orientation to Secondary School Teaching*   1

1 What Do I Need to Know About Today's Secondary Schools?   5

    A. About Orientation and Schedules   6
        Orientation Meetings   6
        Teacher Schedules   7
    B. About Students   8
        Understanding the General Characteristics of Special-Needs Students   9
    C. About Meeting My Students   10
    D. About Teachers   11
    E. About Administrators   12
        Exercise 1.1: Getting Acquainted With My Students   13
    F. About the Overall Picture   15
        Exercise 1.2: Remembering My Own Secondary School Experiences   19
        Exercise 1.3: Interviewing Secondary School Students   20
        Exercise 1.4: Returning to a Secondary School Classroom   23
        Exercise 1.5: Returning to an "Open House" at a Secondary School   25
        Exercise 1.6: Attending a Parent-Teacher Organization Meeting   27
        Exercise 1.7: Interviewing a Teacher Candiate   29
        Exercise 1.8: Interviewing a Teacher   30
        Questions for Class Discussion   31
        Selected Readings and References for Chapter 1   32

2 What Are the Expectations of a Secondary School Teacher?   33

    A. About the Code of Ethics   33
    B. About Instructional Responsibilities   35
    C. About Noninstructional Responsibilities   36
    D. Summarizing the Expectations of a Secondary School Teacher   37
        Exercise 2.1: The Life of a Teacher   39
        Questions for Class Discussion   41
        Selected Readings and References for Chapter 2   41

3 How Do I Develop a Teaching Style?   **43**

A. What Is the Source of One's Teaching Style?   **44**
B. What Are the Basic Theoretical Positions That Determine
Teaching Style?   **44**
Exercise 3.1: Developing a Profile and a Statement About My Own
Teaching Style   **47**
C. What Does Research Offer Toward the Development of My
Teaching Style?   **51**
Exercise 3.2: Analyzing One Teacher, One Style: Teaching Variables That
Affect Student Achievement   **53**
Exercise 3.3: Analyzing Advance Organizers As Used by a Teacher During
My Classroom Observation   **55**
Questions for Class Discussion   **57**
Selected Readings and References for Chapter 3   **57**

4 What Are My Current Skills and Weaknesses?   **59**

Characteristics of the Competent Teacher   **59**
A. Self-Evaluation Assistance: Identifying My Own Competencies   **60**
B. Supervising Assistance: Meeting My Supervisor   **60**
Exercise 4.1: My First Self-Evaluation: What Does It Tell Me?   **61**
Exercise 4.2: My First Self-Evaluation: How Can It Help Me?   **63**
What to Do Before the Supervisor Arrives   **65**
What to Do During the Supervisor's Visit   **65**
What to Do During the Supervisor's Conference   **66**
What to Do After the Supervisor Leaves   **66**
C. Other Sources of Assistance   **67**
Questions for Class Discussion   **67**
Selected Readings and References for Chapter 4   **67**

Part II   Planning for Instruction in a Secondary Classroom   **69**

5 Why Should I Plan?   **73**

A. A Rationale for Planning   **73**
B. The Components of Total Planning   **74**
Exercise 5.1: A Pre-Planning Check   **75**
Exercise 5.2: Lesson Planning Pretest   **77**
Questions for Class Discussion   **79**

6 How Do I Know What to Teach?   **81**

A. What Sources Are Available to Me?   **81**
B. What Public Documents Should I Examine?   **81**
Exercise 6.1: Examining State Curriculum Frameworks   **83**
Exercise 6.2: Examining Curriculum Guides   **85**
C. What Do I Need to Know About Student Textbooks?   **87**
Exercise 6.3: Examining Teacher's Manuals and Student Texts   **89**
D. How Can I Deal with Controversial Issues?   **91**
Exercise 6.4: Teaching About Controversial Issues   **93**
Questions for Class Discussion   **94**

7 What Are Instructional Objectives?   **95**

   A.   How to Write Instructional Objectives   **95**
         Exercise 7.1: Recognizing Instructional Objectives: A Diagnostic Test   **97**
   B.   How to Classify Instructional Objectives   **99**
         Exercise 7.2: How Knowledgeable Am I About Behavioral Objectives?
         A Diagnostic Test   **101**
   C.   How to Judge Whether Instructional Objectives Are Worth the Time   **103**
   D.   How to Select Verbs for Stating Specific Learning Objectives   **103**
         Exercise 7.3: Writing My Own Instructional Objectives   **107**
   E.   A Danger in Over-Objectivity   **109**
       Questions for Class Discussion   **109**

8 How Do I Prepare an Instructional Plan?   **111**

   A.   Preparation for Planning: General Guidelines   **111**
   B.   Preparation of a Unit Plan: Instructions   **112**
         Exercise 8.1: Writing My Unit Plan   **113**
         Exercise 8.2: Evaluating My Unit Plan   **115**
   C.   Unit Plan and Daily Plan: Samples   **117**
       Sample 1: Art   **117**
       Sample 2: Biology   **119**
       Sample 3: Typing   **124**
       Sample 4: Home Economics   **125**
       Sample 5: English   **127**
       Sample 6: Music   **129**
       Sample 7: Physical Education   **131**
       Sample 8: Social Studies   **133**
       Sample 9: Spanish   **135**
       A Model for a Unit Plan Contract   **137**
       Model Lesson Plan   **139**
   D.   Preparation of a Daily Lesson Plan: Instructions   **147**
         Exercise 8.3: Planning a Lesson: Preliminary Action   **149**
         Exercise 8.4: Writing My Daily Lesson Plan   **151**
         Exercise 8.5: Evaluating My Daily Lesson Plan   **152**
       Questions for Class Discussion   **153**

9 How Can I Individualize the Learning Experience for Students?   **155**

   A.   Identifying the Students' Needs in Your Classroom   **156**
       Teaching to Different Needs at the Same Time   **156**
       Teaching Students Who Do Not Receive Special Services   **157**
   B.   Developing the Self-Instructional Package   **159**
       What Is the Self-Instructional Package?   **159**
       How Do I Develop the Self-Instructional Package?   **160**
         Exercise 9.1: Developing My First Self-Instructional Package   **161**
   C.   The Self-Instructional Package Model   **162**
       Questions for Class Discussion   **172**
       Selected Readings and References for Chapters 5 through 9   **172**

Part III *Choosing and Implementing Instructional Strategies in the Secondary Classroom*   **173**

10   What Are Basic Teacher Behaviors That Facilitate Student Learning?   **177**

   A.   Ten Basic Teacher Behaviors   **178**
   B.   About Questioning   **180**
        Recognizing Levels of Classroom Questions   **181**
           Exercise 10.1: Identifying Cognitive Levels of Classroom Questions   **185**
           Exercise 10.2: Observing the Cognitive Levels of Classroom Verbal Interaction   **187**
           Exercise 10.3: Raising Questions to Higher Levels   **189**
           Exercise 10.4: Creating Cognitive Questions   **191**
           Exercise 10.5: Analyzing the Level of Questions in Textbooks   **193**
           Exercise 10.6: Mini Peer Teaching Lesson for Practicing Questioning   **195**
        Ten Guidelines for the Use of Questioning   **196**
           Exercise 10.7: Identifying Basic Teacher Behaviors in Classroom Interaction   **197**
        Questions for Class Discussion   **200**
        Selected Readings and References for Chapter 10   **200**

11   What Are the Guidelines for the Use of Specific Teaching Strategies?   **201**

   A.   Your First Decision in Strategy Selection: The Delivery or the Access Mode?   **202**
   B.   Using the Lecture in Secondary School Teaching   **203**
        Guidelines for Lecturing   **203**
   C.   Using Inquiry and Discovery in Secondary School Teaching   **204**
        Levels of Inquiry   **204**
        Inquiry Cycle Processes   **205**
        Mystery Island: An Inquiry Lesson   **206**
   D.   Using Discussions in Secondary School Teaching   **207**
           Exercise 11.1: Discussion as a Strategy: What Do I Already Know?   **209**
   E.   Using the Demonstration in Secondary School Teaching   **211**
   F.   Using the Textbook in Secondary School Teaching   **212**
   G.   Using Assignments in Secondary School Teaching   **214**
           Exercise 11.2: Analysis of a Teaching Episode   **215**
   H.   Using Games in Secondary School Teaching   **217**
        Why Are Games Used?   **217**
        What Are Educational Games? A Classification   **217**
        What Are Some "Homemade" Games?—Samples   **218**
        Commercially Produced Games   **223**
        Publishers' Addresses   **226**
        Additional Sources of Game Ideas and Materials   **226**
           Exercise 11.3: Creating My Own Game for Teaching   **227**
           Exercise 11.4: Supporting My Instruction: Selecting Guidelines for Teaching Strategies   **229**
        Questions for Class Discussion   **231**
        Selected Readings and References for Chapter 11   **231**

12 **What Other Aids and Resources Are Available to the Secondary School Teacher?** **233**

A. General Guidelines for Selection of Aids and Resources:
The Learning-Experiences Ladder **233**

B. Aids and Resources for Direct and Simulated Experiences **235**

C. Aids and Resources for Vicarious Experiences **235**

D. Aids and Resources for Computer Experiences **235**
Why Use Computers? **235**
What Books Could I Select for My Computer Library? **236**
What Software Could I Preview? **236**
What Computer Periodicals Could I Review? **237**
What Issues Should I Consider? **237**

E. Aids and Resources for Visual and Verbal Experiences **238**
The Chalkboard **239**
Overhead Projection **240**
Sources of Transparency Materials **241**
Exercise 12.1: Using the Chalkboard and the Overhead Projector Creatively **243**
Maps and Globes **245**
Charts, Graphs, and Pictures **245**
Library/Media Resource Center **245**
Audio and Video Tapes **245**
Films, Filmstrips, and Slides **246**
Community Resources and Field Trips **246**
The Spirit Duplicator **246**
Objects **247**
A Bibliography of Free and Inexpensive Resource Materials for
Secondary School Teaching **247**
Questions for Class Discussion **247**
Selected Readings and References for Chapter 12 **248**

13 **What Are Some Motivational Strategies? An Annotated List of 210 Possibilities—
An Idea Bank** **249**

A. General Ideas for Motivation **250**

B. Expressing Encouragement as a Motivator **251**

C. Motivational Ideas Specific to Subject Areas **252**
Art **252**
Business Education **252**
English (Including ESL, Speech, Drama, Journalism) **253**
Foreign Languages **255**
Home Economics **255**
Mathematics **256**
Music **257**
Physical Education **258**
Science **259**
Social Science **260**

D. Professional Periodicals Useful to Secondary School Teachers **262**
Exercise 13.1: Selecting and Experimenting with a Motivational Technique **263**
Exercise 13.2: Developing My Own Bank of Motivational Techniques **265**
Exercise 13.3: Identifying Professional Journals **266**
Exercise 13.4: Beginning My Resource File **267**

Questions for Class Discussion **268**
Selected Readings and References for Chapter 13 **268**

Part IV Classroom Management, Discipline, and Legal Guidelines **269**

14 What Do I Need to Know to Cope with the Daily Challenge of Secondary Teaching? **273**
A. "If I Do Any of These, Please Let Me Know!" **274**
B. Surveying the Physical Environment of the Classroom **276**
   Exercise 14.1: What Should I Do to Maintain the Physical Environment of My Classroom? **277**
C. Achieving Routine Maintenance **279**
   Exercise 14.2: How Can I Maintain Efficiency in Responding to Routines and Clerical Responsibilities? **281**
   Exercise 14.3: Conveying a Positive Message to Parents **283**
D. Reviewing Legal Guidelines **285**
   Exercise 14.4: What Legal Guidelines Are Available to Me? **285**
   The Teacher and the Law **287**
   Student Conduct and Behavior Standards **287**
   Removal of Students from School **288**
   Teacher Liability **289**
   Your Contract **289**
   Exercise 14.5: What Do I Know About Legal Guidelines in My State for the Secondary School Teacher? **291**
   Questions for Class Discussion **293**

15 What Do Some Authorities Suggest as Approaches to Classroom Discipline? **295**
A. What is the Meaning of "Classroom Discipline?" **295**
B. What Do Experts Say? **298**
   General Guidelines for Establishing and Maintaining Classroom Control **303**
   Exercise 15.1: Case Studies for Class Discussion **305**
   Exercise 15.2: Role-Playing Management Problems **311**
C. The Question of Adolescent Smoking, Alcohol, and Drug Use (S-A-D) **313**
   What Can the Classroom Teacher Do? **313**
   What Can the School Do? **314**
   Some Relief on S-A-D **315**
   Questions for Class Discussion **316**
   Selected Readings and References for Chapters 14 and 15 **316**

Part V Evaluation of Teacher Performance and Student Achievement **319**

16 How Do I Evaluate and Report Student Achievement? **323**
A. Evaluating Student Achievement: Some Avenues **324**
B. Evaluating a Student's Verbal and Nonverbal Behaviors **324**
   Guidelines for Evaluating What the Learner Does and Says **324**
C. Evaluating a Student's Written Behaviors (Anecdotal Record) **326**

D. Recording My Observations and Judgments: A Word of Caution About the
Anecdotes I Write   **327**
    Exercise 16.1: An Evaluation of Written Teacher Comments   **329**
E. Constructing Tests   **331**
    General Guidelines for Test-Item Preparation   **331**
F. Analyzing Items for Preparing Written Tests
in Secondary School Teaching   **332**
    I.   Performance Items   **332**
    II.   Identification Items   **333**
    III.   Completion Drawing Items   **333**
    IV.   Essay Items   **334**
    V.   Short Explanation Items   **337**
    VI.   Completion Statement Items   **338**
    VII.   Multiple-Choice Items   **338**
    VIII.   Matching Items   **341**
    IX.   Correction Items   **343**
    X.   Grouping Items   **343**
    XI.   Arrangement Items   **344**
    XII.   True-False Items   **344**
    XIII.   Modified True-False Items   **345**
    XIV.   Sometimes-Always-Never Items   **346**
    Final Guidelines on Testing   **347**
    Exercise 16.2: Preparing My Own Test Items   **349**
G. Grading Student Achievement   **351**
    Guidelines to Prepare You for Grading   **351**
H. Reporting a Student's Achievement   **353**
    Suggestions for Making Out Report Cards   **353**
I. Conferencing with a Parent   **353**
    Guidelines for the Teacher Meeting Parents   **353**
    Questions for Class Discussion   **355**

17   How Can I Continue to Evaluate My Developing Competency?   **357**

A. A Look At My Preservice Skill Development: Micro-Peer Teaching   **357**
    Guidelines for the Use of the MPT   **358**
    Instructions for the MPT Exercise   **358**
    Exercise 17.1: Micro-Peer Teaching: My Preparation   **359**
    Exercise 17.1: Micro-Peer Teaching: My Peer Evaluation   **361**
    What to Look for in Video Playback Session for Your Self-Evaluation   **363**
    Preparing the MPT Packet   **363**
    Exercise 17.1: Micro-Peer Teaching: My Final Evaluation   **365**
    *Exercise 17.2: How Can I Further Analyze My Verbal Interactions
with Students?*   **367**
B. Another Look: My Secondary Teachalogue,
With 20 Teaching Suggestions   **368**
    Secondary Teachalogue Checklist   **368**
C. Still Another Look: Secondary Practice-Teaching Evaluation Form and
Competency Descriptions   **370**
    *Exercise 17.3: Secondary Practice Teaching: What Does My Second
Self-Evaluation Tell Me?*   **373**

D. Looking Ahead: Sample Forms Used by School Personnel to
Evaluate Teachers   **375**
   Teacher Behavior Checklist   **375**
   Teacher Observation Form   **377**
   Classroom Observation   **378**
   Statement of Goals, Objectives, and Assessment Techniques   **380**

E. Looking Within: A Summary of Guidelines That Permeate the
Assessment Component   **381**
   Question for Class Discussion   **383**
   Selected Readings and References for Chapters 16 and 17   **385**

Part VI   *What Should I Know About the Secondary Practice-Teaching Experience and Beyond?*   **387**

18.   What Should I Know About the Secondary Practice-Teaching Experience?   **391**

A. The Paraprofessional Experience   **392**
   Clerical Experience   **392**
   Noninstructional Experience   **392**
   Audiovisual Assistance   **393**
   Some of the Paraprofessional's Duties   **393**

B. The Practice-Teaching Experience   **394**

C. The Practice-Teaching Experience from the Cooperating Teacher's Point
of View: How Can I Help My Student Teacher?   **395**

D. The Practice-Teaching Experience from the Principal's Point of View:
How Can I Help?   **396**
   *Exercise 18.1: The Practice-Teaching Experience from the Student
   Teacher's Point of View: How Can I Continue My Self-Evaluation as a
   Secondary-School Teacher?*   **399**
   Questions for Class Discussion   **401**

19   What Do I Need to Know That May Help Me in Getting My First Teaching Job?   **403**

A. General Guidelines to Help Me in Getting My First Teaching Job   **403**
   My Checklist: How to Look for a Job   **404**

B. Specific Guidelines to Help Me in Getting a Teaching Job   **405**
   My Checklist: How to Write an Eye-Catching Résumé   **407**
   My Checklist: How to Develop Insights About an Interview   **409**
   Exercise 19.1: Making Tough Decisions About "Whom to Hire"   **410**

C. Informational Sources About Credential Requirements State by State   **411**

D. Educational Associations in the United States Related to
Secondary-School Teaching   **413**
   *Exercise 19.2: Completing My Checklist of Competencies as Reviewed
   Through A Resource Guide for Secondary-School Teaching: Planning
   for Competence*   **415**
   Questions for Class Discussion   **419**
   Selected Readings and References for Chapters 18 and 19   **419**

Epilogue   **421**

Index   **423**

A Resource Guide for
Secondary School Teaching

Part I

Orientation to Secondary School Teaching

*Personally I am always ready to learn,
although I do not always like being taught.*
—Sir Winston Churchill

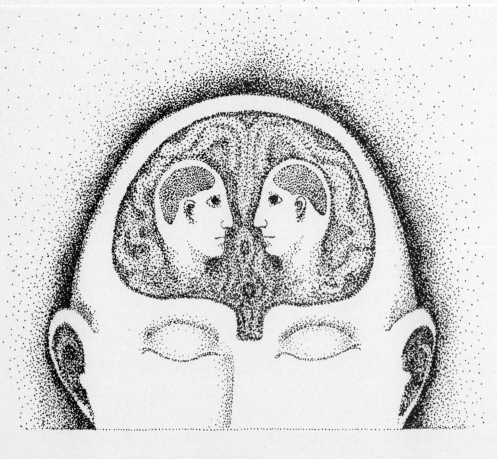

Drawing by Carol Wilson, unpublished material. Reprinted by permission.

Part I deals with your perceptions

- About secondary school teaching.

- About students, teachers, and administrators.

- About the kind of secondary teacher you would like to be.

- And your proposed goals for the development of your teaching style.

1

What Do I Need to Know About Today's Secondary Schools?

One day soon you will likely be offered your first teaching contract, and what an exciting moment that will be for you! But after the initial excitement wears off and you have time to reflect, many questions will begin to take shape in your mind. Which school will I be assigned to? Will it be a high school or a junior high school? Will it be a regular secondary school, or will it be a "magnet" school, or will it be a "fundamentals" school? Will it be a school that has its start in the fall, as is traditional, or will it be a year-round school? Which subjects will I be assigned to teach? Specifically, what grade levels will I have? How many different preparations will I have? What supervision responsibilities might I have? What are the students like? the faculty? What textbooks will I use, and when can I expect to see them? How should I prepare? How *can* I prepare when there are so many unanswered questions? What school district policies are there that I need to learn about now? What support services can I expect? Will my teaching assignment be split between departments? Will the department chairperson like me? How extensive are the school's rules and regulations? Will there be an orientation for new and beginning teachers? How can I prepare for students I know nothing about?

Those questions, and many others, are often the focus of long, concentrated moments of thought by beginning secondary school teachers. To guide you through this initial experience the following informative paragraphs about school organization, about secondary school students, and about teachers and administrators offer a glimpse into the world of secondary education. This bright, active, ever-changing world is so complex that few authors can say all the words that need to be said to every reader. However, you will realize the necessity in starting *somewhere*, and so we begin with certain aspects of school organization.

A. ABOUT ORIENTATION AND SCHEDULES

Orientation Meetings

As a beginning teacher, you will no doubt be invited to participate in an orientation meeting. Some school districts begin their academic year with a district-wide orientation for beginning and new teachers, whereas others schedule on-site orientations at each secondary school. Many school districts do both, with perhaps a district-wide meeting in a morning followed by the beginning of on-site meetings that afternoon. Of course, the ways the orientation meetings are scheduled and planned are going to vary, district by district and school by school. However, the objectives for each orientation meeting should be quite similar. District personnel will encourage the beginning teacher to:

- Meet other teachers and establish the start of new collegial friendships.
- Become familiar with the policies of the school district. These policies are many and will cover a wide range, e.g., policies for procedures relating to students involved in accidents while at school, for procedures involving student medications, for finding dangerous weapons or drugs, for class conduct, for school programs, for off-campus field trips, for parties in the classroom, for students out of the classroom during the school day, grading policies, procedures for completing attendance and tardy forms, for sending students to the office of the vice-principal or to the counselor, and for chaperoning and sponsoring student activities. And those samples are just the beginning!
- Become familiar with courses of study, curriculum guides, resource units, teacher's manuals, student textbooks, and supplementary materials.
- Become familiar with available audiovisual resources and equipment, and procedures for reserving and using them, and to prepare materials for the classroom.
- Become familiar with the school library/resource center, its personnel and procedures.
- Meet district personnel and become familiar with the many services that support you in your classroom.

As a teacher candidate in a secondary teacher education program, you may be asked to participate in an orientation meeting at your college or university. Perhaps this meeting will be a function of one of your college or university courses. You will receive your secondary school assignment (a junior or senior high school, a middle school, an intermediate school, or perhaps some combination of these), the date (with time and specific location) when you should report to your assignment, the name of your cooperating teacher (the experienced teacher who has volunteered or been assigned to work with you), the grade level, the subject(s), the names of the school and the school district, and perhaps the name of your college or university supervisor. You will probably be encouraged to follow the objectives listed at the beginning of this section, meet other teacher candidates and district teachers, become familiar with school and district policies, review the required curriculum materials for your teaching assignment, plan for needed audiovisual materials, and learn what to do in emergencies!

When you arrive at your assigned secondary school and the proper introductions have been made, you should begin to get acquainted with the school campus and the way the school is organized. Know where your classroom is and locate the nearest restrooms, for students and for faculty. Become familiar with the location of such areas as the teachers' workroom, the faculty room (a large comprehensive high school may have more than one), and the faculty lunch room. Determine where the students eat their lunches. Where is the auditorium for student assemblies? Is there a nurse's room? Where are the nearest first-aid supplies? the fire extinguishing equipment? How do you notify maintenance personnel quickly? What is the fire-drill plan? Where is it? Where are the various administrative offices? Where is the library? the media center? the resource room? Where are textbooks stored? How are they checked out and distributed? Where is the attendance office? Are there offices for resource specialists? Have you met your department chairperson? Do you know where he/she can be found at various times during the school day? Where are student records maintained? What access do you have to them? Where are teaching supplies kept, and how do you check them out? Have you located your own faculty mailbox and the place to sign in/sign out? What procedures do you follow if you are absent because of your own illness, or when you are going to be late to school because your alarm failed to awaken you, or your car failed to start, or the local transit authority went on strike? Do you have the necessary phone numbers? And, not least in importance, if you drive to school where do you park? Otherwise, what is the best local transportation available to you to get to school each day?

After you have become acquainted with the campus and have answers to some of your more urgent questions, you will want to focus your attention on the school schedule.

Teacher Schedules

Teacher schedules vary from state to state, from district to district, and from school to school. Junior high school teaching schedules may vary slightly from those of high school teachers, perhaps being slightly shorter each day. The school year for secondary schools will likely begin in late August or early September, and continue through late May or mid-June. Some schools operate a year-round schedule, with each teacher having one quarter off, a practice that began in some schools a number of years ago but that did not catch on as expected. Most secondary schools operate five days a week, although some are open for just four days. The school year, recently lengthened in many states and/or districts, still approximates 180 days.

The school day will begin around 8:00 a.m. and last until around 3:00 or 4:00 p.m. in the many secondary schools that have recently lengthened the school day. In some of these latter schools, the first or last period is optional for students and teachers. For most secondary school teachers the school day consists of six periods, each period lasting 50-60 minutes. One of these periods will be a preparation period, sometimes referred to as the "free" period.

Besides the conventional schedule, some secondary schools have designed a "modular schedule" where each module is usually 15-22 minutes. On a given day you might meet one of your classes for only one or two modules, whereas on another day you might meet the same class for several modules. In the late 1950s and through the 1960s many variations of modular scheduling were tried, and some schools continue the practice today. Having students sometimes for a block of time longer than the usual 50-60 minutes is attractive, particularly to teachers of science, art, home economics, and industrial arts. Teachers in other areas (such as mathematics and foreign languages) often prefer to meet their students for regular periods of time each day for daily drill and practice. Occasionally you may find that a secondary school has successfully combined modular and traditional schedules within the curriculum, thus satisfying the wishes of teachers who prefer modular scheduling as well as those who prefer the traditional schedule.

A typical schedule for a secondary school teacher includes meeting three or four classes before lunch and two or three following lunch. When the teacher's "free" or "prep" period falls during the first or during the final period of the day, or just before or just after lunch, the teacher is still expected to be present on the school campus during that "free" period. Most teachers are quite busy during their preparation periods, reading and grading student papers, preparing materials, conferencing, or checking audiovisual equipment. It is also a time when you sometimes may prefer to sit and relax over a cup of tea or coffee, perhaps in the pleasant surroundings of the faculty room. Teachers need "think time" too!

In addition to the expectation that you be "on duty" throughout the school day, teachers in most districts are expected to be available on campus for a period of time (usually 15-30 minutes) before and after school, a time when students and parents as well as administrators may wish to contact and/or conference with you. You may be expected to sign in upon arrival and sign out upon departure, which is a policy that ensures that the school staff knows you are on duty.

Some secondary schools stagger the start and end of each day so that some teachers (and students) arrive and leave earlier than others. This is a common practice in crowded schools. Some schools even stagger their class times so that each day begins with a different period, a practice common in high schools during final examination week.

Whatever your schedule, you will be busy and your lunch time will seem much too brief for proper rest and digestion. Eat a good breakfast before you leave home in the morning!

It is difficult to generalize about secondary school teachers' schedules, but perhaps we have given you sufficient information to arouse your curiosity about the many variations that can and do exist within America's public secondary schools. Later in this chapter (Exercise 1.4) you will visit a school and learn more at first hand about teacher schedules. For now, let us turn to a discussion about secondary school students.

B. ABOUT STUDENTS

The bell rings for first period to begin and the students enter your classroom—28 of them, "a kaleidoscope of personalities, all unique, each a bundle of idiosyncrasies, different strengths, different attitudes and aptitudes, different needs."[1]

What a challenge to you this is!—to understand and to teach 28 unique individuals all at once, and to do it four more times that day, five days a week, 180 days a year. You must be prepared not only to teach your subject but to do it effectively with students of different cultural backgrounds, of diverse linguistic abilities, of different learning styles, and with certain students who have been identified as having "special needs." Indeed, what a challenge!

What a wealth of information abounds about these young people! And, as a secondary school teacher you are expected to know it all! Certain facts you have learned and accumulated along the way will lodge in your mind. While concerned with the student's cognitive development, you are simultaneously concerned about his/her attitude and value development, social adjustment, emotional health, and physical well-being.

You will be sensitive and understanding about the disadvantaged youth. You will attempt to learn as much as possible about each youngster, aware of who has difficulties in adjusting or developing at school because of socioeconomic and multicultural factors (racial insensitivities, or language-minority characteristics). Your need for background knowledge is increased further because handicapped students are to be educated with their peers in the regular classroom when possible. You will need information and skills unique to teaching any special learners in your classroom.

In 1975, Public Law 94-142 was passed; this law created certain requirements relative to meeting the needs of exceptional children in the regular classroom. The *exceptional child* is defined as

[1] Mary Hatwood Futrell, *Education Week*, April 3, 1985, p. 10.

the child who deviates from the average or normal child (1) in mental characteristics, (2) in sensory abilities, (3) in neuromotor or physical characteristics, (4) in social behavior, (5) in communication abilities, or (6) in multiple handicaps.[2]

The general purpose of P.L. 94-142 was to encourage educators to place these special students in the least restrictive environment possible, in an environment as close to normal as possible. In some cases, this placement is the regular classroom; in others, it is not.

It is beyond the scope of this book to present anything more than some very general guidelines to you in working with these youngsters with special needs. As a regular classroom teacher, you should keep this important fact in mind: when a student with special needs is placed in your classroom, your objective should *not* be to "make the student normal," but, rather, to deal directly with the differences between this student and other students in your classroom.

In order to deal directly with these differences, you should

1. Develop an understanding of the general characteristics of different types of special-needs students. (Most educational psychology courses address this problem.)
2. Attempt to identify and meet the student's unique needs relative to *your* classroom.
3. Design lesson plans that teach to different needs at the same time, as much as possible.

Understanding the General Characteristics of Special-Needs Students

In a regular classroom, there may be students already identified as having specific special needs. These students, when identified, are placed in a particular category, based on their *primary* area of exceptionality. These areas of exceptionality may include:

- The gifted and talented.
- The educable mentally retarded.
- The behavior disordered (also called emotionally disturbed).
- The learning disabled.
- The hearing impaired.
- The visually impaired.
- The speech and language disordered.
- The physically handicapped.
- Students with chronic health problems.

Having been categorized according to one of these specific areas does not necessarily mean that this student will not have strengths and weaknesses in another area. For example, a student identified as being gifted and talented could have some difficulties in speech, or could be visually impaired; or a student identified as being hearing impaired could also be academically gifted. The category of exceptionality under which he/she is identified simply means that that area appears to be the *primary* area of special need, not the only one.

Students who are identified as exceptional may be placed in the regular classroom either for the majority of the school day or only for designated periods. This placement concept is known as "mainstreaming."

---

[2] S. A. Kirk and J. J. Gallagher, *Educating Exceptional Children,* 3rd ed. (Boston: Houghton Mifflin, 1979), p. 3.

It would suffice to say then that the regular classroom teacher's role, in serving students with special needs, is based primarily on two responsibilities:

1. To work as a team member, for those students identified as special-needs students.
2. To serve as a continual source of identification and referral for students not identified as having special needs.

By meeting these two basic responsibilities, a regular classroom teacher will be able to participate in providing an appropriate education for exceptional students.

C. ABOUT MEETING MY STUDENTS

When those 28 students walk into your classroom for the first time, what will you have planned to do? A major contributor to effective classroom management during the school year is the manner by which you *begin* the year: a proper beginning will make your life easier for the entire school year. Consider these *guidelines for getting the year off to a good beginning.*

1. Before the school year begins, spend time getting your classroom organized (if you have your own room), finding out where equipment and materials are and will be kept, and preparing your teaching plans.
2. As soon as you receive your class lists (lists of names of students in your classes), practice pronouncing the students' names.
3. Prepare a seating chart to begin the year, and have students sit in their assigned seats so as to expedite your learning their names. The sound of your own name is one of the most beautiful sounds in the world, and students' awareness that you know them by name will greatly benefit the early establishment of rapport with your classes.
4. Teach your students your CBRs (classroom behavior rules) early, keeping the list of rules brief and enforceable. Among other matters, these might include:
    a. How to correctly obtain your attention and help.
    b. How to properly enter and leave the room.
    c. Tardy and absentee rules.
    d. Procedures for seatwork, for using a pencil sharpener and wastebasket.
    e. How to maintain papers, books, and other class materials in order.
    f. Your policy regarding late assignments, missed tests, and extra credit work.
    g. Your academic and social (school citizenship) grading procedure.
5. As the beginning of the year proceeds, monitor student behavior and respond quickly when necessary, establishing early your expectations and the consequences the students may expect. Remember, your good modeling behavior counts!
6. Use strong communication skills, such as giving directions clearly, listening actively, smiling appropriately, and establishing eye contact with every student in the classroom on the average of about *once every 30 seconds* when addressing the entire class. Be mobile in the classroom. A good teacher is usually tired at day's end because he/she has been so physically active during the school day.
7. Plan carefully what it is you will do on that very first day of class.

One teacher begins with a get-acquainted activity such as going around the room asking each student to answer three or four questions, thus having each member of the class tell a little about his/her self—questions such as "What name would you like to be called by?" "Do you have a job?" "Where did you attend school last year?" "Do you have brothers or sisters?" "What is your favorite hobby?"

Another teacher prefers to start the first day of class by telling students about the course—description, objectives, study hints, assignment expectations, grading procedures—and distributes books, then starts immediately into subject content.

Yet another secondary-school teacher begins the first day with interest-oriented activities such as games or a laboratory investigation, preferring to build students' motivations on the subject itself and leave get-acquainted and/or "housekeeping" activities to a later date. In some secondary schools there are so many student class changes during the first week of school that teachers prefer to neither distribute textbooks nor cover much content until class change has settled down.

What *you* plan to do the first day and the first week of school will be guided by the nature of your school, your students, your subject, and by your own philosophy of education (discussed in Chapter 3). We ask that you consider the guidelines we have set forth, then plan accordingly.

The get-acquainted activity mentioned at the start of Guideline 7 might be especially valuable if you are teaching first-year junior high school students, who may be particularly anxious about their new school experience. Another get-acquainted activity is to provide magazines, newspapers, and catalogs, scissors and paste, and ask each student to prepare a "Get Acquainted Collage," having selected cut-outs of items which mean something to him/her, perhaps with the student's name in the center of the collage. The collages are then shared with the rest of the class. The teacher makes his/her own collage—modeling counts!

Do you like the idea of a get-acquainted session to start the year in your subject field? Can you think of or find other creative "get-acquainted" activities, and share them with members of your class? That is the purpose of the first exercise in this chapter, Exercise 1.1 (p. 13).

D. ABOUT TEACHERS

Secondary school teachers are unique and independent, and represent a myriad of individual personalities—perhaps impossible to generalize about. But let us suppose that a teaching colleague mentions that Ms. Wonderful in Room 17 is a "great teacher," "one of the best we have," "super," and "terrific." What might be some of the teaching characteristics you would expect to see in Ms. Wonderful's teaching behavior in her secondary classroom?

"A large number of researches have investigated teacher behaving styles and a wide variety of trait names have been attached to characteristics that administrators and investigators believe important," writes David G. Ryans in *The Evaluation of Teaching*.[3] In Ryans' article, "Teacher Behavior Can Be Evaluated," the author lists the teacher-behaving styles that are most supported by research. Each of these questions represents one of these teacher-behaving styles:

1. Are you considerate, understanding, warm, sensitive, nurturing, and supportive in your teaching behavior?

2. Are you organized? Can you manage? Are you orderly? Are you responsible and businesslike in your teaching behavior?

---

[3] David G. Ryans, "Teacher Behavior Can Be Evaluated," *The Evaluation of Teaching: A Report of the Second Pi Lambda Theta Catena* (Washington, DC: Pi Lambda Theta, 1967), p. 47.

3. Do you have a stimulating, motivating, and imaginative teaching behavior?
4. Do you maintain expressive, attractive, clear, personally impressive and academically impressive teaching behavior?
5. Do you employ direct teaching behavior? (No beating around the bush in your classroom!)[4]

Returning to our question about what Ms. Wonderful's teaching behaviors might be, we might predict that Ms. Wonderful demonstrates that she accepts *all* the students, is organized, presents interesting lessons, is verbally facile, and knows what she is talking about.

Several times throughout this resource guide we return to this topic of teacher behavior, but for now let us look at the chief administrator in charge of everything, the building principal.

E. ABOUT ADMINISTRATORS

If you are told by another teacher that the principal of your school is a "perfect 10," what will you expect that principal to be like? "Smile, and say 'hello' to every staff member every day" is the first suggestion offered to principals by Penny Hirschman.[5] Hirschman lists several points that contribute to a principal's success with staff members. To achieve a "perfect 10" a principal should

- Promptly follow up recommendations, concerns, or complaints.
- Make sure basic school policies and rules are closely defined and known.
- Keep everyone well informed of school events.
- Give proper recognition to teachers for noteworthy accomplishments.
- Foster the professional growth and development of staff members, with opportunities for intervisitations, demonstrations, conferences, workshops, and research projects.
- Demonstrate a sincere interest in the staff's welfare.
- Spend time each day with students.
- Turn people on by being positive.
- Learn to love himself or herself.

Yes, your "perfect 10" principal has the ultimate responsibility for everything that happens on the secondary school campus, although he/she will have staff vice principals with delegated authority in various school activity areas. Department chairpersons also serve administrative functions in most school districts. One of your tasks as a new teacher is to become familiar with the chain of command within your school and district.

What kind of administrative support should you expect during your beginning year? Support through informal discussions, teachers' meetings, a faculty handbook, and school memos. The principal and the administrative staff will share information with you about many topics:

---

[4] If you are interested in reading more about the characteristics of the teacher, see the early studies reviewed in the *Handbook of Research on Teaching,* edited by N. L. Gage, especially the chapters, "The Teacher's Personality and Characteristics," and "Analysis and Investigation of Teaching Methods." For specific characteristics of beginning teachers, see R. L. Turner's article in *The School Review,* "Characteristics of Beginning Teachers: Their Differential Linkage with School System Types." In addition, David G. Ryans' well-known study of characteristics of effective teachers, "Some Correlates of Teacher Behavior," in *Educational and Psychological Measurement,* and his further clarification in *Characteristics of Teachers: Their Description, Comparison, and Appraisal,* provide an early benchmark for education's response to the question, "What is effective teaching?." This is a topic discussed more thoroughly later in this resource guide.

[5] Penny Hirschman, "A Principal's 'perfect 10' for Staff Success," *Reading '83,* Vol. 1, No. 1 (August 1983), p. 7. International Reading Association membership newspaper.

EXERCISE 1.1: GETTING ACQUAINTED WITH MY STUDENTS

What are some "getting-acquainted" activities you could plan for secondary students? Your educational purpose for this exercise is to select a grade level of your choice and record at least one activity you might use that would enable you and the students to become better acquainted during the first week of school. Share your activity with other teacher candidates.

Subject and grade level: _____

Description of getting-acquainted activity: _____

_____

_____

_____

_____

_____

_____

_____

_____

_____

_____

_____

_____

Notes to myself regarding ideas I received when sharing my activity with other teacher candidates:

_____

_____

_____

_____

_____

_____

_____

_____

_____

1. *Records you are expected to keep.* There are lesson plans, audiovisual forms, supply forms, conference forms, anecdotal records, students' grade report forms, budget request forms, classroom inventory forms, field trip forms, and attendance record forms.
2. *Policies that regulate the school and the district.* There are policies about student conduct, field trips, school assemblies, class parties, before- and after-school activities, and planned school events scheduled during the year.
3. *Opportunities for professional growth and development.* Professional growth and development opportunities will vary from district to district; however, many of these opportunities include: (1) district in-service workshops, classes, and meetings; (2) professional organization workshops and conferences; (3) nearby college or university courses; (4) curriculum improvement committee participation; (5) demonstration teaching for your district; and (6) later in your career, serving as a host teacher for a teacher candidate in a teacher education program. Some of these opportunities may be tied to an increased salary plan in your district. Find out what your district's policies are.
4. *Help from other educators.* Some principals will introduce you to selected resource people and to curriculum coordinators. Other principals will assign one of their teachers as a "big brother" or "big sister," to work with you during this first year—sometimes these teachers have been designated as "mentor" teachers. Still other principals and the department chair will begin some scheduled (or unscheduled) visits to your classroom. This is to be expected and you should not be frightened because this is for your professional growth with follow-up get-together afterwards. Often, conferences with your principal can be scheduled so you can ask all of those questions you have.

F. ABOUT THE OVERALL PICTURE

In the early 1980s no one facet of education received more attention from the media, caused more concern among parents and teachers, or got bigger headlines than that of a decline (factual or fanciful) in students' achievement in the public schools, namely the secondary schools and higher education. Curiously, elementary school education seemed to escape most of that attention. In any case, reports were issued, polls taken, debates organized, dialogues established, and blue-ribbon panels formed. Indeed, the year 1983 may be recorded by historians as "The Year of the Educational Reports." Within a six-month period in that year no less than eight reports or studies of national significance gained public attention. What initiated this attention? We are not sure, but it has never been matched in its political interest and participation. Perhaps never before have so many critical reports about education been published in such a short period of time. Consider this list:

- *Academic Preparation for College: What Students Need to Know and Be Able to Do.* New York: The College Board, 1983.
- *Action for Excellence.* James B. Hunt, Jr. (Chairman), Task Force on Education for Economic Growth, 1983. 1066 Lincoln, #300, Denver, CO 80295.
- Adler, Mortimer J. *Paideia: Problems and Possibilities.* New York: Macmillan, 1983.
- *A Nation at Risk.* National Commission on Excellence in Education. Washington, DC: United States Office of Education, 1983.
- Boyer, Ernest L. *High School: A Report on Secondary Education in America.* New York: Harper & Row, 1983.
- *Educating Americans for the 21st Century.* Washington, DC: National Science Board, 1983.
- Feistritzer, Emily. *The Conditions of Teaching: A State-by-State Analysis.* Princeton, NJ: Princeton University Press, 1983.

- Goodlad, John I. *A Place Called School.* New York: McGraw-Hill, 1983.
- Graubard, Stephen R., ed. "The Arts and Humanities in American Schools," *Daedalus*, 112:3 (Summer 1983).
- *Making the Grade.* Twentieth Century Fund, 41 E. 70th St., New York, NY 10021. (1983).
- Sizer, Theodore R. *Horace's Compromise: The Dilemma of the American High School.* Boston: Houghton Mifflin, 1984.

A 1983 Gallup Poll indicated that most Americans believed that our schools are not working hard enough, that more "basics" should be taught. But that's not all! The poll indicated that the majority of Americans also want the schools to provide information and instruction about Communism, computers, driver education, and parenting. They also want the students to be aware of the dangers of alcohol, drug abuse, and nuclear waste. Needless to say, the poll did not give national, state, or local educators a clear indication of priorities in the desired curriculum changes. So, countless regional, state, and local committees were established and a national reform movement in education was under way.

By 1985 it was well recognized that a severe crisis was developing as too few college students indicated a desire to assume teaching as a career, and it was reported that by 1986 the United States would need at least 31,000 more teacher graduates than it would have. The shortage of qualified substitute teachers has already become an urgent problem for many school districts around the country.

The educational reform movement became centered around two areas of concern: the teacher shortage, and a movement toward increasing standards, both for public school student achievement and for the professional education of teachers. A discussion of possible solutions to the dilemma is beyond the limits of this text, but many of the potential solutions appear on the surface to be mutually antagonistic. Consider these items. During the last half of the 1980s actions in the educational reform movement have included:

- State commitments to upgrade the teaching force.
- Tougher teacher-certification standards.
- Teacher-competency testing.
- Higher salaries for beginning teachers.
- Pay raises for continuing teachers.
- Higher pay for master teachers or mentors.
- Merit pay for schools and teachers (salary tied to performance as indicated by student achievement).
- Extension of the school day and the school year.
- Stricter disciplinary standards for both students and teachers.
- Achievement and competency testing for students.
- Tougher course requirements for high school graduation.
- Tougher course requirements for college entrance.
- New "basics" required for a high school diploma.
- Increasing the number of periods taught daily by each teacher.
- Higher scholastic average and satisfactory marks in citizenship in order to establish and maintain eligibility for cocurricular participation.
- Increasing the amount and quality of homework required of each student.
- Computer classes for students from kindergarten through high school.
- Merit pay for administrators (or for schools) where money received is tied to student scores on standardized achievement tests.

Another issue surfacing and one that is alarming many educators is the national high school dropout rate and the effect the new standards will have for drop-out-prone students. In 1985, despite the national tendency toward improved mean performance of students on standardized tests, the dropout rate in urban areas nationally was over 40 percent. What is the high school dropout rate in your area today? What is it nationally? If there is a discrepancy, how might it be explained?

What other major issues confront the nation's secondary schools today? The exercises that follow will assist you in your effort to come closer to the reality of secondary schools today. You will (1) recall your own secondary school experiences, (2) interview secondary school students, (3) visit a secondary school, (4) visit an "Open House," (5) attend a parent-teacher organization meeting, (6) interview a teacher candidate, and (7) participate in the questions for class discussion that conclude this chapter.

EXERCISE 1.2: REMEMBERING MY OWN SECONDARY SCHOOL EXPERIENCES

Recalling your own secondary school experiences, what are some statements you could share? Your educational purpose for this exercise is to record your thoughts about your own experiences in a secondary school setting, and reflect whether you want your students to repeat such experiences.

UPON REFLECTION

The Profile of "Pluses"   *The Profile of "Minuses"*
(My Likes)   *(My Dislikes)*

_____ My secondary school _____

_____

_____ My teachers _____

_____

_____ My friends _____

_____

_____ A particular class _____

_____

_____ A particular rule _____

_____

_____ A particular test _____

_____

_____ A particular discussion _____

_____

_____ Peer-group pressure _____

_____

_____ Parents and pressures _____

_____

_____ Society and pressures _____

_____

_____ The school schedule _____

_____

EXERCISE 1.3: INTERVIEWING SECONDARY SCHOOL STUDENTS

Use the topics of Exercise 1.2 as your guide to interview secondary school students. Select several students and record their responses as you ask "What do you like/dislike about. . . . ?" Complete the exercise with both junior and senior high school students, compare their responses, then share your interview results with other teacher candidates. (See corollary Exercise 1.4)

A JUNIOR HIGH SCHOOL STUDENT SAYS

I Like   *I Dislike*

_____ My school _____

_____

_____ My teachers _____

_____

_____ My friends _____

_____

_____ A class _____

_____

_____ A rule _____

_____

_____ Tests _____

_____

_____ Discussions _____

_____

_____ Parents _____

_____

_____ Schedule _____

_____

A HIGH SCHOOL STUDENT SAYS

_____ My school _____

_____   _____

_____   _____

_____ My teachers _____

_____   _____

_____   _____

_____ My friends _____

_____   _____

_____   _____

_____ A class _____

_____   _____

_____ A rule _____

_____   _____

_____   _____

_____ Tests _____

_____   _____

_____   _____

_____ Discussions _____

_____   _____

_____   _____

_____ Parents _____

_____   _____

_____   _____

_____ Schedule _____

_____   _____

_____   _____

EXERCISE 1.4: RETURNING TO A SECONDARY SCHOOL CLASSROOM

What will it be like to return to a classroom as a teacher? In most teacher education programs the teacher candidate is expected to visit schools to observe the school plant, the classrooms, the support services, the teaching styles, and the students and their behaviors. Often, the teacher candidate is assigned to participate in the classroom to perform a variety of instructional and noninstructional tasks as part of the teacher education program. (See Chapter 18, Section A for this paraprofessional experience.) If your teacher education program does not require an initial school visit, this exercise provides an opportunity to observe at a school site. (See Chapter 3, Exercises 3.2 and 3.3.)

Your educational purpose is to schedule an observational visit to a nearby secondary school. Of course, you may wish to visit more than one, perhaps a junior high school, a middle school, and a high school, for comparison. Professional courtesy is expected in all of your relationships with school personnel. On the day of your visit, arrive early and check in at the administrative office. If you drove to the school, you should inquire whether you parked properly. A school employee, or perhaps a student, may escort you to the proper classroom or provide you with a map of the campus. Professional courtesy continues as you enter the classroom in a quiet, unobtrusive manner. Please wait until the teacher recognizes you, for the teacher may be in the midst of "that teachable moment."

As an integral part of your observational visit, you may want to use the key words in Exercise 1.2 to complete Exercise 1.3. Plan to share with other teacher candidates the comments of your visits, your observations, and the likes and dislikes mentioned by the secondary school students from the schools you visited.

A gracious "thank you" is appropriate when you leave the classroom at the completion of your visit, and as you stop by the administrative office to notify the staff that you are leaving the campus. Some teacher candidates extend their professional courtesy still further—within the following week, they write brief thank-you notes to the principal and the classroom teacher.

Since time you could spend in length of school day, and in length of class time, varies by state law and/or by district policy, compare your observations with the discussion of schedules as presented earlier in this chapter. How similar were they? How different?

EXERCISE 1.5: RETURNING TO AN "OPEN HOUSE" AT A SECONDARY SCHOOL

What happens at "Open House" or "Back-to-School Night" in a secondary school? As part of your experiences in a teacher education program, you may be expected to participate with your cooperating teacher in the "Open House" activities of your assigned school. This activity will provide an opportunity to observe educational and community-related activities as prepared for this special event.

Your educational purpose is to schedule an observational visit to a secondary school during its "Open House" night. Of course, if you want to observe this activity in more than one school (perhaps a junior high school and a senior high school for comparison), make arrangements to do so. Some schools within the same district schedule their "Open House" activities on different evenings, for the convenience of parents with children enrolled in different schools. You will be attending as an interested school supporter. Record your observational notes on the form that follows.

What school(s) did you visit? _____

_____

What is the total population of the school? _____

What is the average daily attendance (ADA)? _____

If there is a discrepancy between the population and the ADA, how large is it, and how is it

explained? _____

_____

What grades and subject classes did you visit? _____

_____

Are (Were) you the student-teacher of this class? _____

What exhibits did you see? _____

_____

What speeches or presentations did you hear? Who delivered them? Describe each presentation in

terms of effectiveness and assess the audience's reaction. _____

_____

_____

What student work did you see? _____

_____

Whom did you meet? Principal? Vice Principal? Teachers? Parents? _____

_____

_____

What types of questions did parents ask of the teacher? _____

_____

_____

How did the teacher and parents respond to one another? _____

_____

What evidence was there that teachers and students worked together to prepare for this event?

_____

_____

Did the educators demonstrate self-confidence, clarity in school expectations, and did they describe

their programs and goals so the parents understood? _____

_____

Would you like to have been a student in this school? _____

_____

Would you like to be a teacher in this school? _____

_____

Would you be satisfied if your own child were a student in this school? _____

_____

What other observations about this visit would you like to share? _____

_____

_____

EXERCISE 1.6: ATTENDING A PARENT-TEACHER ORGANIZATION MEETING

Parents and teachers are supportive of one another and are linked together by their common interests in youth, in the academic achievements of students, and in the total development—social, physical, emotional, and intellectual growth—of each boy and girl. To demonstrate this support and interest, teachers and parents join together. You will find that each school has a parent-teacher association, organization, or parent's club. Attend one meeting as an interested teacher candidate, and observe (1) the membership; (2) the number of parents attending the meeting; (3) the number of teachers attending the meeting, and what disciplines they are from; (4) the agenda; (5) the interests related to the school; (6) any educational issues; (7) the attitudes of participants; and (8) fundraising projects.

Record your notes about the meeting here. Share and discuss with other teacher candidates.

_____

_____

_____

_____

_____

_____

_____

_____

_____

_____

_____

_____

_____

_____

_____

_____

_____

_____

_____

_____

EXERCISE 1.7: INTERVIEWING A TEACHER CANDIDATE

Let's explore why other teacher candidates have selected secondary school teaching as a career goal. Select one teacher candidate (preferably one who is not in your class) and record that person's responses as you ask the following questions.

1. What motivated you to select secondary school teaching as a career? _____

   _____

2. Even though you indicate secondary school teaching as a goal, do you have a preference as to what level, junior or senior high school, or even elementary? _____

3. What specifically are you preparing to teach? _____

4. Are you looking forward to being free during summer months? Or would you be willing to contract with a year-round school? _____

5. Would you be interested in teaching in a "fundamentals" school, or in a "magnet" school?

   _____

6. Do you know that a nine-month teaching salary is often divided into twelve salary warrants?

   _____

7. How will you plan to spend your vacation months? _____

   _____

8. Would you like to be an administrator or counselor at some future date? _____

   _____

9. Are there any other teachers in your family? _____

   _____

10. What experiences with young people have you had prior to entering this teacher education program? _____

11. In what way did the experiences help or hinder your teaching the secondary school youth?

    _____

12. In a brief statement, how do you really feel right now about secondary school teaching?

    _____

13. What subjects in your discipline do you look forward to teaching? Which ones worry you the most? _____

EXERCISE 1.8: INTERVIEWING A TEACHER

For this exercise you are to interview one (or more) secondary school teachers. You may decide to interview a junior high school teacher who is in his/her first year of teaching, or one who has been teaching for ten or more years; or, you may choose to interview a high school teacher who is in his/her first year, or who has been teaching ten or more years. Your instructor may give further guidance for this exercise, but we suggest the following questions to guide the interview(s).

1. What subject(s) and grade levels do you teach? _____

_____

_____

2. Why are you teaching at this level? _____

3. What training did you have for teaching this subject and this grade level? _____

_____

4. How many years have you been teaching? _____

5. About how many hours a week do you spend on school-related matters? _____

_____

6. What do you like most about teaching secondary school students? the least? _____

_____

_____

_____

7. What advice can you give me with respect to my own preparation? _____

_____

8. Is classroom management a problem for you? Why or why not? _____

_____

_____

_____

9. Do you have any advice for me with respect to professional organizations? _____

_____

10. What kinds of student teaching experience did you have? What advice would you give to

student teachers? _____

_____

_____

In beginning to plan for developing your competencies, you have read an overview of today's secondary schools, made a suggestion for getting acquainted with your students, recorded your thoughts about your own secondary school experiences, returned to a classroom, visited an "Open House," attended a meeting of a parent-teacher organization, interviewed another teacher candidate, and interviewed an experienced teacher. All of these experiences will be useful in your assimilation of the content of the next chapter, "What Are the Expectations of Me as a Secondary School Teacher?" But before proceeding to the next chapter, you and your class may wish to study and discuss the following questions related to topics in this chapter.

QUESTIONS FOR CLASS DISCUSSION

1. Do you recall the teacher who influenced you most during your secondary school years? Why do you suppose that teacher had an influence on you? Were the teacher's behaviors similar to or different from those of Ms. Wonderful as discussed earlier in this chapter?

2. From your point of view, what societal influences affect today's secondary schools and students? How?

3. Of the many activities offered in our secondary schools, which may have the strongest positive influence on students?

4. What evidence have you seen to indicate that secondary school students achieve better the longer the school day or year?

5. What do you see as the main goals of our secondary schools today? Did you observe any indication that the school you visited was working successfully toward those goals?

6. Do you support the point of view that junior high school students should be required to pass a basic competency test before they are promoted to a senior high school? What subjects should be included in a basic competency test if such a test were given to students? What grade levels should be tested? What are the current competency test requirements in your state?

7. Reviewing the teaching behaviors that seem to be important for effective teaching, what evidence do you have that some of these teaching behaviors were occurring during your classroom visit?

8. Recalling the points that may guide a principal toward success with a staff, how would you rate a selected, anonymous principal of your choice? Why?

9. Nobody decides to become a teacher in order to become wealthy; however, salaries for teachers in this country have increased approximately 100 percent during the past decade. Have salaries for teachers kept pace with inflation? What salary can you expect as a beginning teacher in your state? A national report, published in 1983, recommended that teachers' salaries in this nation be increased over "the next three years" by 25 percent. Did it happen?

10. The following is quoted from a major task-force report: "Until we pay teachers at least as well as the middle echelon of executives, we cannot expect the profession to attract its full share of the available range of talents. Salaries must be raised immediately and substantially." Does that strong recommendation sound familiar? It came from the Rockefeller Brothers Fund report of 1958, *The Pursuit of Excellence: Education and the Future of America.* Discuss any feelings this leaves you with, with your classmates.

11. Does your teacher education program require any portion of your experience be completed in an elementary school, even though your training is as a secondary single-subject teacher? What is your feeling on this kind of requirement? Why do you suppose in some teacher education programs this is the case?

12. Can you find any research evidence to indicate that your subject *should* be taught in secondary schools? Is it absolutely necessary that your subject be taught in a secondary school? Why?

13. Do you have any other questions generated by the content of this chapter? How might answers be found?

SELECTED READINGS AND REFERENCES FOR CHAPTER 1

Adler, Mortimer J. *Paideia: Problems and Possibilities*. New York: Macmillan Publishing Company, 1983.

———. *The Paideia Proposal*. New York: Macmillan Publishing Company, 1982.

Boyer, Ernest L. *High School: A Report on Secondary Education in America*. New York: Harper & Row, Pub., Inc., 1983.

Brooks, Douglas M. "The Teacher's Communicative Competence: The First Day of School." *Theory Into Practice*, Vol. 24, No. 1 (Winter 1985), pp. 63-70.

Center for National Policy. *Educating Our Citizens: The Search for Excellence*. Alternatives for the 1980s, No. 9. Washington, DC: Center for National Policy, 1983.

Clark, Burton R. "The High School and the University: What Went Wrong in America, Part 2." *Phi Delta Kappan*, Vol. 66, No. 7 (March 1985), pp. 472-475.

Cleland, Charles C., and Jon D. Swartz. *Exceptionalities Through the Lifespan*. New York: Macmillan Publishing Company, 1982.

Csikszentmihalyi, Mihaly, and Jane McCormack. "The Influence of Teachers." *Phi Delta Kappan*, Vol. 67, No. 6 (February 1986), pp. 415-419.

Doyle, Denis P., and Marsha Levine. "Magnet Schools: Choice and Quality in Public Education." *Phi Delta Kappan*, Vol. 66, No. 4 (December 1984), pp. 265-270.

Evertson, Carolyn M., and Edmund T. Emmer. "Effective Management at the Beginning of the School Year in Junior High Classes." *Journal of Educational Research*, Vol. 74, No. 4 (August 1982), pp. 485-498.

Feistritzer, Emily. *The Conditions of Teaching: A State-by-State Analysis*. Princeton, NJ: Princeton University Press, 1983.

Furth, H. *Piaget and Knowledge: Theoretical Foundations*. Chicago: University of Chicago Press, 1981.

Good, T. L. "Teacher Expectations and Student Perceptions: A Decade of Research." *Educational Leadership*, Vol. 38, No. 5 (February 1981), pp. 415-421.

Goodlad, John I. *A Place Called School: Promise for the Future*. New York: McGraw-Hill Book Co., 1983.

Hart, Verna. *Mainstreaming Children with Special Needs*. New York: Longman, Inc., 1981.

Hirschman, Penny. "A Principal's 'Perfect 10' for Staff Success." *Reading '83*, Vol. 1, No. 1 (August 1983), p. 7.

Keegan, R. *The Evolving Self*. Cambridge, MA: Harvard University Press, 1982.

Litt, Mark D., and Dennis C. Turk. "Sources of Stress and Dissatisfaction in Experienced High School Teachers." *Journal of Educational Research*, Vol. 78, No. 3 (January-February 1985), pp. 178-185.

Reilly, Robert R., and Ernest L. Lewis. *Educational Psychology: Applications for Classroom Learning and Instruction*. New York: Macmillan Publishing Company, 1983.

Robinson, Thomas E. "The Waldtopia School System: A Program for Secondary Schools, 1985." *Phi Delta Kappan*, Vol. 61, No. 7 (March 1980), p. 465.

Sizer, Theodore R. *Horace's Compromise: The Dilemma of the American High School*. Boston: Houghton Mifflin Company, 1984.

Stedman, Lawrence C., and Carl F. Kaestle. "The Test Score Decline Is Over: Now What?" *Phi Delta Kappan*, Vol. 67, No. 3 (November 1985), pp. 204-210.

Wadsworth, Barry J. *Piaget's Theory of Cognitive and Affective Development*, 3rd ed. New York: Longman, 1984.

What Are the Expectations of a Secondary School Teacher?

As a secondary school teacher your professional responsibilities will extend beyond those important ones of working in the classroom from 8:30 a.m. until 3:00 p.m. In this chapter we will guide you through the reality of those responsibilities as they exist today.

A. ABOUT THE CODE OF ETHICS

What do the words "to follow the code of ethics" or "to be ethical" mean? Do they mean to be honorable in your professional actions? virtuous? moral? decent, equitable, and just? Some educators consider the words to mean to portray, as closely as possible, an ideal educator, or to practice certain moral principles inherent in educational pursuits. Others see the terms as meaning to conform to professional standards of conduct. Still others believe they are a way to describe an educator's relationship to action—or performance.

You will see that all of these aspects—the aspects of portrayal, of professionalism, and of performance—stand out in the following code of ethics for the education profession, a code often printed on the reverse side of a teaching credential. The two sections of the code guide your pledge to the students and to the profession.

CODE OF ETHICS OF THE EDUCATION PROFESSION[1]

Preamble

The educator, believing in the worth and dignity of each human being, recognizes the supreme importance of the pursuit of truth, devotion to excellence, and the nurture of

[1] Code of Ethics of the Education Profession, National Education Association, 1975. Reprinted by permission.

democratic principles. Essential to these goals is the protection of freedom to learn and to teach and the guarantee of equal educational opportunity for all. The educator accepts the responsibility to adhere to the highest ethical standards.

The educator recognizes the magnitude of the responsibility inherent in the teaching process. The desire for the respect and confidence of one's colleagues, of students, of parents, and of the members of the community provides the incentive to attain and maintain the highest possible degree of ethical conduct. The Code of Ethics of the Education Profession indicates the aspiration of all educators and provides standards by which to judge conduct.

The remedies specified by the NEA and/or its affiliates for the violation of any provision of this Code shall be exclusive and no such provision shall be enforceable in any form other than one specifically designated by the NEA or its affiliates.

PRINCIPLE I—COMMITMENT TO THE STUDENT

The educator strives to help each student realize his or her potential as a worthy and effective member of society. The educator therefore works to stimulate the spirit of inquiry, the acquisition of knowledge and understanding, and the thoughtful formulation of worthy goals.

In fulfillment of the obligation to the student, the educator—

1. Shall not unreasonably restrain the student from independent action in the pursuit of learning.
2. Shall not unreasonably deny the student access to varying points of view.
3. Shall not deliberately suppress or distort subject matter relevant to the student's progress.
4. Shall make reasonable effort to protect the student from conditions harmful to learning or to health and safety.
5. Shall not intentionally expose the student to embarrassment or disparagement.
6. Shall not on the basis of race, color, creed, sex, national origin, marital status, political or religous beliefs, family, social or cultural background, or sexual orientation, unfairly:
   a. Exclude any student from participation in any program;
   b. Deny benefits to any student;
   c. Grant any advantage to any student.
7. Shall not use professional relationships with students for private advantage.
8. Shall not disclose information about students obtained in the course of professional service, unless disclosure serves a compelling professional purpose or is required by law.

PRINCIPLE II—COMMITMENT TO THE PROFESSION

The education profession is vested by the public with a trust and responsibility requiring the highest ideals of professional service.

In the belief that the quality of the services of the education profession directly influences the nation and its citizens, the educator shall exert every effort to raise professional standards, to promote a climate that encourages the exercise of professional judgment, to achieve conditions which attract persons worthy of the trust to careers in education, and to assist in preventing the practice of the profession by unqualified persons.

In fulfillment of the obligation to the profession, the educator—

1. Shall not in an application for a professional position deliberately make a false statement or fail to disclose a material fact related to competency and qualifications.
2. Shall not misrepresent his/her professional qualifications.

3. Shall not assist entry into the profession of a person known to be unqualified in respect to character, education, or other relevant attribute.
4. Shall not knowingly make a false statement concerning the qualifications of a candidate for a professional position.
5. Shall not assist a noneducator in the unauthorized practice of teaching.
6. Shall not disclose information about colleagues obtained in the course of professional service unless disclosure serves a compelling professional purpose or is required by law.
7. Shall not knowingly make false or malicious statements about a colleague.
8. Shall not accept any gratuity, gift, or favor that might impair or appear to influence professional decisions or actions.

B. ABOUT INSTRUCTIONAL RESPONSIBILITIES

The aspects of portrayal, of professionalism, and of performance take on a very real shape when you consider the instructional related and the noninstructional related responsibilities in secondary teaching.

What Are Some of the Instructional Responsibilities I Will Meet?

The following checklist of questions introduces you to the instructional responsibilities you will have as a secondary teacher. Ask yourself these questions:

1. Have I allotted time each day for planning the daily lessons that are needed?
2. Have I made arrangements for reading papers and for evaluating the papers?
3. Do I take the time to record the necessary grades in the teacher's record book?
4. Do I realize the importance of preparing my classroom for my planned instruction?
5. Do I acknowledge the actual time I spend or devote to classroom instruction?
6. Am I aware of the time I need to devote to professional growth and development that will improve my instruction?
   a. Do I attend courses from a nearby college or university?
   b. Do I attend workshops and presentations offered by the school district or other professional organizations?
   c. Do I read professional journals, magazines, and newspapers?
7. Have I arranged time for preparing all of the materials I will need for my lessons?
8. Have I incorporated my philosophy of education into a "firm but fair" classroom management system?
9. Have I prepared long-range and short-term lesson plans?
10. Have I developed my classroom policies?
11. Am I familiar with the developmental characteristics of this age level?
12. Am I familiar with the background of youngsters with behavior or personality problems, who might cause concerns in the learning environment of the classroom?

C. ABOUT NONINSTRUCTIONAL RESPONSIBILITIES

What Are Some of the Noninstructional Responsibilities I Will Meet?

The following questions will focus your thoughts on the many noninstructional responsibilities you will meet during your first year of teaching. Ask yourself these questions:

1. Am I familiar with the school building and the campus?
2. Do I take the time to become acquainted with the teaching staff and with the nonteaching staff?
3. Am I aware of school and district policies?
4. Am I knowledgeable about the background of all my students?
5. Am I familiar with the community that is served by the school?
6. Am I knowledgeable about such routine procedures as
    a. before-and-after-school events?
    b. restroom regulations?
    c. distribution and collection of school materials and books?
    d. dismissal procedures?
    e. ordering supplies?
    f. established fire-drill routines?
    g. recording daily attendance, tardiness, and absences?
    h. procedures during assemblies?
    i. school and district policies regarding classroom conduct?
7. Have I thought about classroom duties?
    a. Do I maintain a cheerful, pleasant overall classroom environment?
    b. Do I open and close classroom windows as needed?
    c. Do I prepare or locate needed materials and/or supplies for each lesson for each day?
    d. Do I keep the teaching supplies orderly?
    e. Do I clean the chalkboard during the day, as needed?
8. Do I anticipate the many conferences that will be needed, such as between:
    a. teacher and teacher?
    b. teacher and student?
    c. teacher and parent?
    d. teacher and administrator?
9. Have I acknowledged the hours needed for professional meetings, such as
    a. faculty meetings?
    b. other school meetings or committee meetings?
    c. parent-teacher meetings?
    d. meetings and conferences and workshops sponsored by the local, regional, state, and federal professional organizations?

Now that you have reviewed these checklists of questions, turn your attention to the total role of a first-year teacher.

A major continuing role of the teacher is maintaining an awareness of the quality of the interaction within the classroom. Regardless of technological developments of the past 50 years the teacher is still the director of learning, and that learning is dependent upon the quality of classroom interactions. Many times in this resource guide we focus on various aspects of that interaction.

D. SUMMARIZING THE EXPECTATIONS OF A SECONDARY SCHOOL TEACHER

The following list of instructional and noninstructional responsibilities is by no means exhaustive; it does represent the kinds of activities that can exhaust a teacher. Many of these tasks are unavoidable and absolutely necessary for each teacher to perform; others are negotiable. The beginning teacher must first concentrate on the classroom instruction, then move cautiously into those other necessary but more or less optional kinds of activities. Study the list, then proceed with Exercise 2.1, which follows.

A. Responsibilities related to *housekeeping* functions:
   1. Attendance checking and reporting.
   2. Preparation of budget and schedules.
   3. Ordering, using, and maintaining audiovisual materials and equipment.
   4. Ordering, using, and maintaining textbook and curriculum materials and supplies.
B. Responsibilities related to *advising, supervision, and sponsorship.*
   5. Supervision of halls, cafeteria, and student assemblies.
   6. Supervision of homerooms and/or activity periods.
   7. Supervision of intramural contests.
   8. Advising and sponsoring student clubs.
   9. Advising and sponsoring plays, concerts, graduation exercises, and other events and productions.
  10. Advising and sponsoring student government.
  11. Support of the athletic program (e.g., ticket seller or ticket taker, scorer, supervision of stands at ball game, record keeper).
  12. Sponsoring and arranging for guest speaker and campus visitors.
  13. Advising, guiding, and counseling of students.
  14. Responsibility for student safety.
  15. Chaperoning student dances, bus trips, and other student activities.
C. Responsibilities related to *school-community* activities:
  16. Attendance and participation at parent-teacher association meetings.
  17. Attendance and participation in community events.
  18. Support of local bond issues.
  19. Parent conferences.
  20. Representing the school at social gatherings.
  21. Establishing rapport with other adults (e.g., administrators, teachers, paraprofessionals, clerical and custodial staff).
D. Responsibilities related to *professional* activities:
  22. School and district-wide committee work.
  23. Continued study and development in your field.
  24. Support of professional associations—local, state, and national.
  25. Responsibility to professional Code of Ethics.
E. Responsibilities related to *instructional* activities:
  26. Preparation for daily instruction (e.g., long-range planning, daily lesson planning).
  27. Reading and evaluating student work.
  28. Preparing classroom for daily instruction.
  29. Giving your own "think time" about individual students in your classes.
  30. Private consultation time with individual students (e.g., before or after school hours).

EXERCISE 2.1: THE LIFE OF A TEACHER

The educational purpose of this exercise is to assist you in furthering your understanding that teaching is a full-time job. One 24-hour day in the life of a teacher can be safely divided into four categories: time spent in actual classroom instruction; time spent in reading papers, preparing lessons, and generally readying for classes; time spent in the myriad of noninstructional responsibilities; time spent in your own personal life functions.

Instructions: have your class divide into small groups and ask each group to discuss and predict how much of a *beginning teacher's* time is spent in each of the items listed in the chart that follows. Compare your group's predictions with those of the other groups. Visit some teachers and ask them to estimate the time spent in each of the areas, then compare what they say with your group predictions. How similar, how different?

CHART FOR EXERCISE 2.2

Estimated Number of Hours Spent
in One Seven-Day Week

A. *Time spent in clerical and maintenance functions*
    1. attendance checking and reporting . . . . _____
    2. preparation of budgets and schedules . . . . _____
    3. ordering, using, and maintaining AV materials
        and equipment . . . . _____
    4. ordering, using, and maintaining textbook and
        curriculum materials and supplies . . . . _____
    4a. other (specify) . . . . _____

B. *Time spent advising, supervising, sponsoring*
    5. supervision of halls, cafeteria, assemblies . . . . _____
    6. supervision of homerooms and activity periods . . . . . . _____
    7. supervision of intramural contests . . . . _____
    8. advising and sponsoring plays, concerts, other
        events and productions . . . . _____
    9. advising and sponsoring student government . . . . _____
    10. support of athletic program (e.g., ticket taker,
        supervision, serving as scorer) . . . . _____
    11. sponsoring and arranging for guest speakers and
        campus visitors . . . . _____
    12. advising, guiding, and counseling of students . . . . _____
    13. responsibility for student safety . . . . _____
    14. chaperoning student dances and bus trips . . . . _____
    15. other (specify) . . . . _____

C. *Time spent in school-community activities*
    16. attendance-participation at PTA . . . . _____
    17. attendance-participation in community events . . . . _____
    18. supporting local bond issues . . . . _____
    19. parent conferences . . . . _____
    20. representing the school at social gatherings . . . . _____

21.   establishing rapport with other adults (e.g., administrators, teachers, paraprofessionals, clerical and
custodial staff) .... _____

21a.   other (specify) .... _____

D.   *Time spent in professional activities*

22.   school and district-wide committee work .... _____

23.   continued study and development in your field ...... _____

24.   support of professional associations—local, state,
and national .... _____

25.   responsibility to professional Code of Ethics .... _____

25a.   other (specify) .... _____

E.   *Time spent in instructional activities*

26.   preparation *and implementation* of daily
instruction .... _____

27.   reading and grading student work .... _____

28.   preparing classroom .... _____

29.   giving time for individual students outside of
regular class time .... _____

29a.   other (specify) .... _____

Total hours per week = _____

We estimate an approximate average of 52 hours per week. How do your averages compare?

In this chapter, you reviewed the instructional related and noninstructional related responsibilities facing a beginning secondary school teacher. In the next chapter we focus on the identification of teaching styles.

QUESTIONS FOR CLASS DISCUSSION

1. How do you now feel about being a secondary school teacher—motivated, excited, enthusiastic, befuddled, confused, depressed? Explain and discuss your current feelings with your classmates. Sort out common concerns or anxieties, and design avenues for correcting any negative attitudes or feelings you might have.
2. Which instructional responsibilities excite you the most? Which concern you most?
3. Which noninstructional responsibilities interest you most? Which frighten you most?
4. About a quarter of a century ago a publication entitled *Six Areas of Teacher Competence*[2] detailed six roles of the teacher: director of learning, counselor and guidance worker, mediator of the culture, link with the community, member of the school staff, and member of the profession. Are all of these of equal importance for the secondary school teacher of today?
5. Teaching involves interaction between teacher and students, but most research studies in this area have been limited to observations of the teacher while working with the entire class. Teachers frequently work with individuals or small groups of students. What research can you find that has studied the interaction of the teacher with individual students or with students in small groups?
6. How possibly can failure be viewed by a student as positive feedback?
7. Is it possible for a teacher to be sending two separate and contradictory messages to a student? If so, what are the ramifications for teacher education?
8. When should and can "controlled silence" be used by a teacher?
9. Teachers' use of strong praise to an individual within a group should be used sparingly and for specific content-related matters. Why do you suppose this is the case?
10. What other questions would you like to have discussed? How might answers be found?

SELECTED READINGS AND REFERENCES FOR CHAPTER 2

Feistritzer, Emily. *The Conditions of Teaching: A State-by-State Analysis*. Princeton, NJ: Princeton University Press, 1983.

Flanders, Ned A. *Analyzing Teaching Behavior*. Reading, MA: Addison-Wesley Publishing Co. Inc., 1970.

Reilly, Robert R., and Ernest L. Lewis. *Educational Psychology: Applications for Classroom Learning and Instruction*. New York: Macmillan Publishing Company, 1983.

Segal, J. W., S. F. Chipman, and R. Glaser, eds. *Thinking and Learning Skills, Volume I: Relating Instruction to Research*. Hillsdale, NJ: Lawrence Erlbaum Associates, 1985.

Smith, Howard A. "The Marking of Transitions by More and Less Effective Teachers." *Theory Into Practice*, Vol. 24, No. 1 (Winter 1985), pp. 57-62.

[2] California Teachers Association, "Six Areas of Teacher Competencies." Burlingame, CA, 1964.

3

How Do I Develop a Teaching Style?

You will hear teaching styles (teachers' distinctive mannerisms, behaviors, and methods) described by secondary teachers and teacher candidates in a variety of ways. While sitting in the teachers' lounge at a nearby school, one teacher candidate hears teachers describe their teaching styles to one another with an emphasis on *the way they instruct*. This teacher candidate hears about

- A discussion style.
- A lecture style.
- An inquiry style.
- A discovery style.
- A social interaction style.

Another teacher candidate tells you that teaching styles can be described *from a contrastive point of view* and says these are some of the definitive contrasts the candidate has found from several readings:

- An integrative style versus a dominative style.
- A democratic style versus an autocratic style.
- A student-centered style versus a teacher-centered style.
- A progressive style versus a traditional style.
- An informal style versus a formal style.
- An indirect style versus a direct style.
- A didactic style versus an inquiry style.

Still another teacher candidate mentions hearing of teaching styles being identified by *categories,* and describes these examples:

- A behavior-modification style.
- A social-interaction style.
- An informational-processing style.
- A personal-source style.

There have been pages and pages in volume after volume devoted to research that investigates these various styles of teaching. Where do teaching styles come from and what does research have to tell us about what is an appropriate style for teaching?

That question is what we will help you with as you progress through this chapter.

A.   WHAT IS THE SOURCE OF ONE'S TEACHING STYLE?

Teaching styles develop from tradition, research, and personal experience. Each style is based on certain philosophical and psychological assumptions about children and their development, complemented by the teacher's own personality characteristics.

Although it is beyond the scope of our intent to explore deeply into the philosophy and psychology of educational learning theories we will share with you what we consider to be three major theoretical positions and recent research findings that may help you better understand the basis of your own emerging teaching style.

B.   WHAT ARE THE BASIC THEORETICAL POSITIONS THAT DETERMINE TEACHING STYLE?

Each of the three positions that follows is based upon certain assumptions. Each suggests different ways of working with students. We believe that most teachers today use a style that is an amalgamation of these three positions. "Traditional education as practiced in the United States . . . . is rooted in the concept that the job of education is the direct transmission of bodies of information, skills, and the value of the culture to the child."[1] It is our belief that this traditional approach stems from these assumptions:

1. That the learner's mind is neutral-passive to good-active and that the main focus in teaching should be the addition of new ideas to a subconscious mental store of old ones (tied to the theoretical position of *Romanticism-Maturationism*).
2. That the learner's mind is neutral-passive with innate reflexes and needs, and the main focus in teaching should be successive, systematic changes in the learner's environment to increase the possibilities of desired behavioral responses (tied to the theoretical position of *Behaviorism*).
3. That the learner is a neutral-interactive purposive individual in simultaneous interaction with his/her physical and biological environments, and the main focus in teaching should be to facilitate the learner's gaining of new perceptions which then lead to desired behavioral changes, and that ultimately lead to the learner's becoming a more self-realized individual (tied to the theoretical position of *Cognitive-Experimentalism*).

If we are correct in what we have said about teachers today using a combination of thought from three separate theoretical positions, then indeed each teacher's style will likely be eclectic. But, before continuing that line of thought let's take a closer look at the three theoretical positions.

---

[1] From Barry J. Wadsworth, *Piaget's Theory of Cognitive and Affective Development,* 3rd ed., p. 215. Copyright © 1971, 1979, 1984 by Longman Inc. Reprinted by permission of Longman, Inc., New York.

THREE THEORETICAL POSITIONS

Position	Assumptions	Key Persons
Romanticism-Maturationism	Development is genetically determined, although it can be arrested by experience. "What comes from within the child is the most important aspect of development; therefore, the pedagogical (educational) environment should be permissive enough to allow the inner 'good' to unfold and the inner 'bad' to come under control."[2]	Jean Jacques Rousseau Sigmund Freud Maria Montessori
Essentialism-Behaviorism-Connectionism	"The mind is a machine and there are environmental 'inputs' and behavioral 'outputs'—the environment is responsible for development."[3] "Learning, due to its nature, involves hard work and often unwilling application."[4] "The initiative in education should lie with the teacher rather than the pupil."[5] "The heart of the educational process is the absorption of prescribed subject matter."[6] "The school should retain traditional methods of mental discipline."[7] (This last one is a carry-over from older theories connected with Plato and Aristotle.)	John Locke Ivan Pavlov B. F. Skinner A. H. Thorndike John Watson
Cognitive-Experimentalism	"Mental development is the product of the interaction of the learner and the environment and the learner plays a major role in his/her own development, which is neither fixed by genetics nor completely controlled by external factors."[8] "Education should be related directly to the interests of the child."[9] "Learning through problem solving should replace inculcation of subject matter."[10] "Education should be life itself rather than a preparation for living."[11] "The teacher's role is not to direct but to advise."[12] "The school should encourage cooperation rather than competition."[13]	John Dewey Jerome Bruner Jean Piaget Arthur W. Combs

[2] Ibid., p. 215.
[3] Ibid., p. 215.
[4] Lloyd Duck, *Teaching With Charisma* (Boston: Allyn and Bacon, 1981), p. 46. Reprinted by permission.
[5] Ibid., p. 47.
[6] Ibid., p. 48.
[7] Ibid., p. 49.
[8] Wadsworth, op. cit., p. 216.
[9-13] Duck, op. cit., pp. 77, 79, 81, 82, 83 respectively.

Emerging from these basic theoretical positions are a variety of theories of learning.[14] The educational philosophies and practices of many teachers and administrators include suggestions from more than one learning theory, sometimes contradictory in nature. It could be a problem for a student teacher or a new teacher if her/his educational style did not match with the philosophy/ practice of the school where he/she had been assigned.

It is our belief that a competent teacher develops a teaching style that is consistent with her/his own personal assumptions about children and learning.[15] Indeed, that style might well be eclectic. Our own position as we have taught and as we have prepared this resource guide is to provide an eclectic approach with a bent toward Cognitive-Experimentalism with its greater emphasis on divergent thinking. But before exploring this further let us now turn your attention to Exercise 3.1, which is designed to help you develop a profile of your own philosophical position.

[14] See Morris L. Bigge, "Theories of Learning," *NEA Journal,* Vol. 55, No. 3 (March 1966), pp. 18-19.
[15] For further study of this position we recommend Lloyd Duck, *Teaching With Charisma* (Boston: Allyn and Bacon, 1981).

EXERCISE 3.1: DEVELOPING A PROFILE AND A STATEMENT ABOUT MY OWN TEACHING STYLE

The educational purpose of this exercise is to help you clarify and articulate your own assumptions about teaching and learning. You will develop a profile of your emerging teaching style, and from that, a statement that is representative of your current philosophy about teaching and learning.

Proceed with the following four steps.

Step 1. Read each of the 50 statements and rate your feeling about each, giving a 1 to those with which you strongly agree, a 2 to those for which you feel neutral, and, a 3 to those with which you strongly disagree.[16]

Remember: 1 = agree; 2 = neutral; 3 = disagree

____ 1. Most of what students learn, they learn on their own.

____ 2. Students should be primarily concerned with other students' reactions to their work in the classroom.

____ 3. An important part of schooling is to learn to get along with other people.

____ 4. Students learn more by working on their own than by working with other students.

____ 5. Students should actively participate in all aspects of class planning and implementation.

____ 6. I think that grades are inappropriate in an effective learning environment.

____ 7. Most students seem to enjoy working in a class that has clearly defined learning objectives and evaluative criteria.

____ 8. I favor the use of classroom methods that maximize the student's independence to learn from his/her own experiences.

____ 9. Most of what students learn, they learn from other students.

____ 10. Students should be primarily concerned with getting good grades.

____ 11. An important part of class is to learn how to work in an independent manner.

____ 12. I feel that a teacher should not usually be contradicted by a student in the classroom.

____ 13. I think that an exciting interchange between students and the teacher often provides ideas about content that are better than those in a textbook.

____ 14. In order for students to get the most out of a class, they must be aware of the primary concerns and biases of the teacher.

____ 15. I do not think that students should be given high grades unless they have clearly earned them.

____ 16. A student's learning should help her/him become an independent thinker.

____ 17. Most of what students learn, they learn from their teachers.

____ 18. A teacher who makes students do things they don't want to do is not doing his/her job well.

____ 19. Learning takes place most effectively under conditions in which students are in competition with one another.

____ 20. I feel that a teacher should try to persuade students that particular ideas are valid and exciting.

____ 21. I think students have to be assertive to do well in school.

____ 22. In general, I have found that the facts presented in textbooks are accurate.

____ 23. I favor the use of classroom methods which maximize student-teacher and student-student interaction.

---

[16] This list of statements was adapted by us from William H. Berquist and Steven R. Phillips, *A Handbook for Faculty Development* (Washington, DC: The Council for Independent Colleges, June, 1975), pp. 25-27. Used by permission.

___ 24. Most of what students learn, they learn from books.

___ 25. A teacher who lets students do whatever they want is not doing his/her job well.

___ 26. Students can learn more by working with an exciting teacher than by working by themselves.

___ 27. I favor the use of classroom methods which maximize the student's learning of basic content.

___ 28. The ideas of other students are useful for helping a student understand class material.

___ 29. A student should study what the teacher says is important and not necessarily what is important to himself/herself.

___ 30. A teacher who does not increase the student's interest in subject matter is not doing his/her job well.

___ 31. An important part of education is to learn how to perform under testing and evaluation conditions.

___ 32. Students can learn more by sharing their ideas than by keeping their ideas to themselves.

___ 33. Teachers often give students too many trivial assignments.

___ 34. I think that the ideas contained in a good textbook should be the primary sources of content in a class.

___ 35. I think that students should be given high grades as a means of motivating them and increasing their self-esteem.

___ 36. I think that the ideas a student brings into a class are useful for helping her/him understand material.

___ 37. A student should study what is important to him/her and not necessarily what the teacher says is important.

___ 38. Learning takes place most effectively under conditions in which students are working independently of one another.

___ 39. Teachers often give students too much freedom of choice.

___ 40. I think teachers should clearly state what they expect from students.

___ 41. I think that a student's ideas about content are often better than those in a textbook.

___ 42. In general, I have found that classroom discussions are exciting learning experiences.

___ 43. A student's education should help him/her become a successful member of our society.

___ 44. Learning takes place most effectively under conditions in which students are working cooperatively with one another.

___ 45. Teachers often are too personal with their students.

___ 46. I think a teacher should encourage students to disagree with him/her in a classroom.

___ 47. I think students have to be able to work effectively with other people to do well in school.

___ 48. In order for students to get the most out of school, they must take at least part of the responsibility.

___ 49. Most students seem to enjoy discussing their ideas about learning with the teacher and other students.

___ 50. A student's education should help him/her become a more sensitive human being.

Step 2. From the list of 50 items now write the items in two columns, those with which you held strong agreement in one column, those with which you strongly disagreed in the other column, ignoring those items for which you gave a 2 (neutral).

Step 3. In groups of three or four, discuss your lists (from Step 2) with your classmates. From the discussion you may re-rank any items you wish.

Step 4. You now have a finalized list of those items with which you were in agreement, and those with which you disagreed. Now write a paragraph that summarizes your present philosophy about teaching and learning. It should be no longer than one page in length. This statement is a representation of your present teaching style.

  Compare your statement with the theoretical positions as outlined earlier in this chapter. Can you clearly identify your position? Name it. _____

_____

_____

_____

Reason: _____

_____

_____

_____

  You may wish at the completion of this book (course) to revisit your philosophical statement, perhaps even to make revisions in it. Also, it might be useful to have it firmly implanted in your memory during teaching job interviews at a later date.

C. WHAT DOES RESEARCH OFFER TOWARD THE DEVELOPMENT OF MY TEACHING STYLE?

In the preceding we have reviewed certain theoretical positions that have historically given a philosophical and psychological base to the development of teaching styles. Also affecting a teacher's style are certain teaching variables that have been shown by recent research to have a relationship with student learning. Four of these variables will be discussed now: classroom environment, lesson planning, teaching delivery, and the student. Within each of these there are certain actions that seem to have a *positive* relationship with student achievement.

The *classroom learning environment* in which learning takes place is crucial as the best learning takes place when:

1. The student perceives an involvement and an affiliation with what is happening.
2. The student perceives the teacher as friendly, understanding, and sympathetic.
3. The student perceives that she or he is in a demanding but rewarding learning environment.

Within the category of *lesson planning,* research tells us that the following actions make a positive contribution to student learning:

1. The teacher provides lesson introductions.
2. The teacher provides practice, reinforcement, and review.
3. The teacher provides content-relevant information.
4. The teacher provides advance organizers (links between what the students already know and the material they are about to learn. See Exercise 3.3.).
5. The teacher provides behavioral expectations, i.e., specific learning objectives.

The following actions are positive contributors within the third category—*teaching delivery:*

1. The teacher presents objectives and lessons clearly.
2. The teacher poses questions that are clearly understood.
3. The lessons and the class, as an entity, are well organized.
4. The teacher allows "think-time" and/or "brainstorming time" on the cognitive challenges.
5. The teacher is business-like in classroom behavior.
6. The teacher demonstrates enthusiastic teaching behaviors.
7. The teacher uses gestures and variations in speech inflections.
8. The teacher initiates sincere and low-keyed praise for a student's work.
9. The teacher asks questions frequently and pauses for responses.
10. The teacher provides a variety of questions designed to lead students through higher levels of cognitive thought.
11. The teacher changes his/her teaching style according to the students' learning activities.
12. The teacher is aware that the maximum level of effectiveness for each teaching style will differ according to the students' learning activity.

The fourth and final variable in our discussion is the *student variable.* A major variable affecting teaching style (or that should affect it) is the nature of the learner. Some of the most exciting (to us) research in education today is coming from two, but perhaps related, areas: right/left brain hemispheric research and learning modality preference research. We think that research in these areas is lending further support to our hypothesis that the teacher's best teaching style choice is an eclectic one, at least until the day arrives when students with certain modality strengths are matched with teachers with particular teaching styles. As stated by Dunn et al., "The case for matching learning and teaching styles grows stronger every year . . . many researchers have evidenced that both achievement and attitudes toward school improve significantly when instructional methods or resources complement the way individuals learn."[17]

Historical and traditional education in the United States has shown a "pragmatic bias" toward the rational, logical functioning hemisphere and has tended to "demean" the metaphoric, intuitive half of our brain."[18] It appears that some learners have a right-hemispheric preference (i.e., think in pictures, prefer deductive reasoning) while others have a left-hemispheric preference (i.e., think in words, prefer inductive reasoning).[19] To teach using only one single approach would therefore cheat a portion of the learners who learn better another way. Future research should shed further light on the exact relationship, if any, between hemispheric learning and what we already are beginning to learn about modality strengths.

From the research of Barbe and Milone regarding modality strengths and learning come these findings.[20]

1. Young children enter school with stronger auditory strengths. "When they enter school, however, the situation changes drastically. For much of their waking day, they are expected to use the visual modality (through reading) and the kinesthetic modality (through writing). Teachers suppress audition, sometimes actively, in an effort to maintain an orderly classroom."

2. Children with auditory-oriented strengths do better with the spoken word than with the printed word, and probably do less well on standardized tests, which tend to favor children of mixed or visual modality strengths.

3. A shift in modality strength occurs between kindergarten and sixth grade. "Vision becomes the dominant modality, and kinesthesia overtakes audition."

4. Between late elementary and adulthood another shift takes place as audition becomes more important than kinesthesia, but vision remains dominant.

5. Modality integration (using all three) has been found to contribute to success in reading in the early grades.

6. "There is no difference between the modality characteristics of boys and girls."

7. "Handedness and modality strengths do not seem to be related."

8. Race and modality strengths are independent.

9. Teachers tend to teach the way they learn best (modality strength) but students may have modality strengths different from the teacher. This difference can affect student achievement.

10. Supervisors (i.e., the university supervisor of a student teacher or the principal supervising a teacher) need to be aware that their "perceptions of a teacher's effectiveness may be clouded by their own modality strengths."

Now, considering what you have learned from this chapter, put it to work in an analysis of what you have observed in a real classroom as you proceed with Exercises 3.2 and 3.3.

[17] Rita Dunn, David P. Cavanaugh, Betty M. Eberle, and Robert Zenhausern, "Hemispheric Preference: The Newest Element of Learning Style," *The American Biology Teacher,* Vol. 44, No. 5 (May 1982), p. 291. The National Association of Biology Teachers.

[18] Robert E. Samples, "Are You Teaching Only One Side of the Brain?" *Learning,* Vol. 3, No. 6 (February 1975), p. 25.

[19] Dunn et al., op. cit., p. 291.

[20] Walter B. Barbe and Michael N. Milone, Jr., "What We Know About Modality Strengths," *Educational Leadership,* Vol. 38, No. 5 (February 1981), pp. 378-380.

EXERCISE 3.2: ANALYZING ONE TEACHER, ONE STYLE: TEACHING VARIABLES THAT AFFECT STUDENT ACHIEVEMENT

Return your thoughts to the secondary classroom you visited for Exercise 1.4, "Returning to a Secondary School Classroom." From any of the teaching variables identified in this chapter, note those you observed in action during your visit. Record them in the spaces here and discuss with your class members.

Grade level and subject I visited: _____

Classroom learning environment variables: _____

_____

_____

_____

_____

_____

_____

Lesson planning and delivery variables: _____

_____

_____

_____

_____

_____

_____

_____

Student variables: _____

_____

_____

_____

_____

_____

Could you identify the teacher's teaching style according to the theoretical positions discussed in this chapter? Which and why? _____

_____

_____

_____

_____

EXERCISE 3.3: ANALYZING ADVANCE ORGANIZERS AS USED BY A TEACHER DURING MY CLASSROOM OBSERVATION

This exercise may be completed concurrently with Exercises 1.4 and 3.2.

Advance organizers are the links a teacher makes between material that students already know and that they are about to learn—techniques for introducing new material and helping students learn it either by arranging the material and providing key concepts and terms (an *expository organizer*), or by helping students see similarities and differences between what they already know and what they are about to learn (a *comparative organizer*).

Your educational purpose in this exercise is to observe a teacher and how that teacher introduces new material. Record the advance organizer used and identify whether it was an expository organizer or a comparative organizer.

Share your observations with students in your class who are in the same discipline area.

Grade level and subject I visited: _____

Advance organizer(s) observed and type(s): _____

_____

_____

_____

_____

_____

_____

_____

_____

_____

_____

_____

_____

_____

_____

_____

_____

_____

_____

_____

_____

In this chapter we have defined "teaching style" as meaning *the teacher's distinctive mannerisms complemented by the teacher's choice of classroom teaching behaviors and methods.* We stated that a teacher's style develops from tradition, research, and from personal experiences, and we illustrated the philosophical and psychological origins of that tradition and discussed some of the most recent research findings.

Many variables affect a teacher's style, some of which we know little about. In this chapter we discussed certain of these variables—learning environment variables, delivery variables, student and teacher modality strengths, and hemispheric preferences—all of which to us seem to indicate that the competent secondary school teacher today needs an eclectic style to effectively reach all of the students. But that is our bias. While research continues, teachers must teach. We hope that they do it with "style."

The next chapter is designed to help you identify some of your teaching skills and weaknesses, an important step in the development of your own teaching style.

QUESTIONS FOR CLASS DISCUSSION

1. Have educational researchers been able to provide a definitive answer to the question, "Which teaching style is most effective in helping students increase their academic achievement?"
2. If a certain teaching style correlates with student achievement, can we conclude that this teaching style causes this greater achievement?
3. What environmental variables can teachers use to improve their teaching effectiveness? How?
4. Is an eclectic style a legitimate teaching style? How would you define and characterize such a style?
5. What do you think "business-like" in the classroom means?
6. What teaching variables do you think might be *destructive* to the learning process? Why?
7. Teachers tend to teach the way they learn best, but is that the way they *should* teach?
8. What recent research can you find to add to the information in this chapter regarding hemispheric preferences? about modality strengths and preferences?
9. Is hemisphericity more or less important to teaching/learning in your specific teaching field? Why?
10. What questions do you have? How might answers be found?

SELECTED READINGS AND REFERENCES FOR CHAPTER 3

Barbe, Walter B., and Michael N. Milone, Jr. "What We Know About Modality Strengths." *Educational Leadership,* Vol. 38, No. 5 (February 1981), pp. 372-375.

Crossett, Betty. "Using Both Halves of the Brain to Teach the Whole Child." *Social Education,* Vol. 47, No. 4 (April 1983), pp. 266-269.

Davis, Dorothy S., and Phyllis Chasson. "Style-A Manner of Thinking." *Educational Leadership,* Vol. 38, No. 5 (February 1981), pp. 376-377.

Haglund, Elaine. "A Closer Look at the Brain as Related to Teachers and Learners." *Peabody Journal of Education,* Vol. 58, No. 4 (July 1981), pp. 225-234.

Johnson, Virginia R. "Myelin and Maturation: A Fresh Look at Piaget." *The Science Teacher,* Vol. 49, No. 3 (March 1982), pp. 41-49.

Kane, Martin. "Cognitive Styles of Thinking and Learning: Part One." *Academic Therapy,* Vol. 19, No. 5 (May 1984), pp. 527-536.

Myers, John T. "Hemisphericity Research: An Overview with Some Implications for Problem Solving." *Journal of Creative Behavior,* Vol. 16, No. 3 (Third Quarter 1982), pp. 197-211.

Stellern, John, Mike Marlowe, and Ace Cossairt. "Cognitive Mode and Classroom Behavior." *Psychology in the Schools,* Vol. 21, No. 1 (January 1984), pp. 103-111.

Sylwester, Robert, Jeanne S. Chall, M. C. Wittrock, and Leslie A. Hart. "Symposium: Educational Implications of Recent Brain Research." *Educational Leadership,* Vol. 39, No. 1 (October 1981), pp. 6-15.

Webb, Gertrude M. "Left/Right Brains, Teammates in Learning." *Exceptional Children,* Vol. 49, No. 6 (April 1983), pp. 508-515.

Yellin, David. "Left Brain, Right Brain, Super Brain: The Holistic Model." *Reading World,* Vol. 23, No. 1 (October 1983), pp. 36-44.

4

What Are My Current Skills and Weaknesses?

Throughout this text we identify and discuss teacher competencies. The following is a compilation of those characteristics we believe to be most important for teacher competence. Some of these are addressed in this text; others are beyond its parameters. We suggest that you compile your own list as you go through this course and, with the help of exercises such as Exercise 4.1, 17.3, and 19.2, keep an account of how you are doing in building your competencies.

Characteristics of the Competent Teacher[1]

We believe that the competent teacher:

1. Has a comfortable understanding of the subject matter.
2. Understands the process of learning.
3. Is an "educational broker," knows where and how to find information.
4. Practices modeling behaviors, behaviors consistent with his/her beliefs.
5. Is open to change, and willing to take risks and to be held accountable.
6. Is aware of his/her changing and emerging style.
7. Has a developing understanding of the dynamics of behavioral change (learning).
8. Is unbiased and unprejudiced with regard to race, color, creed, national origin, or sex.
9. Plans thoroughly, is resourceful, creative, and motivating.
10. Is protective of the health and safety of students.
11. Is optimistic and hopeful.
12. Continues to develop a strategy repertoire.

[1] The list of 20 competencies may be substituted by a list of teacher competencies from your own local district, college, university, or state.

13. Is skillful and fair in assessment of learning.
14. Is skillful in working with colleagues and parents.
15. Provides a constructive and positive environment for learning.
16. Has a continued interest in professional responsibilities and opportunities.
17. Maintains ethical standards in professional relationships.
18. Has a wide range of interests, including those activities of students.
19. Has a wide range of coping skills.
20. Maintains a sense of humor.

A. SELF-EVALUATION ASSISTANCE: IDENTIFYING MY OWN COMPETENCIES

No matter what grade level or what subject you want to teach, it is important to find out how much you know about yourself. This will help you (1) understand your students better in dealing with them, (2) understand your colleagues better in working with them, and (3) help beginning teachers prepare better for a job interview. For these purposes let us begin with a personal assessment of yourself and share it with others in the class with respect to your secondary school teaching skills (proceed with Exercises 4.1 and 4.2).

B. SUPERVISING ASSISTANCE: MEETING MY SUPERVISOR

When is the supervisor coming? Is the supervisor going to be here today? Do you perceive a university or a college supervisor's observation of your teaching as a pleasant experience or a painful one? Do you realize that classroom observations of your teaching continue during your beginning years of teaching? Being observed and evaluated doesn't have to be a painful, nerve-racking experience for you! And no—you don't have to become a bundle of raw nerve endings when you realize the supervisor is coming to see you.

In fact, some teacher education programs, cooperatively with school districts, have developed their practice teaching around a *clinical supervision* model: the essence of such a model is that supervision of practice teaching is a collegial process, involving the student teacher, the cooperating teacher, and the college or university supervisor, in a triad. The members of this triad are involved together in a preobservation planning conference, observation of the practice teaching, a cooperative analysis of the observational data, feedback conferencing, and finally, an analysis of the cycle. There are usually a minimum of five such cycles during the course of a semester of practice teaching.

Research data are inconclusive about the ultimate benefits of clinical supervision over the traditional approach to supervision (with its greater emphasis on the evaluative aspect), but preservice teachers seem to prefer the more direct approach of traditional supervision. As inservice teachers prefer clinical supervision because of its collegial, rather than evaluative, focus, many school districts have developed their own versions of clinical supervision for the continued skill development of their teachers. Whichever the approach within your own program, the suggestions that follow on page 65 may help you to turn supervision visits into useful, professionally satisfying experiences.

EXERCISE 4.1: MY FIRST SELF-EVALUATION: WHAT DOES IT TELL ME?

Your educational purpose for this exercise is to read the list of skills of the competent secondary teacher and indicate your own level for each. You will see a scale of I through V to the right of each skill. If you mark "I," you are indicating that this skill is one you will be able to accomplish or portray in a secondary school teaching environment; if you mark "V," you are saying that this is a skill that may be a difficult one for you. There is a scale from I through V, so you may sometimes mark "III," indicating that at this particular time, you believe you are some distance from making a judgment about that particular skill. Marking these skills may generate new thoughts in your mind about secondary teaching. Later, when you have completed the list, share those thoughts with your classmates.

IDENTIFYING THE SKILLS OF THE COMPETENT SECONDARY TEACHER

	I can do this.		I may find this difficult to do.		

The Classroom Environment Variables:

1. I am able to help each student perceive that he or she is involved in my classroom and is affiliated with the teaching-learning activity. I II III IV V
2. I am able to help each student perceive that she or he is in a challenging yet satisfying learning environment. I II III IV V

The Lesson Planning Variables:

3. I am able to provide lesson introductions. I II III IV V
4. I allow time to review during my lessons. I II III IV V
5. I provide content-relevant information during my lessons. I II III IV V
6. I plan behavioral, or performance, objectives. I II III IV V
7. I include mental, or advance organizers about the lesson. I II III IV V
8. I can design lessons that require critical thinking. I II III IV V

The Teaching-Delivery Variables:

9. I present the aims (goals, objectives) for my lessons quite clearly. I II III IV V
10. I ask questions that are quite clear. I II III IV V
11. My lessons and the class as an entity are well-organized. I II III IV V
12. I allow "think-time" for the cognitive challenges that appear during my lessons. I II III IV V
13. I am businesslike in my classroom teaching behavior. I II III IV V
14. Although businesslike, I exhibit stimulating teaching behavior. I II III IV V
15. I use gestures and variations in speech inflections. I II III IV V
16. I provide sincere, teacher-initiated praise. I II III IV V
17. I ask questions frequently. I II III IV V
18. I ask questions that lead toward improved student responses. I II III IV V
19. I ask a variety of questions, questions that require different cognitive levels of thought from students. I II III IV V
20. I formulate and ask questions that give students practice in developing their reasoning skills. I II III IV V

EXERCISE 4.2: MY FIRST SELF-EVALUATION: HOW CAN IT HELP ME?

Your first self-evaluation will assist you in discussing competencies.

Now that you have completed marking the list of skills (Exercise 4.1), share your thoughts about the skills with other teacher candidates in your class.

Your first self-evaluation will provide information about your competency development.

After sharing your thoughts with others, return to the list of skills, and reread all the statements you checked with a "I" and then take a few minutes to generalize your thoughts about these statements and write your generalizations in a short paragraph. This paragraph will reflect your most competent areas and/or skills in secondary teaching. Now return to the list and reread all the statements you marked with a "V." Form your thoughts into a second paragraph, one that indicates what you may need to work on during your time in a teacher-education program.

_____

_____

_____

_____

_____

_____

Your first self-evaluation will assist in planning your agenda.

In Exercise 4.1, identify the skills that you marked with a "V," a mark that signifies that this skill might be difficult for you. Select one. Do you believe you will be able to learn this skill? Or do you believe that this skill is an inborn one? If this skill is one that you will be able to learn, or develop, what class activities would you suggest for this course to assist you in developing this skill?

_____

_____

_____

_____

_____

_____

Your first self-evaluation will assist you in future evaluations.

You can duplicate this checklist. Select a calendar date at midterm, and, during your final week, duplicate this checklist and remark the skills again. Compare your midterm list and your final list with this first self-evaluation. What growth did you make in your teaching skills? Yes, you can check yourself with this list as often as you wish. Your first self-evaluation form will give you helpful feedback about your growth in competency development, any time you want to use it!

What to Do Before the Supervisor Arrives

You may not know when your supervisor is going to visit your class, and if such is the case you can be assured that on the day you are visited Murphy's Law will apply: if anything can go wrong, it will! The best way to forestall unfortunate events during your supervisor's visit is for you to *always plan well* your lessons for each day, and do so *with the guidance* of your cooperating teacher. Plan each and every lesson with the help and approval of your cooperating teacher. Here are some more hints.

- Always plan well, using your best choice of teaching strategies.
- Plan a neat, orderly classroom.
- Practice the use of any media equipment prior to class so that you won't falter when using the equipment during your teaching.
- Use an overhead projector rather than the chalkboard. Its use will help keep your nerves calmer, and you will retain more eye contact with your students.
- If, in the past, your supervisor has targeted some of your weak skill areas, plan to demonstrate growth in those teaching skills.
- Make sure your students are aware of potential visitors to the classroom and of the purpose of those visits.

What to Do During the Supervisor's Visit

Some supervisors choose to preannounce their visits. This is certainly true for clinical supervision practices. In those instances you will know when the supervisor is coming, and if it is truly clinical supervision you will probably look forward to the visit because of the rapport that has been established among members of your triad.

However, in other instances your supervisor may drop in unannounced. When that happens, we urge you to consider taking a deep breath, counting to ten (quietly), and then proceeding with your teaching. You will undoubtedly do just fine if you have followed our suggestions from the previous section.

Now here are some hints for what you might do during the supervisor's visit.

- Allow the supervisor to enter the room and sit wherever he/she wishes.
- Do not, repeat, *do not* interrupt your teaching to introduce the supervisor (unless, of course, your supervisor wants you to).
- Your supervisor may or may not know much about the subject matter at hand, so do not, repeat, *do not* put the supervisor on the spot by suddenly involving him/her in the lesson (unless this has previously been approved by your supervisor).
- Without "missing a beat" in your teaching you may walk over and quietly hand the supervisor a copy of the textbook, opened to the appropriate page, a copy of your lesson plan (Yes! always have an extra copy on hand for that purpose), and a copy of any other appropriate printed materials.

The "supervisor" who comes to dinner—Whoops! We mean who comes to visit—might be a college or university supervisor, a cooperating teacher, a departmental chairperson, a vice principal, the principal, or even the superintendent. Or, heaven forbid, it could be all of those people at the same time! If that should ever happen to you, don't faint! It might just be by accident. In Exercise

17.1 we prepare you for peer evaluation "in chorus," and although we admit that it's not quite the same thing, it does come close to bridging the gap between teaching to secondary students and teaching to "peers."

What to Do During the Supervisor's Conference

Some university supervisors will arrange to have a conference with you, to discuss the classroom observation and to begin to resolve any classroom teaching problems. As a teacher candidate, you should be professional during this conference. For instance, one teacher candidate asks for help by requesting resources. Another takes notes and suggests developing a cooperative plan with the supervisor to improve teaching competencies. Still another teacher candidate discusses visiting other classrooms to observe certificated teachers.

During other supervisor-teacher conferences, some teacher candidates ask permission to select a future date, during which the teacher candidates view films, filmstrips, or videotapes of selected teaching styles or methods, listen to audiotapes, visit an outside educational consultant, or visit a nearby resource center.

Almost all supervisors conclude their evaluative conferences by leaving something in writing with the beginning teacher or teacher candidate. This written record usually includes (1) teaching strengths or weaknesses, and a review of class management; (2) the supervisor's recommendations; and (3) perhaps some steps in an overall plan for the beginning teacher's or teacher candidate's growth and development of teaching competencies.

What to Do After the Supervisor Leaves

In addition to observing the classes of other teachers, attending workshops, signing up for conferences, and conferencing with college and university authorities, Lee[2] suggests the following ways to implement your plan for improvement:

- Do what you and the evaluator have agreed on. Document your activities with a record or diary with dated entries.
- Get help if you need it. Ask colleagues you trust to help you by visiting your class or demonstrating skills.
- Write comments to parents about students' progress, and leave a space for a return message. Keep positive responses from parents and present them at your next evaluation conference.
- If your problem is discipline or organization, seek information on class management skills from others or from articles in the professional literature.
- Sometimes the answer lies simply in more self-discipline and hard work; sometimes *smart* work is better than hard work.
- Many beginners are unaware that they need to debug their lesson plans by walking through them in advance.

---

[2] Helen C. Lee, "Evaluation Without Tears," *Educational Horizons*, Vol. 61, No. 4 (Summer, 1983), p. 201. Bloomington, IN: Pi Lambda Theta.

C. OTHER SOURCES OF ASSISTANCE

Indeed, there are many resources to help you develop your competencies as a teacher candidate and as a continuing secondary teacher:

- Your professional texts, journals, and other publications.
- Nearby college and university workshops, courses, seminars, and conferences.
- District in-service programs.
- Professional presentations supported by educational organizations.
- Your colleagues, consultants, district personnel, and college or university professors.
- Your former college instructor or university supervisor assigned to be your educational consultant during a teacher education program.

QUESTIONS FOR CLASS DISCUSSION

1. What are some of the teaching behaviors that seem easy for you?
2. Which teaching behaviors will you want to develop? Can you identify sources in this book that will help?
3. What are some ways you can turn a supervisor's visit into a positive experience for you?
4. What are your suggestions for classroom action during a supervisor's visit?
5. What should you remember to do during a supervisor's conference?
6. How can you design and implement your own teaching improvement plan?
7. What can you do if you do not get along with or respect your supervisor?
8. What questions do you have about this chapter? How might you find answers?

SELECTED READINGS AND REFERENCES FOR CHAPTER 4

Acheson, K. A., and M. D. Gall. *Techniques in the Clinical Supervision of Teachers: Preservice and Inservice Application.* New York: Longman, 1980.

Costa, Arthur L. (ed.). *Developing Minds: A Resource Book for Teaching Thinking.* Washington: Association for Supervision and Curriculum Development, 1985.

Costa, Arthur L., and Robert Garmston. "Supervision for Intelligent Teaching." *Educational Leadership,* Vol. 42 (February 1985), pp. 70-80.

Lee, Helen C. "Evaluation Without Tears." *Educational Horizons,* Vol. 61, No. 4 (Summer 1983), Bloomington, IN: Pi Lambda Theta, pp. 121-125.

Part II

Planning for Instruction in a Secondary Classroom

Once upon a time the animals decided they must do something to meet the problems of the "New World," so they organized a school. They adopted an activity curriculum consisting of running, climbing, swimming, and flying and to make it easier to administer, all animals took all subjects.

The duck was excellent in swimming, better in fact, than his instructor, and made passing grades in flying, but he was poor in running. He had to stay after school and also drop swimming to practice running. This was kept up until his web feet were badly worn and he was only average in swimming.

The squirrel was excellent in climbing, until he developed frustration in the flying class, where his teacher made him start from the ground up instead of from treetop down. He also developed charlie-horse from overexertion and then got a "C" in climbing and a "D" in running.

At the end of the year, an abnormal eel, who could swim exceedingly well, and also run, climb and fly a little, had the highest average and was valedictorian.

The prairie dogs stayed out of school and fought the tax levy because the administration would not add digging and burrowing to the curriculum. They apprenticed their children to a badger and later joined the groundhogs and gophers to start a successful private school.[1]

Part II responds to your needs about

- Why you should plan.

- What you should plan.

- How to prepare a plan.

- How to prepare instructional objectives.

- How to individualize the learning experience.

[1] Reproduced by permission of the publisher, F. E. Peacock Publishers, Inc., Itasca, IL. From George H. Reavis, "Animal School," in *Catcher in the Wrong: Iconoclasts in Education*, ed. by Billy L. Turney, 1968, pp. 188-189.

5

Why Should I Plan?

A. A RATIONALE FOR PLANNING

Professional teachers plan! Their daily lessons are parts of a larger picture of their long-range goals for the year. A teacher who ignores this broader context, or who does not take into account where the students have been or where they are going, is doing a disservice to students. The students deserve better. Administrators, parents, and students expect better.

The daily plans are representative parts of teaching units (Chapter 8), which in turn reflect the teacher's comprehension of the total curricular organization. Daily student learning experiences—affective, cognitive, and psychomotor—are carefully planned and orchestrated by the teacher who understands the rationale for their particular place in the total curriculum. What the teacher is doing at any particular moment has been carefully thought out with a goal-direction in mind. Of course, this does not preclude an occasional diversion from preplanned activities.

The foregoing emphasizes the major reason for planning—*to provide program coherence.* There are other reasons why a teacher must plan, listed as follows:

1. To insure program continuation, your plans are available for a substitute teacher.
2. To evaluate your teaching, your plans may be a criterion recognized and observed by the administration.
3. To provide mechanism for vertical (K-12) articulation, i.e., scope and sequence curriculum development.
4. To prepare for the individual differences of the students within your class.
5. To prevent classroom-control problems: the teacher who has planned carefully is less likely to have severe discipline problems.
6. To serve as a criterion for self-evaluation by the teacher.

Unfortunately there are teachers who ignore careful planning, rationalizing that teaching never proceeds in the way a teacher has planned; therefore planning is a waste of time and energy. We abhor such an attitude, which can only result in teaching that is sloppy, indecisive, chaotic, and without direction or clear purpose. As a true professional you must plan carefully before you begin your teaching. Let us now review the components of total planning.

B. THE COMPONENTS OF TOTAL PLANNING

The seven components of a total plan are:

1. A *philosophy* about how students learn. (Refer to Chapter 3.)
2. A *perception of the needs of society and its learners,* with an appreciation for the cultural plurality of this nation.
3. A *goals and objectives* statement consistent with the needs assessment. (Refer to Chapter 7.)
4. A curriculum that is *articulated vertically* (grades K-12) and *horizontally* (integration of disciplines). (Refer to Chapter 6.)
5. A collection of *sequentially planned learning objectives* appropriate for the subject, and for the age and diverse abilities of the students.
6. A listing of *resources,* e.g., books, speakers, field trip locales, materials needed.
7. An *assessment* strategy. (Refer to Chapter 16.)

Textbooks provide the basis for many high school curriculum programs. A textbook series is often the basis for middle and junior high programs. For a textbook series the content is easily determined by examining a scope and sequence chart, frequently found in the teacher's edition. Textbooks and other curriculum resources are the topic of the next chapter, where we also start you on the development of your own teaching plans. Let us now focus your attention on the following table entitled "Schema of Planning" to review the important considerations for the three planning phases: pre-instructional, implementation (or instructional), and post-instructional.

SCHEMA OF PLANNING

Phases	Considerations		
	Subject-matter Contents	Student	Community
Pre-instructional stage	Philosophy/goals objectives	Cognitive ability Affective ability Psychomotor ability	Cultural/ethnic traits Occupational status Rural/urban settings
Instructional stage	Teacher goals Student objectives	Approaches Procedures Techniques Materials Evaluations	Community reactions Parents' input Support from professional organizations
Post-instructional stage	Assessment of goals and objectives	Assessment of student output	Assessment by community and professional organizations

EXERCISE 5.1: A PRE-PLANNING CHECK

Instructions: Let us review this chapter by completing the following.

1. List at least four reasons you should plan carefully what you are going to do.

   Reason 1 _____

   Reason 2 _____

   Reason 3 _____

   Reason 4 _____

   Reason 5 _____

   Reason 6 _____

   Reason 7 _____

2. Identify the seven components of a total curricular plan.

   Component 1 _____

   Component 2 _____

   Component 3 _____

   Component 4 _____

   Component 5 _____

   Component 6 _____

   Component 7 _____

EXERCISE 5.2: LESSON PLANNING PRETEST

Instructions: Without looking ahead to subsequent chapters, list five major components of a daily lesson plan.

1. _____

2. _____

3. _____

4. _____

5. _____

    Now look at the suggested inclusions inverted at the bottom of this page. How did you do? The chapters that follow will aid you in planning for your teaching. But before you can plan, you need to know how one decides what to teach. Chapter 6 will provide this information.

Did you include the following? objectives; set induction; lesson content procedure with time planning; closure; materials and audiovisual needs.

QUESTIONS FOR CLASS DISCUSSION

1. Which characteristics of students have an effect on curricular planning? Describe the effects.
2. How do you discover which books are appropriate for a particular group of students? What characteristics define a book as appropriate?
3. What is the importance of scope and sequence in the secondary subject you intend to teach?
4. Can you describe the difference between vertical and horizontal curriculum articulation? How important is each in your subject field?
5. Why should you plan your teaching day?
6. Identify, in order, each of the components of total planning.
7. Share an example of how a teacher's lack of careful planning affected a classroom situation.
8. What does a substitute teacher do if no lesson plans have been left for the substitute to follow?
9. How do you distinguish between what is curriculum and what is instruction?
10. "Historically in this country schools focused on broadly stated aims (principally committees of the National Education Association in 1893, 1899, and again in 1913; and, the Educational Policies Commission in 1938 and again in 1961), but today the focus seems more on student achievement of specific competencies." Do you agree with this statement? What is the evidence to support or reject the statement? If you agree, how is this shift accounted for?
11. Do you have a question you would like to introduce for class discussion? How might the answer be found?

6

How Do I Know What to Teach?

A. WHAT SOURCES ARE AVAILABLE TO ME?

There are three general sources to help you discover what to teach: documents, colleagues, and yourself.

1. You will examine school and other public documents for mandates and guidelines.
2. You will talk with other professionals and learn something of school and community expectations. As a new teacher you will find other teachers at the school cooperative in offering helpful suggestions.
3. You will probe, analyze, and translate your own convictions, knowledge, and skills into behaviors that will foster the development of your students.

This chapter will focus on the first source, the resource documents.

B. WHAT PUBLIC DOCUMENTS SHOULD I EXAMINE?

State department of education curricular publications, district courses of study, and school-adopted textbooks are the sources you will now examine, with the guidance of the exercises that follow.

EXERCISE 6.1: EXAMINING STATE CURRICULUM FRAMEWORKS

Instructions: Find whether your State Department of Education publishes a curricular framework. Addresses of State Departments of Education are provided in the final chapter of this text. State frameworks can provide valuable information pertaining to content and process, and teachers need to be aware of these documents. Frameworks for the State of California, for example, are:

> *California Curriculum Framework: A Handbook*
> *English Language Framework*
> *Foreign Language Framework*
> *Health Instruction Framework*
> *History-Social Science Framework*
> *Mathematics Framework*
> *Physical Education Framework*
> *Reading Framework*
> *Science Framework*
> *Visual and Performing Arts Framework*
> *Program Descriptions for Bilingual-Bicultural and ESL Instructional Materials*
> *Guide for Multicultural Education*
> *Nutrition Education—Choose Well, Be Well: A Resource Manual for Secondary Teachers*

QUESTIONS FOR CLASS DISCUSSION FOR EXERCISE 6.1

1. Is there a state curricular document available to teachers for your state in your subject field? _____ If so, what is its title? _____

2. If so, is it free to teachers, or how much does it cost? _____

3. Is the document specific as to subject-matter content, showing a scope and sequence articulation for various grade levels? _____

4. Does the document offer specific process strategies? _____

5. Does the document distinguish between what you *shall* teach and what you *can* teach? _____ _____

6. Does the document offer suggestions for specific resources, such as supplementary books, films, microcomputer programs? _____

7. Does the document offer suggestions to the teacher for dealing with students with special needs? _____

8. Does the document offer suggestions or guidelines for dealing with controversial topics? ____ _____

EXERCISE 6.2: EXAMINING CURRICULUM GUIDES

A primary resource for what to teach is referred to as the *curriculum guide,* or the *course of study.* Samples may be available in your university library or in a local district resource center. Examine how closely these documents follow the components listed in Chapter 5, Section B. An analysis of several documents will give you a good picture of expectations. Compare documents from several school districts, using the format that follows.

Title of document _____

District or school _____

Date of document _____

I. Does the document contain the following components?

		Yes	No
1.	Statement of philosophy	( )	( )
2.	Evidence of preassessment (regarding needs)	( )	( )
3.	Goals and objectives	( )	( )
4.	Scope and sequence (vertical and horizontal articulation)	( )	( )
5.	Recommended procedures (learning activities)	( )	( )
6.	Recommended resource materials	( )	( )
7.	Evaluation procedures (assessment strategy)	( )	( )

II. Answer the following questions regarding your document, then share with members of your class.

1. Does the document list expected learning outcomes? _____

2. Does the document contain detailed unit plans? _____

3. Does it contain initiating activities? _____

   Does it contain learning activities? _____

   Does it contain enrichment activities? _____

   Does it contain culminating activities? _____

   Does it contain evaluating activities? _____

   Does it provide activities for learners with special needs? _____

4. Does it provide bibliographic entries for:

   the teacher? _____

   the students? _____

5. Does it list audiovisual and other materials needed? _____

6. Does it provide information regarding resource ideas? _____

7. Does the document clearly help you understand what you are expected to teach? _____

   How to do it? _____

8. Are there questions you have that are not answered by your examination of this document? List them for class discussion. _____

_____

_____

_____

_____

C. WHAT DO I NEED TO KNOW ABOUT STUDENT TEXTBOOKS?

Probably as much as two thirds of a secondary student's time in the classroom is spent using textbook and related written materials. Considerable national attention is currently being given to a discussion of the improvement of the quality of student textbooks, with particular attention to the need to better develop student critical thinking skills. There seems to be a gap between what is needed in textbooks and *what is available for student use in many classrooms.* Many school districts have experienced bad economic times and have not been able to maintain current textbooks and/or a variety of books to better address the varying reading levels of students within a class. From 1974 to 1984 the amount of money spent on school textbooks nationally declined by 50 percent. Indeed, the books you will be using may be several years old. In this chapter you will become familiar with some of the textbooks you are likely to be using. In a later chapter (Chapter 11, Section F) we provide guidelines for the use of your textbook.

Some states have statewide textbook adoption policies; others rely on local committees; yet others have a statewide process that provides a list from which local committees make the final selection. In some high schools, the teacher can make the initial decision as to what book he/she wishes to use; that decision is then approved by others, perhaps beginning with the departmental chairperson, then the principal, and finally, perhaps, a district textbook approval committee, which may be comprised of laypersons from the community and teachers and administrators from the district. Whichever the case, today's textbooks represent the *de facto* curriculum in many secondary schools, and the books used by the students may be outdated, in which case you will need to provide supplementary and current material to the students.

The exercise that follows is designed to help you analyze textbooks and their accompanying teacher's editions. (See also Exercise 10.5 in Chapter 10.)

EXERCISE 6.3: EXAMINING TEACHER'S MANUALS AND STUDENT TEXTS

Textbooks are usually accompanied by a teacher's edition, which will contain specific objectives, teaching techniques, learning activities, test items, and suggested resources. Again, your university library or local schools may be your source for locating these.

Instructions: Select a textbook that is accompanied by a teacher's edition and examine the contents using the following format. *If there are no standard textbooks available for your teaching field (i.e., music, physical education, art), then select a field in which there is a possibility you might teach. Beginning teachers are often assigned to teach in more than a single field.*

Title of book: _____

Author(s): _____

Publisher: _____

Date of publication: _____

I. Does the teacher's manual contain the following elements?   Yes   No
   1. Goals that are consistent with those of local guides and/or state guides? (   )   (   )
   2. Specific objectives for each lesson?   (   )   (   )
   3. Units and lessons sequentially developed with suggested time
      allotments?   (   )   (   )
   4. Suggested provisions for individual differences? Reading levels,
      learners with special needs?   (   )   (   )
   5. Specific techniques and strategies?   (   )   (   )
   6. Listings of helpful aids, materials, and resources?   (   )   (   )
   7. Suggestions for extension activities?   (   )   (   )
   8. Specific guidelines for assessment of student learning?   (   )   (   )

II. Analyze the student textbook as follows:
   1. Does it treat the content in adequate depth?   (   )   (   )
   2. Does the book treat ethnic minorities and women in a fair manner?   (   )   (   )
   3. Is the format attractive?   (   )   (   )
   4. Does the book have good quality binding with suitable type size?   (   )   (   )
   5. Are illustrations and visuals attractive and useful?   (   )   (   )
   6. Is the reading level clear and appropriate?   (   )   (   )

III. Would you like to use this textbook? Give reasons.

   _____

   _____

   _____

   _____

   _____

IV. Share your book and this analysis with your class members.

As you review current textbooks available for secondary school students in your subject field you will undoubtedly find most of them well organized and quite useful. Textbooks may be accompanied by sequentially designed *resource units* from which you will select and build your specific *teaching units.* A resource unit usually consists of an extensive list of objectives, a large number and variety of kinds of activities, suggested materials, and extensive bibliographies for teacher and students, from which the teacher will select those that best suit his/her needs to build an actual teaching unit.

As you may have discovered from your work with Exercise 6.2, some curriculum guides consist of actual teaching units that have been prepared by teachers from a particular school district. An important question asked by most student teachers is: How closely must the student teacher follow the school's curriculum guide, whether it is a textbook or a curriculum written by teachers within that school or district? *It is a question you need to have an answer to before you begin teaching.*

In summary, your final decisions as to what content to teach will be guided (perhaps even dictated) by all of the following:

- Discussions with other teachers.
- State curricular documents.
- Local school courses of study.
- Your personal convictions, knowledge, and skills acquired in teacher education.
- The cultural backgrounds, interests, and abilities of your students.

After discovering what you will teach comes the process of preparing the plans. The remaining chapters of this part of the text will guide you through the planning process. Teacher's textbook editions and curriculum guides make the process easier *but should never substitute for your own specific planning.*

D. HOW CAN I DEAL WITH CONTROVERSIAL ISSUES?

Controversial issues (usually involving matters of religion, politics, and/or sex) abound in certain disciplines, particularly English (e.g., controversial books), social studies (e.g., political issues), and biology (e.g., origin of life, evolution). Within your teaching career, particularly if you teach in any of these disciplines, you undoubtedly will have to make a decision regarding what you will do in your own teaching with respect to a particular controversial subject. Here are our guidelines for your consideration.

- *To the student teacher:* Maintain a perspective with respect to your own personal objective, which is to complete your credential so that you can then go out and obtain your first paid teaching assignment. Student teaching is *not* the time for you to "make waves," and to get yourself involved in a situation that could lead to a lot of embitterment. If you maintain close communication with your cooperating teacher and your college or university supervisor, you should be able to prevent any major problems dealing with controversial issues. Sometimes, during normal discussion in the classroom, a controversial subject will emerge spontaneously, perhaps from the students asking you a question. When this occurs, *think before you say anything!* You may wish to postpone further discussion until you have a chance to talk over the issue with your supervisors, including the department chairperson. Controversial issues can seem to come from nowhere for *any* teacher, and that is perfectly normal while teaching secondary school students. These students are developing their own moral and value systems and they *need* to know how adults, particularly adults they hold in esteem, feel about things important to them.

- *To the inservice teacher:* We believe that secondary school students need discussions about issues that are important to society, and we see absolutely nothing wrong with dealing with those issues so long as the following guidelines are established:

    1. Students should learn about all sides of an issue (an *issue* differs from a problem in that *a problem generally has a solution, whereas an issue has many opinions and several alternative solutions*).

    2. Like all lesson plans, one dealing with a controversial issue should be well thought out ahead of time. Problems are most likely to occur when the plan has been underprepared. Potential problem areas, and resources must be carefully considered in advance.

    3. All involved have a right to input—parents, students, community leaders, other faculty members, and so forth. Parents and students should have the right to nonparticipation without academic penalty.

    4. We see nothing wrong with students knowing how you, the teacher, feel about an issue *as long as you make it clear that students may certainly disagree without reprisal or academic penalty,* but your opinions should perhaps be reserved until after students have had full opportunity to study other sources.

In our opinion, what makes this country so great is the freedom members of society have to speak out on issues, to express their opinions. That freedom should not be omitted from the classroom of our public schools. Teachers and students should be allowed to express their feelings and attitudes about the great issues of today, encouraged to *study* the issues, to collect data, to form reasoned opinions after suspending judgment. *Teachers must understand the difference between teaching truth, values, and morality, and teaching* about *truth, values, and morality.*

To you, the teacher candidate, who may still be taking college or university courses in your subject field, it is not unusual in those classes to have experienced a professor who *pontificates* on a certain controversial issue—perhaps on the right-to-life issue, or on the liberation movement of a specific group of individuals in our society, or on the position of our government in Central America, or on the use of live animals in medical research, or on the issue of safety of nuclear power plants, or on "arms buildup," or on any other of the long list of important issues in society today—*but as a teacher in a secondary school you do not necessarily have the same academic freedom* and it is important that you understand this difference. The junior or senior high school students with whom you will be working are not yet adults and they must be protected from dogmatism while allowed the freedom to learn and to develop without coercion from those who have power over their lives.

Now that we have expressed our opinion and offered our guidelines, what do you think about this topic, which will be quite important to you as a teacher? For this development and expression of your opinion we offer the exercise that follows, Exercise 6.4.

EXERCISE 6.4: TEACHING ABOUT CONTROVERSIAL ISSUES

The educational purpose of this exercise is for you to discover *before* teaching what some of the possibilities are for controversial issues in your subject field, and for you to consider what you can and will do with the issues. This exercise should first be completed by you, then shared with and completed by all members of your class who share your discipline interest.

1. Your subject (discipline) field: _____

2. Spend some time in the library studying current periodicals in your subject field, and also talk with your colleagues in the schools, and list two or three potential controversial issues that are likely to come up during your teaching.

   Issue   *Source*

   _____

   _____

   _____

3. Take one of these issues and identify "sides" and "current resources."

   _____

   _____

   _____

4. Identify your own position on this issue with a statement of your rationale.

   _____

   _____

   _____

5. How accepting can you be of students who take an opposing position?

   _____

   _____

6. Share the above with other teacher candidates from your subject field. Note any comments of theirs that you find helpful or enlightening.

   _____

   _____

   _____

   _____

QUESTIONS FOR CLASS DISCUSSION

1. Do the psychologies of Piaget, Bruner, Gagné, or others, show up in the curricular documents you have examined? Which and how?
2. Reading seems to be more effective when it has a purpose. In what ways can you make your students' content reading more purposeful?
3. Can you define and describe the differences among these terms: resource unit, textbook unit, teaching unit?
4. How will *you* really decide what to teach? How will you know if this is the proper content to be taught?
5. When we have sought original lessons and/or teaching units from experienced secondary school teachers, they frequently reply that they do not write them. Why do you believe this is the case when, in fact, we will be teaching *you* how to write lesson and unit plans?
6. Ask experienced teachers if they like the books they are using. Share their replies with others from your class. Are the majority of teachers happy with their textbooks?
7. Are the textbooks being used in your subject field too hard, too easy, or about right?
8. What distinguishes a good student textbook from a bad one?
9. Specifically how does a teacher attend to the individual differences of all the students?
10. Would you have any personal conflict using any of the documents you have examined?
11. What would be some of your options if you had to use a student textbook that you did not like?
12. Do you have a question you would like to introduce for class discussion? How might the answer be found?

7

What Are Instructional Objectives?

An instructional objective is *an intent communicated by a statement describing a proposed change in the learner*—a statement of what the learner is to be able to do upon completion of the learning experience. You will notice that this description of an instructional objective dictates a demonstrable behavioral change in the learner. This is consistent with our interpretation of *learning* as being an *observable and desired behavioral change*. In other words, we can tell that learning has occurred only when we observe a change in behavior.

Instructional objectives are also referred to as *behavioral* or *performance objectives* (we consider these terms to be synonymous). Instructional objectives are elements crucial to effective planning, which are written for the student, stating what the child is to be like as a result of the learning experience.

Instructional objectives are different from "teacher intention" or "teacher goals," which tell what the teacher intends to do. Instructional objectives are also different from "course description" or "course goals," which tell, generally, what the course is like and about. Instructional objectives are much more specific and are student-centered. Let's explore how they are written.

A. HOW TO WRITE INSTRUCTIONAL OBJECTIVES

When preparing your instructional objectives, you should ask yourself the primary question, "How should the learner indicate that the objective has been achieved?" In other words, what will the student be able to *do* as a result of the learning experience? The best objective is one that is open to the fewest interpretations. For example, although the following might be an appropriate goal, it is *not* a good instructional objective: "The student will enjoy science." It is not a clearly stated instructional objective. Even though "will enjoy science" is a student-centered phrase, it is ambiguous; it does not state how the intended behavioral change will be demonstrated; there are too many possible interpretations of what "enjoy science" means. What we can do is to expand the statement to include *what* learner behavior will indicate the intended enjoyment. We might write it in this way: "The student will demonstrate enjoyment of science by volunteering to participate as a new member of the school science club." We can only *trust our assumption* that the students joining the science club does reflect the increased enjoyment we are looking for.

The example objective described in the preceding paragraph represents a "responding" objective in the affective domain (see next section). Objectives in that domain are more complicated when it comes to evaluation because they represent behaviors involving attitudes and feelings, which are more difficult to measure than are cognitive areas. This is the reason we need the "trust our assumption" statement at the end of the preceding paragraph.

Success in writing behavioral objectives rests with the selection of a performance word that is measurable. Calvin K. Claus has provided a list of illustrative verbs that are representative of acceptable performance words (Section D of this chapter). The anticipated acceptable performance is the first ingredient of the well-stated instructional objective.

The second ingredient is the condition(s) in which the performance will be demonstrated, and the third and final ingredient is the level of the performance. Let's see how this all fits together in the making of a complete instructional objective. Suppose you are teaching mathematics, and *your* goal is to teach your students to solve quadratic equations. Your instructional *objective* might read as follows: "When given ten quadratic equations (the conditions), the student will solve them (the behavioral performance) with 80 percent accuracy (the performance level.)"

The objective now has the three ingredients necessary for a completely stated instructional objective:

1. The *acceptable performance* (terminal behavior).
2. The *conditions* in which the behavior will be demonstrated (thus observed by the teacher).
3. The *level of performance* (primarily for the purposes of evaluation).

Now, with Exercise 7.1, try your skill at recognizing instructional objectives that are measurable. Conditions and performance level may be absent, but is the objective measurable?

EXERCISE 7.1: RECOGNIZING INSTRUCTIONAL OBJECTIVES: A DIAGNOSTIC TEST

Instructions: Place an X before each of those in the following list that is a measurable instructional objective.

_____   1.   To develop critical thinking.
_____   2.   To identify those celestial bodies that are known planets.
_____   3.   To provide worthwhile experiences for the students.
_____   4.   To recognize subject and verb in a sentence.
_____   5.   To focus the microscope without damaging the objective lens.
_____   6.   To write a summary of the factors that led to World War II.
_____   7.   To fully appreciate the value of art.
_____   8.   To prepare a critical comparison of the two major political parties in the United States.
_____   9.   To illustrate an awareness of the importance of balanced ecology by supplying relevant newspaper articles.
_____   10. To know all the rules of spelling and grammar.

Check your answers with this key:

2, 4, 6, 8, 9

How did you do? If you scored 100 percent correct, please disregard what follows and go on to Section B. Numbers 1, 3, 7, and 10 of the exercise are inadequate because of their ambiguity. Number 3 is not even a student objective; it is a teacher goal. "To develop," "to fully appreciate," and "to know," are open to too many interpretations.

With correctly worded objectives, it is easy to see how the teacher can tell if the objective has been reached. When writing instructional objectives, verbs that are vague, ambiguous, and not measurable should be avoided. (See Section D for acceptable verbs.)

Verbs to Avoid When Writing Instructional Objectives	
to appreciate	to grasp
to believe	to know
to comprehend	to learn
to enjoy	to like
to familiarize	to understand

Although the conditions are not present, numbers 2, 4, 5, 6, and 8 are clearly measurable. The teacher would have no difficulty knowing if the learner had reached these objectives, whereas in number 9, which is in the affective domain, our "trust assumption" must be put to work. Discussions with your classmates and instructor should alleviate any further difficulty you may have had with this exercise. Read on when ready.

B. HOW TO CLASSIFY INSTRUCTIONAL OBJECTIVES

There are three domains of instructional objectives useful in planning:

- *Cognitive objectives* involve mental processes, from simple recall of information to complex evaluation of processes.
- *Psychomotor objectives* involve manipulation of materials through motor control.
- *Affective objectives* involve feelings, attitudes, and values.

Each of the three domains is further divided into hierarchies.

COGNITIVE-DOMAIN HIERARCHIES, WITH EXAMPLES

1. *Knowledge.* Example: The learner will recall when Columbus arrived in the Americas.

2. *Comprehension.* Example: The learner will give examples, in his/her own words, of recent legal decisions regarding equal rights.

3. *Application.* Example: When provided with fractions, the learner will apply the rules to change to decimal numbers.

4. *Analysis.* Example: The learner will detect discrepancies between magazine advertisements and the actual quality of "junk foods."

5. *Synthesis.* Example: The learner will create from trash an environment for an imaginary animal.

6. *Evaluation.* Example: The learner will write a critical appraisal of his/her essay on the use of public money for space exploration.

PSYCHOMOTOR-DOMAIN HIERARCHIES, WITH EXAMPLES

1. *Accuracy.* Example: The student will demonstrate the ability to catch and pass the ball accurately while in motion during a basketball game.

2. *Coordination.* Example: The student will blow the trumpet skillfully to produce a high F for a duration of 1 minute.

3. *Manipulation.* Example: The student will use the power saw safely to cut out a desired form for a bookstand.

AFFECTIVE-DOMAIN HIERARCHIES, WITH EXAMPLES

1. *Attending.* Example: The student will illustrate an awareness of the importance of ecology by supplying pertinent newspaper clippings.

2. *Responding.* Example: The student will demonstrate enjoyment of the subject by volunteering to join in the role playing of the King Arthur story.

3. *Valuing.* Example: The student will demonstrate a continuing desire to learn to use the microscope by volunteering to work with it after school hours.

4. *Value Development.* Example: The student will, in a class discussion, freely express his/her opinion about the importance of sex education.

Most of the objectives used by teachers seem to be in the cognitive domain, although there is undoubtedly an equal interest in the affective. Perhaps too frequently our attention is on the cognitive, and we assume the affective will develop simultaneously. Our concern here is that you direct your planning so that the learners are guided from the lowest to higher levels of operation, and that equal attention be given to cognitive and affective development. Learning that is solely at the lowest cognitive level of operation can get pretty boring. Undoubtedly, you can recall classes during your own education where the instructor's expectations went no further than the lowest cognitive level—simple recall of isolated bits of information. Effective learning must go beyond the mere recall of memorized facts. Indeed, to develop student skills in reasoning and in critical thinking, such must be the case. Competent teachers provide educational objectives in all three domains that are designed to raise the levels of student thinking and behaving in the classroom. Now, let us practice recognizing objectives from each of the domains.

EXERCISE 7.2: HOW KNOWLEDGEABLE AM I ABOUT BEHAVIORAL OBJECTIVES? A DIAGNOSTIC TEST

I. Write an X by any of the following objectives that are stated in performance (behavioral) terms, and that are measurable.

_____ 1. The student will learn the major parts of speech.
_____ 2. The student will appreciate the significance of the Gettysburg Address.
_____ 3. The student will be able to construct an isosceles triangle with a protractor.
_____ 4. Given a model of a hypothetical cell, the student will identify the cellular structures.
_____ 5. The student will read and understand the chapter on civil rights.
_____ 6. The unit on chemical oxidation-reduction reactions will be reviewed.
_____ 7. The student will write an essay in which he develops an argument for or against family planning.
_____ 8. The student will volunteer to visit a pre-school program.
_____ 9. The student will become aware of the significance of supermarket shelving practice.
_____ 10. The students will translate the song "Hey Jude" into Spanish.
_____ 11. The student will correctly operate the duplicating machine.
_____ 12. From a list of ten substances, the student will identify those that are compounds and those that are mixtures.
_____ 13. The student will write the Spanish alphabet from memory.
_____ 14. The student will know the Mendelian laws.
_____ 15. The learner will show an appreciation of outdoor sports.
_____ 16. The learner will list the major causes of the Civil War.
_____ 17. Given three hypothetical situations, the student will decide which one best represents the posture of the Republican Party.
_____ 18. The student will learn to recognize differences between the music of Beethoven and of Bach.
_____ 19. The student will learn ten French verbs.
_____ 20. The student will create in miniature a model environment for an imaginary animal.

II. Classify each of the following objectives by writing the correct letter in the blank provided according to the following domains: Cognitive (C); Affective (A); or Psychomotor (P). Answers at the end of the test. Check your answers (after).

_____ 1. The student will correctly focus the microscope.
_____ 2. The student can summarize the histories of the origin of the two major political parties.
_____ 3. The student will identify from a list those items that are Spanish cognates.
_____ 4. The student will anonymously indicate in writing that this course has improved his confidence.
_____ 5. The student will volunteer to remain after class to help clean up the classroom.
_____ 6. The student will be able to identify the respective poets after reading and analyzing several poems.
_____ 7. The student will translate a French poem into English.
_____ 8. The student will accurately predict the results of combining equal quantities of any paired combination of secondary colors.
_____ 9. The student will voluntarily read outside material related to current events.
_____ 10. The student will make a goal in basketball a minimum of seven times in ten attempts.

III. For the following cognitive objectives, identify by the appropriate letter the highest level within that domain (one subdomain which will be the highest within a given objective): Knowledge (K); Comprehension (C); Application (Ap); Analysis (An); Synthesis (S); Evaluation (E).

____ 1. When given a new poem, the student will recognize it as one of Shelley's.
____ 2. The student will underline from a list those words that are spelled correctly.
____ 3. The student will read a pattern and correctly select the amount of material and equipment necessary to make a dress.
____ 4. The student will create a poem using the style that is designated.
____ 5. The students will write critical appraisals of their essays on capital punishment.

Part I: The following objectives should be marked X: 3, 4, 7, 8, 10, 11, 12, 13, 16, 17, and 20.
Part II: (1) P, (2) C, (3) C, (4) A, (5) A, (6) C, (7) C, (8) C, (9) A, (10) P.
Part III: (1) C, (2) K, (3) Ap, (4) S, (5) E.

C. HOW TO JUDGE WHETHER INSTRUCTIONAL OBJECTIVES ARE WORTH THE TIME

It is clear from surveys that often teachers do not schedule the time (nor trouble their busy hours) to write specific objectives for all the learning activities they plan. But it is also clear from research studies that, when teachers do prepare specific objectives (by writing them themselves, or by borrowing them from other sources), and teach toward those objectives, their teaching is more effective. Some school districts require their teachers to use objectives that are quite specific. There is no question that clearly written instructional objectives are worth the time, especially when the teacher evaluates students' progress against them. It is not imperative that you write all the instructional objectives that you will need. As a matter of fact, they are usually already available in the textbooks teachers use, and in other places as well.[1]

D. HOW TO SELECT VERBS FOR STATING SPECIFIC LEARNING OBJECTIVES

Arranged according to disciplines, here is a list of performance verbs recommended for use in writing instructional objectives.[2]

1. "Creative" Behaviors

Alter	Generalize	Question	Regroup	Rephrase	Rewrite
Ask	Modify	Rearrange	Rename	Restate	Simplify
Change	Paraphrase	Recombine	Reorder	Restructure	Synthesize
Design	Predict	Reconstruct	Reorganize	Retell	Systematize

2. Complex, Logical, Judgmental Behaviors

Analyze	Combine	Contrast	Designate	Formulate	Plan
Appraise	Compare	Criticize	Determine	Generate	Structure
Assess	Conclude	Deduce	Discover	Induce	Suggest
		Defend	Evaluate	Infer	Substitute

3. General Discriminative Behaviors

Choose	Describe	Discriminate	Indicate	Match	Place
Collect	Detect	Distinguish	Isolate	Omit	Point
Define	Differentiate	Identify	List	Order	Select
				Pick	Separate

4. Social Behaviors

Accept	Answer	Cooperate	Forgive	Laugh	Reply
Admit	Argue	Dance	Greet	Meet	Smile
Agree	Communicate	Disagree	Help	Participate	Talk
Aid	Compliment	Discuss	Interact	Permit	Thank
Allow	Contribute	Excuse	Invite	Praise	Visit
			Join	React	Volunteer

[1] One such source is described in *Phi Delta Kappan,* Vol. 52, No. 3 (1970), pp. 174-175.
[2] Calvin K. Claus, National College of Education, Evanston, IL. From revision (1983) of text of paper read at February 10, 1968, meeting of National Council on Measurement in Education, in Chicago. Reprinted by permission of Calvin K. Claus.

5. Language Behaviors

Abbreviate	Call	Indent	Punctuate	Speak	Tell
Accent	Capitalize	Outline	Read	Spell	Translate
Alphabetize	Edit	Print	Recite	State	Verbalize
Articulate	Hyphenate	Pronounce	Say	Summarize	Whisper
			Sign	Syllabicate	Write

6. "Study" Behaviors

Arrange	Cite	Diagram	Itemize	Mark	Record
Categorize	Classify	Find	Label	Name	Reproduce
Chart	Compile	Follow	Locate	Note	Search
Circle	Copy	Gather	Look	Organize	Sort
			Map	Quote	Underline

7. Music Behaviors

Blow	Clap	Finger	Hum	Pluck	Strum
Bow	Compose	Harmonize	Mute	Practice	Tap
			Play	Sing	Whistle

8. Physical Behaviors

Arch	Climb	Hit	March	Ski	Swim
Bat	Face	Hop	Pitch	Skip	Swing
Bend	Float	Jump	Pull	Somersault	Throw
Carry	Grab	Kick	Push	Stand	Toss
Catch	Grasp	Knock	Run	Step	Walk
Chase	Grip	Lift	Skate	Stretch	

9. Arts Behavior

Assemble	Cut	Frame	Mold	Roll	Stamp
Blend	Dab	Hammer	Nail	Rub	Stick
Brush	Dot	Handle	Paint	Send	Stir
Build	Draw	Heat	Paste	Saw	Trace
Carve	Drill	Illustrate	Pat	Sculpt	Trim
Color	Fold	Melt	Polish	Shake	Varnish
Construct	Form	Mix	Pour	Sketch	Wipe
			Press	Smooth	Wrap

10. Drama Behaviors

Act	Direct	Enter	Imitate	Pantomime	Respond
Clasp	Display	Exit	Leave	Pass	Show
Cross	Emit	Express	Move	Perform	Sit
				Proceed	Turn

11. Mathematical Behaviors

Add	Compute	Estimate	Integrate	Plot	Subtract
Bisect	Count	Extrapolate	Interpolate	Prove	Sum
Calculate	Cumulate	Extract	Measure	Reduce	Tabulate
Check	Derive	Graph	Multiply	Solve	Tally
Circumscribe	Divide	Group	Number	Square	Verify

12. Laboratory Science Behaviors

Align	Conduct	Dissect	Keep	Plant	Set
Apply	Connect	Feed	Lengthen	Prepare	Specify
Attach	Convert	Grow	Limit	Remove	Straighten
Balance	Decrease	Increase	Manipulate	Replace	Time
Calibrate	Demonstrate	Insert	Operate	Report	Transfer
				Reset	Weigh

13. General Appearance, Health, and Safety Behaviors

Button	Comb	Eat	Fill	Taste	Unzip
Clean	Cover	Eliminate	Go	Tie	Wait
Clear	Dress	Empty	Lace	Unbutton	Wash
Close	Drink	Fasten	Stack	Uncover	Wear
			Stop	Untie	Zip

14. Miscellaneous

Aim	Erase	Hunt	Peel	Scratch	Store
Attempt	Expand	Include	Pin	Send	Strike
Attend	Extend	Inform	Position	Serve	Supply
Begin	Feel	Kneel	Present	Sew	Support
Bring	Finish	Lay	Produce	Share	Switch
Buy	Fit	Lead	Propose	Sharpen	Take
Come	Fix	Lend	Provide	Shoot	Tear
Complete	Flip	Let	Put	Shorten	Touch
Correct	Get	Light	Raise	Shovel	Try
Crease	Give	Make	Relate	Shut	Twist
Crush	Grind	Mend	Repair	Signify	Type
Develop	Guide	Miss	Repeat	Slip	Use
Distribute	Hand	Offer	Return	Slide	Vote
Do	Hang	Open	Ride	Spread	Watch
Drop	Hold	Pack	Rip	Stake	Weave
End	Hook	Pay	Save	Start	Work

EXERCISE 7.3: WRITING MY OWN INSTRUCTIONAL OBJECTIVES

Instructions: Complete the format below, as you begin writing your own instructional objectives. (You may wish to use these later for Exercises 8.1, 8.4, 9.1, and 16.2.)

1. Select a grade level, subject, and content topic you will likely teach.

    Grade level _____ Subject _____ Content topic _____

2. Write nine specific instructional objectives for the topic, including both *performance* and *conditions,* as follows:

    Cognitive knowledge _____

    _____

    _____

    Cognitive comprehension _____

    _____

    _____

    Cognitive application _____

    _____

    _____

    Cognitive analysis _____

    _____

    _____

    Cognitive synthesis _____

    _____

    _____

    Cognitive evaluation _____

    _____

    _____

    Psychomotor _____

    _____

    _____

    Psychomotor _____

    _____

    _____

Psychomotor _____

_____

_____

Affective _____

_____

_____

Affective _____

_____

_____

Affective _____

_____

_____

Upon completion of this exercise, exchange papers with your classmates, discuss the objectives with them, and make any corrections necessary.

E. A DANGER IN OVER-OBJECTIVITY

Once again, let us make it clear that we expect you to plan—to plan well and specifically—what it is that you intend to teach; to convey your specific expectations to your students, and *to evaluate their learning against that specificity*. But we cannot conclude this chapter without emphasizing a danger inherent in this kind of performance-based teaching. The danger is that it is highly objective and *over-objectivity can have a negative effect upon students' learning*. The danger in over-objectivity is that the students are treated as objects, and the relationship between teacher and learner becomes impersonal and counterproductive to *real* learning, learning that establishes the kinds of ultimate goals we addressed in the Preface to this resource guide. In objective teaching, when the teacher has clearly specified expected outcomes, and the conditions for learning are proper, then the teacher will get exactly that performance expected. Highly specific teaching may not allow for serendipity, creativity, and the excitement of real discovery. The source for student motivation for performance-based teaching is largely extrinsic, i.e., teacher expectation, grades, parental expectation, and peer pressures. As a teacher in our secondary schools, your challenge is to be competent and effective, to teach with performance-based criteria, while simultaneously developing a teaching style that encourages *intrinsic* sources of student motivation. As stated elsewhere: "When the affective is served, the cognitive is inevitable."

QUESTIONS FOR CLASS DISCUSSION

1. What observable behaviors would enable you to know whether a student is learning?
2. Do you believe you should place a greater emphasis in your teaching on the cognitive or the affective? Explain.
3. Can you clearly distinguish the three major types of objectives available in your planning?
4. Could you write a short critical appraisal of how writing instructional objectives will help or hinder you in your teaching?
5. What caution do you need to remember about "highly specific teaching?"
6. Do you agree with the definition of learning as presented in this chapter? Why? Why not?
7. Can you clearly distinguish among the following: instructional objectives; teacher goals; teacher intentions; course description; course goals; performance objectives; terminal objectives; behavioral objectives? Some of the terms are synonymous. Which?
8. Do you understand the authors' use of the term "trust assumption" as used in this chapter?
9. What performance level would be appropriate if the teacher uses mastery learning? Why isn't mastery learning more widely used?
10. Do you have a question you would like to introduce for class discussion? How might an answer be found?

8

How Do I Prepare an Instructional Plan?

As we stated earlier in the text, teacher's manuals and resource materials will expedite your planning but should not substitute for it. We want you to learn how to create a good plan for teaching. Here are some guidelines for preparation of your own instructional plan.

A. PREPARATION FOR PLANNING: GENERAL GUIDELINES

1. *There is no single best format* for lesson and unit plans. We provide in this chapter alternative plans from which you may work.
2. *Know what you are expected to teach* by consulting the "course of study" as discussed in Chapter 6. From that you will likely still need to make decisions regarding scope and sequence.
3. *Prepare long-range plans.* You need to know where you intend the class to be months from now.
4. *Prepare unit and daily plans* that generate the greatest amount of learning involvement and motivation.
5. *Organize the learning experiences from the learners outward,* rather than from the content. You begin with where the learners are and move them into new horizons.
6. When dealing with concepts,[1] try to develop the learner's understandings *from the concrete to the abstract,* rather than the reverse. (See Chapter 12, Section A.)
7. *Know the interests and abilities of your students* as you start your plans.
8. *Keep in mind your own interests, skills, knowledge, and biases.* Your enthusiasm for a topic and activity is contagious and will most certainly enhance the learning of the students.
9. *The best prepared lesson plan may go untaught* as the teacher is diverted from the plan in order to follow the interest and activity of the students. You must not allow yourself to get frustrated when the lesson plan you spent all night working on must be modified. The plan is

---

[1] *Concepts,* as used by the authors, refer to generalizations that organize the world of objects and events into a smaller number of categories.

your guide, but the students of your class are the key to what actually happens. The beginning teacher is advised to try to stick to the plan; only after hours in the classroom will your experience provide the skill to effectively deviate from it.

10. *Plans are revised.* Your students and experiences should demand that your plans never be "set in concrete," but always be subject to revisions from year to year.

B. PREPARATION OF A UNIT PLAN: INSTRUCTIONS

We now ask you to prepare a unit plan for a grade level and subject topic you are likely to teach, perhaps during your practice teaching. Here are two general points we emphasize regarding the preparation of a unit plan:

1. There is *no single best format for a unit plan*. Particular formats may be best for specific disciplines and/or topics, and for that reason we have included sample units in this chapter for nine disciplines—art, business, English, foreign language, home economics, music, physical education, science, and social studies. Whereas we have not included a unit plan for mathematics, we have included as our model of a *complete lesson plan* one in mathematics.

2. Theoretically there is *no set time duration for a unit plan,* although most of the curriculum guides may indicate *suggested time durations.* Some units may extend for several days or weeks depending on the subject, interest, and abilities of the students. We will be suggesting that your unit plan for Exercise 8.1 be written for a five-day sequence. Your instructor may alter the guidelines for that exercise (8.1) and for its evaluation (8.2).

EXERCISE 8.1: WRITING MY UNIT PLAN

Instructions: Prepare a five-day unit plan for a grade level, subject, and topic you are likely to teach. Follow the Long Form Format unless your instructor directs otherwise.

UNIT PLAN: LONG FORM

Grade Level and Subject _____ Topic _____

Teacher _____ Time Duration _____

1. Rationale for plan (State the significance or justification for the unit) _____

   _____

2. Instructional objectives (List the expected behavioral outcomes)

   Cognitive _____

   _____

   _____

   _____

   Psychomotor _____

   _____

   _____

   _____

   Affective _____

   _____

   _____

   _____

3. Content and processes to be emphasized (List the major content ideas and related processes to be taught) _____

   _____

   _____

   _____

4. Motivational ideas and techniques to be used _____

   _____

   _____

5. Daily lesson plans (To be attached; see samples for formats)

6. Materials and resources needed (List items needed and where located) _____

_____

_____

7. Evaluation (assessment) strategies (Specific test items should be included with daily lesson plans and should match the stated behavioral objectives) _____

_____

_____

_____

_____

8. Special provisions for individual differences (State how you will attend to varying reading levels, cultural backgrounds, needs of special students) _____

_____

_____

_____

9. Technique for assessment of unit effectiveness (State how you will determine the success of this unit) _____

_____

10. Plans for modification of unit (To be completed after unit is taught, so unit can be improved before using again) _____

_____

_____

EXERCISE 8.2: EVALUATING MY UNIT PLAN

Instructions: This exercise provides a form to be used by you and your classmates to evaluate your unit plans. The form should be duplicated so each teacher candidate's unit plan is evaluated by at least three other members of the class. Circle the appropriate criteria descriptions.

CRITERIA

1.	RATIONALE	clearly stated	acceptable	unacceptable
2.	OBJECTIVES	clear and measurable	acceptable	inadequate
3.	IDEAS AND PROCESSES	appropriate coverage	adequate	inadequate
4.	MOTIVATIONAL STRATEGIES	good ideas	adequate	inappropriate
5.	METHODS AND TEACHING SEQUENCE	appropriate, good variety and balance	acceptable	inadequate
6.	MATERIALS (RESOURCES)	well planned, individual students considered	acceptable	inadequate
7.	EVALUATION	provision good, matches objectives, well-balanced	acceptable	inadequate

Evaluator's comments: _____

_____

_____

_____

After you have received evaluations of your unit plan make appropriate changes prior to implementation.

C. UNIT PLAN AND DAILY PLAN: SAMPLES

Included in this section are sample unit plans (long range) and their corresponding representative daily lesson plans (one for each unit) to serve as guidelines for your lesson planning. Sample plans are arranged in the following order: art, biology, business education, consumer education, English, music, physical education, social studies, Spanish, and a sample Contract Plan for biology. A model lesson plan for geometry follows.

UNIT AND DAILY LESSON PLAN—Sample 1

Grade: _____ 7 and 8 _____ Subject: _____ Art (ceramics) _____

Unit Topic: _____ Forming clay—hand building[2] _____ Duration: _____ three weeks _____

1. *Introduction:* The purpose of this unit is to acquaint the students with the methods of forming clay through hand-building techniques.

2. *Behavioral Objectives:* Upon completion of this unit the student will be able to:
   a. Name five different techniques for forming clay with the hands.
   b. Demonstrate forming clay over objects to create an interior form.
   c. Demonstrate forming clay inside objects to create an exterior form.
   d. Demonstrate creating a form using hand-rolled clay coils.
   f. Demonstrate creating a form using clay slabs.

3. *Content Outline*
   a. Using objects to create a form with clay (1st week)
      (1) Forming clay over objects (2 sessions).
      (2) Forming clay inside objects (2 sessions).
      (3) Pushing objects into clay (2 sessions).
   b. Coil technique of handbuilding (2nd week): rolling coils; making small pots; making large objects.
   c. Slab technique of handbuilding (3rd week): making slabs; making small boxes; making larger objects.

4. *Procedures and Activities*
   Informal lecture combined with demonstration by teacher;
   Studio experiences working in classroom studio or home studio;
   Studio demonstration.

5. *Materials and Equipment*
   clay, objects, sticks, rocks, molds, equipment, wheel, kiln, glazes, wedging table.

6. *Evaluation*
   a. Each student will show a representative sample of each technique in forming clay, rolling coils, and making slabs.
   b. Each student will demonstrate at least one other technique.

---

[2] John Meeks, unpublished material. Reprinted by permission.

UNIT AND DAILY LESSON PLAN—Sample 1 *(Continued)*

Daily Lesson Plan

Class: _____ Art Grade 7 & 8 _____ Topic: _____ Handbuilt Coil Pots _____

1. *Objective:* The student will make a small pot using hand-rolled clay coils.
   Skills to be learned: how to determine clay consistencies; to roll coils; to adhere clay coils to make pot shapes; to score clay coils for strengthening pot; to burnish clay for a surface.

2. *Teaching points:* Teacher will demonstrate and give an informal lecture about each step of construction. Students will then recreate sequences with individual help from teacher.

3. *Materials needed:* Each student will need:
   1 lb. of clay, fork for scoring, sponge for dampening; smooth block of wood for burnishing.

UNIT AND DAILY LESSON PLAN—Sample 2

Unit Plan

Subject: _____ Biology _____ Teacher: _____ D. Grobman _____

Unit Topic: _____ Microorganisms—Viruses and Bacteria[3] _____

Text: _____ Biological Science, An Inquiry Into Life _____

Topics	*Time Estimates in Periods*	*Learning Activities*
A. Viruses		
1. Discovery	$\frac{2}{5}$	T lectures
2. Electron Microscope	$\frac{3}{5}$	Ss read Chapter 9 in class and complete at home.
3. Structure	1	Lab—Inquiry 9-1 Microbiological techniques.
4. Life Cycle	1	Lab—Inquiry 9-2 A disease of bacteria.
5. Diseases	$\frac{3}{5}$	Oral participation, Q/A on previous labs.
	$\frac{2}{5}$	T goes over Quiz questions for tomorrow, SS read and study for Quiz.
6. Review	$\frac{3}{5}$	Written Quiz.
	$\frac{2}{5}$	Ss Oral Q/A at end of Chapter 9. Ss to read Chapter 10 at home.
7. Epidemic—Bubonic Plague	$\frac{1}{10}$	T explains approach and assigns groups.
Occurrence Today	$\frac{1}{10}$	Role-playing by students. T conducts Q/A on results.
B. Bacteria		
1. Discovery	$\frac{1}{5}$	T lectures on Chapter 10.
	$\frac{1}{10}$	T introduces Lab—Inquiry 10-1. Distribution of Microorganisms.
	$\frac{7}{10}$	Ss work on lab.

[3] Deborah Grobman, unpublished material. Reprinted by permission.

UNIT AND DAILY LESSON PLAN—Sample 2 *(Continued)*

Topics	Time Estimates in Periods	Learning Activities
2. Structure		
3. Shapes		
4. Reproduction Growth, Colonies	1	Ss do lab—Inquiry 10-2. Staining and observing Bacterial cells.
5. Cultures	$\frac{9}{10}$	Ss work on Labs—Inquiry 11-1.
6. Diseases		Descendents of a single cell and Inquiry 11-2, War on Bacteria.
	$\frac{1}{10}$	Q/A on quiz tomorrow.
7. Evaluation	1	Written quiz.

OBJECTIVES AND SAMPLE TEST ITEMS

Instructional Objectives	Test Item
A. *Viruses*	
1. Describe the discovery.	What is the piece of equipment that made it possible to study viruses?
2. State evidence for the hypothesis that viruses are similar to the earliest forms of life.	Propose a theory explaining why viruses could not have been the first life on earth.
3. Identify the structure of a virus.	Draw and label the parts representing a typical virus.
4. Diagram the reproductive cycle of a virus.	Draw and label the stages in reproductive cycle of a virus.
5. Explain how a virus infects and affects another living cell.	Predict what would happen when a virus enters a healthy cell.
6. Identify equipment used in dealing with microorganisms.	Given various pieces of lab equipment: microscope, Petri dish, agar, inoculating loop, etc., identify each item and state its use.
7. List aseptic techniques in handling and growing microorganisms.	List aseptic techniques in handling and growing microorganisms.
8. State diseases caused by viruses, their prevention, and cure.	What are some of the diseases caused by viruses? Do these have cures? How can you be protected against them?

UNIT AND DAILY LESSON PLAN—Sample 2 *(Continued)*

Instructional Objectives	*Test Item*
9. Postulate the occurrence of a viral epidemic happening today.	See Lesson Plan that follows.
10. Describe the discovery of bacteria.	List several conditions under which bacteria survive. What helps them survive these conditions?
11. Identify the structure of a generalized bacterium.	Given a diagram of a generalized bacterium, label the parts.
12. Identify 3 bacterial shapes.	Shown various bacteria, classify each according to correct shape.
13. List the principal steps of the Lederberg-Tactum experiments of the effects of X-rays on bacteria.	List the principal steps of the Lederberg-Tactum experiments of the effects of X-rays on bacteria.
14. Explain the transforming principle.	Fill in the partially completed chart on transduction in bacteria.
15. Explain Koch's postulates.	State Koch's postulates in your own terms.
16. List ways bacteria benefit us.	Name several ways man benefits from bacteria.

UNIT AND DAILY LESSON PLAN—Sample 2 *(Continued)*

A Daily Lesson

Unit Topic—*Microorganisms, Viruses, and Bacteria*
Topic for this lesson—*Plague today, A reality?*
Class/Period—Biology 10, Period 4

Instructional Objectives

1. Postulate the occurrence of a viral epidemic happening today.
2. Identify the steps leading to the identification of the disease.
3. Explain the difference between bubonic and pneumonic plague.
4. State the animal vectors of the disease.
5. Recall and state symptoms of the plague.
6. List the defense systems of the body.
7. Trace the spread of the epidemic.
8. Propose the procedures for containment and elimination of the plague.
9. Criticize the public's reaction to the epidemic.

Content Item	Special Material or Equipment	Instructional Strategies	Routines		Time Est.
			1. Take attendance via seating chart as students enter.		

Content Item	Special Material or Equipment	Instructional Strategies	Feedback Strategies			Time Est.
			Get	Give		
Recall concept of viruses, pathogens		T reviews Chapter 9 and conducts Q/A on viruses and diseases. "How many cases of Bubonic Plague were there in U.S. this year, 10 years ago, 50 years ago, and 100 years ago?" "Can viral diseases be controlled?"		Ss raise hands to answer. T calls on several to confirm replies.		5 min.
Bubonic Plague is thought to be a disease of the past. Is this a true statement?	Prepared profiles on specific roles: 1. Initial single plague victim. 2. Police-found victim and try to trace where it was contracted.	T explains that the class will be simulating an outbreak of Bubonic Plague in New York City. T breaks Ss up into groups and assigns each for role-playing. T hands out character sketches to each group and asks for questions.		T takes straw vote to confirm understanding of assignment. Ss break into groups and ask questions.		5 min.

UNIT AND DAILY LESSON PLAN—Sample 2 (Continued)

Content Item	Special Material or Equipment	Instructional Strategies	Feedback Strategies		Time Est.
			Get	Give	
Role-playing cont.	3. Health Dept. and Disease prevention and control. 4. People victims contacted. 5. Nurses and Doctors associated with the case. Try to trace victim's contacts. 6. Government officials: Mayor, etc.		Tour and look for errors. Answers Qs.	Ss start working in groups and try to solve their particular problem.	30-40 min.
Comparing results and generalizing in their cases.		T leads Q/A on class results. T asks for class agreement of proposed actions of the various groups. T shares group progress with class.	T writes results on board. T takes straw vote.	Ss respond and vote on feasibility of each group's conclusions.	5 min.
Relating a similar model.		T relates the theory proposed by Gwyneth Cravens and John S. Marr in *The Black Death*, a novel.	T asks Ss to list the similarities and differences and to justify their theory.	Ss discuss the results. T confirms correct proposals. T praises thoughtful responses.	5 min.
Look ahead		T instructs Ss to work on the write-up of the results of their group's and the class' activity.	Compliment class on good work of today (to extent this proves true).	Ss write their parts and bring to class the next day.	5 min.

If the Role-playing part of the lesson takes longer than the time allotted, the remainder of the lesson plan can be carried over to the next class period and finished then.

UNIT AND DAILY LESSON PLAN—Sample 3

Subject: _____Business Education_____ Teacher: _____Christy Scofield_____

Unit Topic: _____Typing—Modified Block[4]_____ Duration: _____5 days_____

1. *Introduction:* Relate business letter to personal letter which students have already written. Show similarities and differences. Talk about the importance of proper form in a business letter.

2. *Instructional Objectives:* Given a business letter in an unorganized form, the student will produce it in the proper form in 20 minutes.

3. *Unit Content:* Introduction of the 60-space line; use of the bell cue; proper spacing in the rest of the letter; use of typist's initials.

4. *Procedures and Activities*
   a. Show example of proper format in book.
   b. Review by drawing letter and format on chalkboard.
   c. Give practice by doing letters in typing book.
   d. Have papers turned in for suggestions and corrections.
   e. Work with individuals as necessary.

Lesson Plan—Daily

Subject: _____Business Education (Typing I)_____ Date: _____

Teacher: _____Christy Scofield_____ Duration: _____55 minutes_____

1. *Warm-up:* Conditioning practice, p. 86, 55A.

2. *Topic for This Lesson:* Business letter in modified block form.

3. *Instructional Objective:* The student will produce two letters with proper format by the end of the period.

4. *Skills to be Learned:* Correct form of a business letter; correct setting of right margin by listening for bell cue.

5. *Specific Teaching Points*
   Review bell cue;
   Review use of typist's initials;
   Review centering and use of 60-space line.

6. *Assignment:* Type letter problems 1 and 2 on page 87.

7. *Evaluation:* The letters completed and turned in at the end of the period should have the proper format; maximum errors, 12.

---

[4] Christy Scofield, unpublished material. Reprinted by permission.

UNIT AND DAILY LESSON PLAN—Sample 4

Course and Subject: _____ Home Economics—Consumer Education _____

Grade: _____ 12 _____

Unit Topic: _____ Coping with a Cashless Society _____

Unit Duration: _____ 10 days _____

1. *Introduction:* The purpose of this unit is to acquaint the student with checking accounts, usage of credit, and current Electronic Funds Transfer systems (EFT).

2. *Instructional Objectives:* Upon completion of this unit the student will
   a. explain in his/her own words how a checking account works,
   b. demonstrate the process of writing, entering, and balancing a checking account,
   c. explain in his/her own words a brief history of credit,
   d. demonstrate the ability to fill out a credit application,
   e. state what the EFT system is,
   f. identify the possible effects the EFT system will have on the consumer.

3. *Unit Content*
   a. Introduction of the computer revolution (1 session)—forerunners of EFT system: courtesy cards, credit, checking accounts
   b. Checking accounts (2 sessions)—writing, entering, and balancing a checking account
   c. Credit (2 sessions)—brief history, how to select credit appropriate for you, basic laws concerning billing and applying for credit, the effects of credit on consumer behavior
   d. Perspectives on EFT systems (2 sessions)—the components of EFTs, EFT issues, implications of EFT
   e. EFT and the consumer (1 session)—legal issues

4. *Procedures and Activities*
   Informal lecture on each of the above topics and discussion will follow based on:
   a. Charts to be made: timetable of technological revolution, enlarged check book and balance statement
   b. Transparencies to be used: the student will be able to follow the route at which information travels in an EFT system (customer-seller-local bank-central switch-board—yes/no switchboard)
   c. Dittos to be used: How a Checking Account Works, Filling Out a Credit Application, Benefits and Problems of the EFT Systems, You Are the Computer (directions to game), What Do You Think? (preliminary to classroom discussion)
   d. Game: You Are the Computer

5. *Instructional Aids and Resources*
   Overhead projector, dittos, game

6. *Evaluation*
   Participation in classroom discussion, quiz on checking account, unit test, dittos to be handed in

UNIT AND DAILY LESSON PLAN—Sample 4 *(Continued)*

Daily Lesson Plan

Class: _____12_____ Topic: _____Coping with a Cashless Society_____

Theme for the Day: _____What Do You Think?_____ Time: _____1 hour_____

Objective

The student will be able to explain his/her own feelings about the effects of EFT on society and on him/herself. The student will demonstrate the ability to participate in group discussion and decision making.

Motivation

A statement, "You don't need cash in your life."

Discussion

Key Question 1: What do you think about a cashless society?
   a. How do you feel about a computer handling your money?
   b. What are some good reasons for having a checking account?
   c. When would it be difficult to use cash?

Key Question 2: How do you think the EFT will change consumer behavior?
   a. How will people budget their money?
   b. What changes will take place in buying habits?
   c. Why will they take place?

Key Question 3: Where do you think EFT systems will have the greatest impact?
   a. How will it affect banks and stores?
   b. Will it increase or decrease the possibility of errors?
   c. Will it increase or decrease the possibility of getting credit?

UNIT AND DAILY LESSON PLAN—Sample 5

Grade: _____7th_____ Course: _____English_____ Teacher: ___Ms. Sue Morgan___

Unit Topic: _____How to Correctly Punctuate with Commas[5]_____

Duration: _____Three weeks; two sessions each week_____

Introduction: The purpose of this unit is to introduce the correct use of the comma through student application of the comma use rules found in the grammar text to practice sentence exercises, assigned literature readings, and most importantly, to their own writing.

2. *Instructional Objectives:* Upon completion of this unit the students will
   a. correctly punctuate with commas in test exercises and passages with at least 70 percent accuracy.
   b. correctly punctuate with commas in their own writing compositions with at least 80 percent accuracy.
   c. recognize the value of correct comma use to produce clear and comprehensible writing.

3. *Unit Content Concepts*
   a. Comma use in specific occasions (Rules 1-6). Two class sessions.
   b. Comma use to separate works in direct address (Rules 7-10). One class session.
   c. Comma use to separate appositives (Rule 11). One class session.
   d. Comma use in compound and complex sentences (Rules 13-15). Two class sessions.

4. *Procedures*
   a. Students complete pre-test of ten sentences (Grammar text, p. 19).
   b. Students write descriptive compositions, letters, narrative paragraphs, and a dialogue.
   c. Informal lectures introducing comma use rules.
   d. Students practice sentence and paragraph exercises orally and in writing.
   e. Students edit classmates' compositions.
   f. Class discussion of application of comma rules to the practice exercises and to student compositions.

5. *Aids*
   a. Text: Dawson, Elwell, Johnson, and Zollinger, *Language for Daily Use,* Silver Level (New York: Harcourt Brace Jovanovich, Inc., 1973).
   b. Students' compositions.
   c. Dittos of sentence and paragraph exercises.
   d. Overhead projector.

6. *Evaluation:* Three objective tests and three student compositions
   a. Pre-test: Ten test sentences; one student-written letter.
   b. Midterm: Review of comma use skills, Rules 1-10.
   c. Final: Review of comma use skills, Rules 1-15.
   d. Writing: Narrative paragraph, Descriptive paragraph, and Dialogue.

[5] Sue Morgan, unpublished material. Reprinted by permission.

UNIT AND DAILY LESSON PLAN—Sample 5 *(Continued)*

Lesson Plan—Daily

Subject: _____ English _____ Unit Topic: _____ Correct Comma Use _____

Lesson Topic: _____ How to Use Commas to Separate Words or Phrases Within a Series _____

1. *Instructional Objectives*
   a. Students will apply the comma use skill requiring the separation of items in a series by commas to their classmates' descriptive paragraphs.
   b. From the above editing activity, the students will recognize the need for proper comma use to achieve sentence clarity in their own writing.

2. *Contents*
   a. Teacher explanation of the comma rule.
   b. Examples.
   c. Practice application of rule with sentence exercises.
   d. Application of rule to student writing.
   e. Group review for correction.

3. *Motivation*
   Reading and editing their classmates' writing will stimulate the students' interest and appreciation for the value of this lesson.

4. *Procedure:* Teacher will:
   a. Give short lecture introducing grammar rule regarding comma use within a series of words or phrases.
   b. Lecture using test examples and exercises displayed on the overhead projector.
   c. Assign ditto of three student paragraphs and request the class to edit the paragraphs for proper comma use within items of a series. Paragraphs done day before.
   d. Lead class discussion of the correct answers to Exercise D. Stress to the class that commas are necessary to produce clear, easily understood sentences.

5. *Instructional Aids and Materials*
   a. Overhead projector.
   b. Copy of grammar text for each student.
   c. Student copies of classmates' descriptive paragraphs.

6. *Evaluation:* Objective Test
   Given two descriptive passages from two already assigned short stories, in which the commas between series of items have been removed. Students will correctly punctuate with commas with at least 70 percent accuracy.

UNIT PLAN—Sample 6

Grade: _____8_____ Subject: _____Music_____ Teacher: _____John Skorich[6]_____

Unit Topic: _____Music for Fun_____ Duration: _____2 Months_____

1. *Introduction:* This unit will help students to get acquainted with basic concepts of music reading, singing, and instrument playing.

2. *Instructional Objectives:* Students will:
    a. Read basic rhythmic patterns using quarter and eighth note values with their rests.
    b. Recognize differences in sound—high, low, loud, soft, short, long—and its movement up and down by step or skip.
    c. Learn basic techniques of singing.
    d. Recognize different instruments by sight and sound.

3. *Procedures/Activities/Methods*
    Singing, instrument playing, body movements, clapping, reading, game playing.

4. *Instructional Aids or Resources*
    Basic collection of percussion instruments, records, record player, overhead projector, piano or resonator bells, guitar or autoharp.
    Text: Eunice Boardman, *Exploring Music* (New York: Holt, Rinehart and Winston, Inc., 1976).

5. *Evaluation:* Everyday performance. See following page.

[6] John Skorich, unpublished material. Reprinted by permission.

UNIT PLAN—Sample 6 (Continued)

UNIT TOPIC: MUSIC FOR FUN
EVALUATION

Date:

Musical Learning	Listening Selection or Song	Teaching Procedures	Materials	Evaluation
Rhythm: Long/short		1. a. Echo clapping: T claps, Ss repeat.		Clapping accurately?
		b. Rotate some of the examples.		
	Text: *Exploring Music*, p. 38	2. a. Sing "Scotland's Burning." b. Rhythm read:	Text Guitar	Reading accurately?
Duration: Short/Long Form: Round Harmony: Round		c. Rhythm read as a round (divide class in half). d. Sing as a round (divide class in half).		Sing in the round?
Timbre		3. a. Introduce violin as a member of string family—demonstrate different parts & play.	Violin	Recognize violin by sight and hearing?
Melody High/Low Sound		b. Play high/low sounds and let students identify by raising their hand.		Recognize high/low sounds by raising their hands?
Dynamics: Soft/Loud (*p*) (*f*)		4. Clap the following using dynamic levels as indicated.	None	Different dynamic levels?

UNIT AND DAILY LESSON PLAN—Sample 7

Grade: _____9_____ Subject: _____Physical Education_____

Unit Topic: _____Beginning Track and Field[7]_____ Duration: _____2 weeks; 55 minutes/day_____

1. *General Objective:* For students to realize and experience an increased level of cardio-vascular efficiency through skill instructions and drills in the track and field unit.

2. *Specific Objectives:* The student will be able to:
   a. Demonstrate proper techniques in each of the following areas: springs, long jump, high jump, distance runs.
   b. Observe the proper safety procedures during class while pursuing the objectives above.

3. *Unit Content:* See master calendar that follows.

4. *Evaluation:* Written test and skill demonstrations.

5. *Equipment:* (for 32 students) three sets of high jump standards; three cross bars; two 18-lb. shots; two 12-lb. shots; four flights of hurdles.

MASTER CALENDAR

Monday	*Tuesday*	*Wednesday*	*Thursday*	*Friday*
		First Week		
Introduction to unit and class procedures	WU: stretch and jog	WU: Astronaut drill	WU: stretch and jog	WU: stretch and form running
WU: stretch and jog	SI: sprint start	SI: relay techniques	SI: long jump	SI: review with station work
SI: running form	SD: start	SD: hand-offs	SD: pop-ups	SD: stations
SD: form running	CA: 10-yd sprints	CA: relay race 100 yd 4 x 25	CA: group jump relay	1. start
CA: 20-yd sprints				2. hand-offs
				3. long jump
				4. form running

[7] David Shipp, unpublished material. Reprinted by permission.

UNIT AND DAILY LESSON PLAN—Sample 7 *(Continued)*

MASTER CALENDAR *(continued)*

Monday	Tuesday	Wednesday	Thursday	Friday
Second Week				
WU: astronaut drill SI: distance running SD: 100-yd runs with correct form CA: 1320 run for time	WU: stretch SI: high jump SD: approach and take-offs CA: low jump	WU: stretch and short jog SI: high jump SD: jump and landing CA: jump for maximum height	WU: upper body stretching SI: shot put SD: circle moves; put itself CA: group relay	WU: upper body stretching SI: discus SD: circle moves throw CA: group relay

KEY: WU: warm up   SI: skill instructions   SD: skill drills   CA: culminating activity

Daily Lesson Plan

Class: ___Physical Education___   Topic: ___Beginning Track and Field—day 1___

Objectives
1. Students will demonstrate correct arm movement while running.
2. Students will demonstrate correct leg action while running.

Procedure	Time	Formation	Teaching Points
1. Introduce unit and class procedures.	5 min.	x x x x x x x x x x x x x x x x	1. Listen attentively to teacher; follow instruction.
2. Warm up.	5 min.	x x x x x x x x	2. Static stretching.
3. Gather students and demonstrate form running.	4 min.	same	3. Arms moving up and down. High knee action. Push off toes.
4. Have students find a place and practice form running.	3 min.	same	4. High knee action. Arms moving up and down.
5. Have students line up in 8 lines and stride out.	5 min.	x x x x x x x x x x x x x x x x x x x x x x x x x x x x x x x x	5. High knees. Point out students with this and up and down arm motion.
6. Remain in same formation and bound out 10 yds.	5 min.	same	6. Exaggerate points in Step 5.

UNIT AND DAILY LESSON PLAN—Sample 8

Grade: _____8th_____ Course/Subject: _____Social Studies_____ Teacher: _____Therese Feeney_____

Unit Topic: _____The Energy Crisis and Your Environment[8]_____ Unit Duration: _____5 days_____

Introduction

Americans today are realizing that the nation has been facing an environmental and energy problem since the 1950s. To combat these problems, several measures have been implemented. With these in mind, this five-day unit will focus on the following:

a. The students will identify the general nature of the energy crisis and how it has influenced their world.
b. The students will compare and contrast personal ideas and opinions about the energy crisis with classmates, the teacher, and the guest speaker.
c. The students will initiate and evaluate the energy-saving device that they set up in their homes.

Day 1: Objectives and Activities

a. The students are asked to define the term energy crisis in their own words (content).
b. Students will tell the class what they have heard and/or know about energy crisis (content).
c. The students are asked to list ten terms they might use to describe oil companies, and place a plus sign next to each term which has a positive connotation, a minus sign next to each negative term, and a zero next to each term that is neutral. The results are tabulated on the chalkboard totaling the plus, minus, and zero symbols. They are then asked to analyze their results and write a paragraph explaining what the exercise reveals about their own attitudes toward oil companies (inquiry).

Day 2: Objectives and Activities

a. The students will openly discuss the ways in which the energy is used in their homes (content).
b. The students will decide on an appropriate energy-saving device for their homes (decision-making).
c. Students will decide in their own minds what energy-saving devices that they like and might use in their future in their community (inquiry).

[8] Therese A. Feeney, unpublished material. Reprinted by permission.

UNIT AND DAILY LESSON PLAN—Sample 8 *(Continued)*

Day 3: Objectives and Activities

a. The class will have the opportunity to hear about the need for conservation from a state official, a guest speaker (content).
b. The students will ask questions about the energy crisis and other areas of concern that the guest speaker is able to answer and explain (inquiry).

Day 4: Objectives and Activities

a. The students will critique and apply the lecture presented by the guest speaker to what they are studying in class and at home while carrying out an energy-saving program (content).
b. The students will evaluate the information and experience the guest speaker shared with the class. They will also make suggestions that they can use in their home projects and in their future contacts in the real world (inquiry).
c. Through the use of the simulation game (Recycling the Resources) the students will express their own feelings, emotions, and values when placed in the various roles within the context of the game (valuing).

Day 5: Objectives and Activities

a. The students will listen carefully to their fellow classmates when they explain and discuss their home energy-saving devices (content).
b. Students will do the follow-up exercise which essentially involves the comparison of history with the energy crisis and conservation (inquiry).

Reading Assignments

1. Go to the library and consult the book reviews of the following books: *Silent Spring* by Rachel Carson and *The Quiet Crisis* by Stuart L. Udall.

   After reading the reviews you are asked to decide if the book would be worth your while to read. Does it appear to relate to our topic of discussion this week?

or

2. Review the section in your textbook about the Native Americans. Then tell me if you think they had an "energy crisis" in their time.

Evaluation

1. The homework from Day 1 (10 percent of your grade).
2. Group participation and sportsmanship (15 percent of your grade). It will basically measure how well you work with your fellow classmates and how cooperative you are within the group setting.
3. The Home Energy-Saving Project (50 percent of your grade). This is based on the fact that you decide on a certain project and then set it up within your home environment. Lastly, you will be asked to explain your project to the class and turn in a brief summary.
4. The follow-up exercise (25 percent of your grade).

UNIT AND DAILY LESSON PLAN—Sample 9

Subject: _____ Spanish 4 _____ Teacher: _____ Gloria Rodriguez _____

Unit Topic: _____ The Uses of *Ser* and *Estar*[9] _____ Unit Duration: _____ 8 days _____

1. *Introduction: Ser* and *estar* are verbs which both mean "to be." These two verbs, however, are widely different in their concepts, and they can never be interchanged without a basic change of meaning. It is important that a student automatically know when to use these two verbs, considering the frequency with which they are used in the language. This unit is designed as an extensive review of the uses of these two verbs.

2. *Instructional Objectives*
    The student will:
    a. Identify the rules governing the uses of *ser* and *estar*.
    b. Complete substitution and fill-in oral and written drills involving the uses of the two verbs.
    c. Translate correctly the English sentences containing forms of "to be" into their Spanish equivalents.
    d. Spell correctly the vocabulary words presented in the chapter.
    e. Compose short oral presentation correctly using the new vocabulary and using the correct forms of *ser* and *estar*.

3. *Content Outline*
    a. Read and discuss the *Enfoque* at the beginning of the chapter (3 days).
       1. New vocabulary words (Estudio de vocabulario).
       2. Topic for discussion (the law).
    b. *Estructura* (3 days).
       1. General view of *ser* and *estar*.
       2. *Ser* and *estar* with adjectives.
       3. Other uses of *ser* and *estar*.
    c. Read and give presentations on *"Creación"* to reinforce vocabulary words and grammatical concepts (2 days).

4. *Procedures/Activities*
    a. Read and discuss *"Enfoque-Usted y la ley."*
    b. Handouts on vocabulary words to be learned and *ser* and *estar* drills.
    c. Have students prepare short oral presentations about their opinions and solutions to the situations given in the *"Creación."*

5. *Instructional Aids or Resources*
    a. Zenia Sacks da Silva, *On with Spanish,* Harper & Row.
    b. Handouts on *ser/estar* drill.

[9] Gloria Rodriguez, unpublished material. Reprinted by permission.

UNIT AND DAILY LESSON PLAN—Sample 9 *(Continued)*

6. *Evaluation*
   a. Students' answers to oral and written homework drills.
   b. Content of students' oral presentation.
   c. Vocabulary quiz.
   d. Unit test.

Daily Lesson Plan

Grade: _____12_____ Subject: _____Spanish 4_____

Unit Topic: ___The Uses of *Ser* and *Estar*___ Topic for This Lesson: ___Other Uses of *Estar*___

1. *Instructional Objectives*
   The student will:
   a. Complete the exercises, both oral and written, on the uses of *ser* and *estar* with a minimum of teacher help.
   b. Identify circumstances other than those already studied in which the verb *estar* is used.

2. *Assignment*
   Finish worksheet. Read *"Creación"* on pp. 148-149 and be prepared to discuss in class.

3. *Procedure*
   a. Review previously learned uses of *ser* and especially *estar*.
   b. Review homework on "Other uses of *ser*."
   c. Explain other uses of *ser*.
   d. Give oral drills, including Ejercicio 1 (drill on other uses of *ser*).
   e. Have class work on worksheet in class.

4. *Instructional Materials*
   On with Spanish text, ditto.

5. *Evaluation*
   Student answers to homework, performance on drills and on worksheet.

A MODEL FOR A UNIT PLAN CONTRACT

Growing in popularity in recent years has been the use of "teacher-learner contracts." Here is a sample Unit Plan Contract.

Biology: Photosynthesis[10]

Read through the following items and check those you would like to do. Then decide what grade you would like to contract for. Grades will be given as follows:

D—The starred items plus one more from each group
C—The starred items plus two more from each group
B—The starred items plus three more from each group
A—The starred items plus four more from each group

Discuss your choice with your teacher and then sign your name in the proper place on the other side of this sheet.

★ Prepare a title page for the section on photosynthesis in your notebook.
★ Introduce your unit with a brief description of the energy conversion process that takes place during photosynthesis.
★ Write a paragraph explaining why photosynthesis is a vital process in regard to life on earth.

Group I

★ Diagram a "typical" chloroplast and identify its organelles and components.

1. Explain why a high percentage of photosynthesis occurs in the ocean. State what organisms make this possible.
2. Read about Van Niel's experiment with photosynthetic bacteria. Explain where the liberated O_2 comes from during photosynthesis.
3. Set up an experiment to show how different wavelengths of light affect the rate of photosynthesis.
4. Examine *Spirogyra*, *Mougeotia*, and *Zygnema* under the light microscope. Locate the chloroplast in each and make a drawing of it.

Group II

★ State the probable origin of the chloroplast in the higher plants.

1. Identify the "process" that replenishes the CO_2 content of the atmosphere.
2. Explain why Ruben used $^{18}O_2$ (a stable isotope of oxygen) in his famous experiment in 1941. Write a chemical equation showing the reaction Ruben proved.
3. Extract and separate by paper chromatography the photosynthetic pigments from fresh spinach leaves. Identify the pigments on the chromatogram.
4. Examine *Mougeotia* under a microscope. Move a bright light source around the microscope in different positions and write down what you observe about the chloroplast.

[10] Targe Lindsay, Jr., unpublished material. Reprinted by permission.

A MODEL FOR A UNIT PLAN CONTRACT *(Continued)*

★ Explain the role of chlorophyll in photosynthesis.

1. Tell how stomatal activity and CO_2 concentrations are related to photosynthesis.
2. Make a collection of leaves from different plants. Examine the stomatiferous areas of the leaves. Try to draw some conclusions regarding the size, number, and location of stomata on the different leaves.
3. Identify five accessory pigments and explain their role in photosynthesis.
4. Explain the manometric method of detecting photosynthesis.

Date	Pupil's Signature
Grade Contracted	Teacher's Signature

MODEL LESSON PLAN

Subject: _____ Geometry _____ Teacher: _____ Janice Wong _____

Lesson Topic: _____ Geometry theorems pertaining to alternate interior angles, corresponding _____

_____ angles, and interior angles on the same side of the transversal.[11] _____

Preassessment Strategies: Short quiz after going over questions on previous night's homework assignment on identifying interior, exterior, alternate interior, alternate exterior, and corresponding angles.

Quiz: Use the picture at the right to identify the following angles by

1. alternate interior angles

2. exterior angles

3. corresponding angles

4. interior angles

5. alternate exterior angles

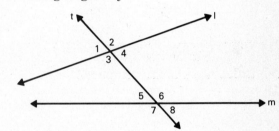

Quizzes are corrected in class and collected. The purpose of the quiz is to check to see if the students have a solid background in identifying types of angles before moving on to today's lesson on theorems pertaining to these angles.

Behavioral Objectives

1. Given two parallel lines crossed by a transversal, students will identify two out of three congruent angles and state which theorem justifies that the angles are congruent.
2. Given two parallel lines crossed by a transversal, students will identify two out of three supplementary angles and state which theorem justifies that the angles are supplementary.
3. Given the degree measures of specific angles in a figure, students will find the measures of at least four out of seven angles.
4. Given specific conditions, 50 percent of the students will successfully apply the theorems about vertical, supplementary/complementary, alternate interior, interior, alternate exterior, exterior, and corresponding angles to prove that specific angles are congruent (or supplementary/complementary).

[11] Janice Wong, unpublished material. Reprinted by permission.

MODEL LESSON PLAN *(Continued)*

Type of Set

1. *Evaluation set:* Quiz to evaluate previously learned material.
2. *Orientation set:* Group work allows student to visualize the content of the presentation (lecture).
3. *Transition set:* Groups report back to the entire class the "rules" or theorems they have discovered; class as a whole decides which theorems actually work; lecture on applying these theorems to solve for missing angles and to write formal proofs.

Lesson Body

Activity	*Stimulus Variation*	*Classroom Control Techniques*
1. Quiz		frequent quizzes immediate, specific feedback to all students
2. Group Work	*Kinesic Variation* (I walk around and visit groups) *Shifting Interaction* (Students go from independent to group learning) *Shifting Senses* (Hands-on type of activity)	discovery learning ad hoc small group cluster chairs facing the center high content participation and practice change my position in the room periodically induce total group participation and effort
3. Lecture	*Shifting Interaction* (Students go from group learning to independent learning) *Pausing* (Use of silence to maintain control) *Focusing*	give clear advance organizers followed by relevant examples desks auditorium-style during lecture name-dropping and eye contact change voice volume for content effects vary voice pitch look at all students as lesson goes on point to lesson object move continually and constantly during lesson ask question, wait, call on volunteer, wait ask higher level questions on content identify source of error, ask again use name dropping/use target student's name

Type of Closure

1. *Review Closure:* Recapitulate main points of lecture.
2. *Transfer Closure:* Homework assignment will permit students to practice what they have learned.

MODEL LESSON PLAN *(Continued)*

Evaluative Items

Behavioral Objectives 1 and 2

Use the Figure (lines T, L, M) to answer the following questions:

A. Fill in the blank with the letter of the correct answer.
B. Write the theorem that justifies why the angles are supplementary (or congruent).

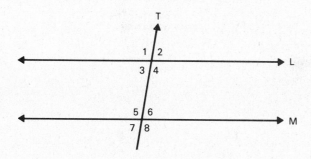

Given: Line L ‖ Line M

1. ∠2 ≅ ∠ _____   a. ∠6   b. ∠8   c. ∠5   d. ∠1

   Reason: _____

2. ∠5 ≅ ∠ _____   a. ∠4   b. ∠7   c. ∠3   d. ∠6

   Reason: _____

3. ∠4 is supplementary to ∠ _____   a. ∠5   b. ∠1   c. ∠6   d. ∠8

   Reason: _____

4. ∠1 ≅ ∠ _____   a. ∠6   b. ∠3   c. ∠4   d. ∠2

   Reason: _____

5. ∠1 is supplementary to ∠ _____   a. ∠7   b. ∠5   c. ∠4   d. ∠8

   Reason: _____

6. ∠7 is supplementary to ∠ _____   a. ∠3   b. ∠6   c. ∠8   d. ∠2

   Reason: _____

MODEL LESSON PLAN *(Continued)*

Behavioral Objective 3

Use the figure at the right to answer the following questions.

Find:

1. m ∠ 2
2. m ∠ 3
3. m ∠ 4
4. m ∠ 5
5. m ∠ 6
6. m ∠ 7
7. m ∠ 8

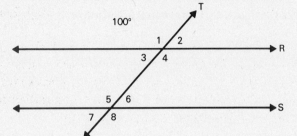

Given: Line R ‖ Line S
  m ∠ 1 = 100°

Behavioral Objective 4

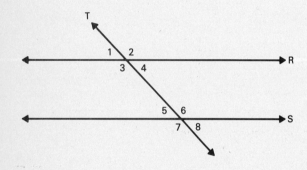

Given: Line R ‖ Line S
Prove: ∠ 8 and ∠ 3 are supplementary

Statements	Reasons

MODEL LESSON PLAN *(Continued)*

Group Work

1. Break up into groups of four.
2. Work individually when you measure the angles for Problems 1-4 and compare your answers with others in your group before proceeding to the next step. Remeasure if there are any disagreements!
3. Answer (a)-(e) for Problems 1-4, then compare your answers with those of others in your group. Everyone should agree on the answers before you proceed to the next step!
4. Discuss with others in your group about generalizations you can make from your answers to Problems 1-4 and complete a "group theorem" for each generalization. Be ready to share your theorems with the rest of the class when we regroup.
5. HAVE FUN!!!!!!!

Name _____

(1)

$\overset{\leftrightarrow}{a} \parallel \overset{\leftrightarrow}{b}$

(2)

$\overset{\leftrightarrow}{a} \parallel \overset{\leftrightarrow}{b}$

MODEL LESSON PLAN *(Continued)*

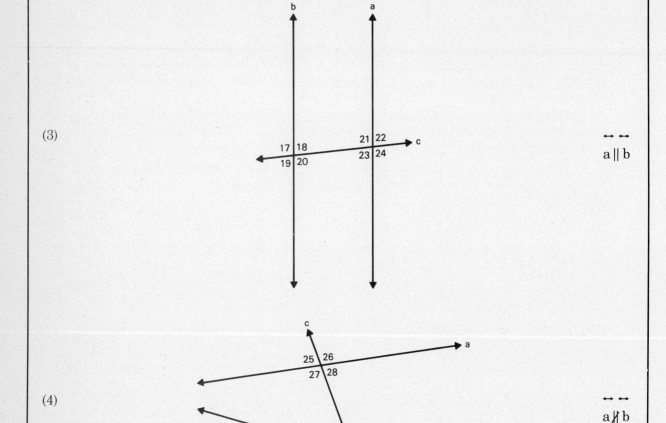

(3)

$a \parallel b$

(4)

$a \nparallel b$

For Problems 1 2, 3, and 4 do the following:

a. Find the measure of each numbered angle.
b. Identify the alternate interior angles and compare their measures.
c. Identify the alternate exterior angles and compare their measures.
d. Identify the corresponding angles and compare their measures.
e. Identify the interior angles on the same side of the transversal and compare their measures.

1. a. m ∠ 1 = _____ m ∠ 2 = _____ m ∠ 3 = _____ m ∠ 4 = _____
    m ∠ 5 = _____ m ∠ 6 = _____ m ∠ 7 = _____ m ∠ 8 = _____

    b.

    c.

    d.

    e.

MODEL LESSON PLAN *(Continued)*

2.   a. m ∠ 9 = _____   m ∠ 10 = _____   m ∠ 11 = _____   m ∠ 12 = _____
       m ∠ 13 = _____   m ∠ 14 = _____   m ∠ 15 = _____   m ∠ 16 = _____

     b.

     c.

     d.

     e.

3.   a. m ∠ 17 = _____   m ∠ 18 = _____   m ∠ 19 = _____   m ∠ 20 = _____
       m ∠ 21 = _____   m ∠ 22 = _____   m ∠ 23 = _____   m ∠ 24 = _____

     b.

     c.

     d.

     e.

4.   a. m ∠ 25 = _____   m ∠ 26 = _____   m ∠ 27 = _____   m ∠ 28 = _____
       m ∠ 29 = _____   m ∠ 30 = _____   m ∠ 31 = _____   m ∠ 32 = _____

     b.

     c.

     d.

     e.

From the above answers, make a generalization about the following:

1. alternate interior angles.

     _____

2. alternate exterior angles.

     _____

3. corresponding angles.

     _____

4. interior angles on the same side of the transversal.

     _____

MODEL LESSON PLAN *(Continued)*

5. Do your lines have to be parallel in order for your generalizations to work?

    _____

6. Write a theorem in "if-then" form for each generalization.

    _____

Lecture

1. Allow each group to report about their findings.
2. Read the actual theorem in the textbook.

Theorem: If two parallel lines are cut by a transversal, then the alternate interior angles are congruent.

Theorem: If two parallel lines are cut by a transversal, then the alternate exterior angles are congruent.

Theorem: If two parallel lines are cut by a transversal, then the corresponding angles are congruent.

Theorem: If two parallel lines are cut by a transversal, then the interior angles on the same side of the transversal are supplementary.

Stress that the lines have to be parallel in order to use these theorems!

3. Do an example on the board applying these theorems to find the measures of missing angles.

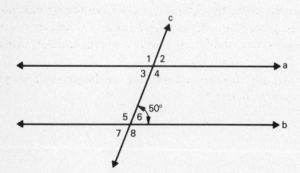

Given: Line a || Line b
            m ∠ 6 = 50°

Find: m ∠ 1, m ∠ 2, m ∠ 3, m ∠ 4,
          m ∠ 5, m ∠ 7, m ∠ 8

4. Do an example of a formal proof applying these theorems, using student input.

Statement	Reason
1. Line a || Line b	1. Given
2. m ∠ 1 = m ∠ 5	2. Corresponding angles are ≅ if lines are ||
3. m ∠ 5 = m ∠ 6	3. Vertical angles are ≅
4. m ∠ 1 = m ∠ 8	4. Transitive property of equality

Given: Line a || Line b

Prove: ∠ 1 ≅ ∠ 8 (without using the alternate exterior angle theorem)

5. Go over oral exercises with class.

In summary, the format of your own lesson plan may vary from our model depending upon subject content, types of activities, and the nature of your students. A guideline we suggest in evaluating the care given to your lesson plan is to ask the question: "Is the plan detailed enough so that a substitute teacher could follow it?"

Review the daily plans of the previous pages, then begin preparation of your first lesson plan as you follow the guidelines of Exercise 8.3.

D. PREPARATION OF A DAILY LESSON PLAN: INSTRUCTIONS

The process of designing a lesson plan is important in getting you to think the lesson through, and will result in a more effective learning experience for the students. Going through the process will prevent the "crime" of greeting your class with "Okay, kids, what shall we do today?" *There is no greater assurance of teacher failure than going into class unprepared, underprepared, or poorly prepared.*

As you prepare your lesson plans, keep in mind these three key ingredients:

1. How you introduce the lesson—*the orientation set induction.*
2. The methods and content—*the lesson body.*
3. How you wrap it up—*the closure.*

Give careful consideration to the preparation of your orientation set and to the lesson closure, as well as the normal careful attention to the content and strategies for teaching that content. Prepare every lesson as carefully as if you were a trial attorney preparing a court case, as if the school principal were scheduled to visit your class.

Within the lesson body, you need to give special attention to how you will make *transitions* from topic to topic, activity to activity. You need to plan your *stimulus variation* techniques, i.e., your body movements, gestures, interaction strategies, use of silence, and sense stimulation variations. These are all important to effective delivery of the lesson body.

As you complete the body of your lesson plan, give final consideration to the *procedures* you will use for effective classroom management (Chapters 14 and 15).

EXERCISE 8.3: PLANNING A LESSON: PRELIMINARY ACTION

Instructions: The educational purpose of this exercise is to start the process that will lead to the preparation of an actual lesson plan. Complete this exercise now.

Grade Level and Subject: _____ Teacher: _____

Topic: _____

1. List the instructional objectives for this lesson.

    Cognitive _____

    _____

    _____

    Psychomotor _____

    _____

    _____

    Affective _____

    _____

    _____

2. What specific learning activities I will provide.

    _____

    _____

    _____

    _____

3. What teaching strategies I will use.

    _____

    _____

    _____

4. What materials and resources I will need.

    _____

    _____

    _____

5. Describe the set induction I will use.

_____

_____

_____

6. What closure I will use.

_____

_____

_____

7. What classroom control techniques I will use.

_____

_____

_____

8. How I will deal with individual differences.

_____

_____

_____

9. How I will determine whether objectives have been met.

_____

_____

_____

10. (Note: your assessment strategy should correspond directly with Item 1 of this exercise.) Share this exercise with your classmates and instructor for useful feedback before you convert it into a lesson plan.

11. From the feedback, what modifications will I make as I convert this into a lesson plan?

_____

_____

_____

_____

EXERCISE 8.4: WRITING MY DAILY LESSON PLAN

Instructions: Prepare a lesson plan you are likely to teach. Follow these steps:

1. From your work for Exercise 8.3 and your study of the Model Lesson Plan (pp. 139-146), prepare a detailed lesson plan that includes the following ingredients.

    Grade level: State the grade and subject for which the lesson is intended.

    Lesson topic: State the lesson topic.

    Preassessment: State what preassessment technique is used.

    Lesson objectives: State the behavioral objectives for this lesson.

    Orientation set: State the set, trying to choose a set that stimulates all modalities—visual, auditory, and kinesthetic.

    Lesson body: Develop your lesson to meet the following criteria:

      Content that meets the behavioral objective(s) and presented in logical order.
      Stimulus variation techniques.
      Logical transitions.

    Closure: Identification of type and means of implementation.

    Evaluation: Statement of how lesson will be evaluated; include items.

    Materials and resources: List of items needed and where obtained.

    Individual needs: Identification of attention you will give to learners with special needs.

2. Have your plan evaluated by members of your class, using Exercise 8.5.

3. Make appropriate modifications in your plan.

4. If possible, try your plan (perhaps during practice teaching), then make further modifications as warranted.

EXERCISE 8.5: EVALUATING MY DAILY LESSON PLAN

Instructions: This exercise provides a form to be used by you and your classmates to evaluate your lesson plans. The form should be duplicated so each teacher candidate's lesson plan is evaluated by three others from the class.

	(Check one)		
	Good	Weak	None
1. Is it clear for what grade level, subject, and topic the plan is designed?			
2. Are the instructional objectives clearly stated?			
3. Are the content and procedures spelled out clearly enough so that a substitute teacher could follow the plan?			
4. Is it clear what materials and instructional resources are to be used, and where obtained?			
5. Are motivators planned for and clearly indicated?			
7. Does the procedure clearly lead to attainment of the objectives?			

LESSON PLAN EVALUATION CODE
(to be completed after evaluation)

	(Circle one)		
	Good	Weak	None
1. Grade level, subject, topic	1	0	—1
2. Objectives	2	1	—2
3. Content and procedures	6	3	0
4. Materials and instructional aids	2	1	—1
5. Advance organizers, set induction, motivators	1	0	—1
6. Closure	1	0	—1
7. Procedure consistent with objectives	2	1	—1

Total _____

Scoring Key:

15 = excellent plan
13-14 = Good lesson plan, review potential weaknesses
11-12 = acceptable, but improvements suggested
less than 11 = unacceptable, do again

QUESTIONS FOR CLASS DISCUSSION

1. Which guidelines for planning do you feel positive about? Negative?
2. Do you have any concerns about daily planning? What are they?
3. Many experienced teachers report they do not write original unit or daily plans. What do you think about this?
4. What is meant by "developing your plan from the concrete to the abstract?" Give a specific example.
5. What can you find in research literature about modality strengths of secondary school students?
6. What are some ways you can individualize your teaching when you have a class of 30 students? Identify at least ten things you could do.
7. What dangers are inherent in using an unmodified lesson plan year after year?
8. Have you ever been a substitute teacher? If so, how useful were the lesson plans left for you to use? Strengths? Weaknesses?
9. Give several reasons why both a student teacher and a first-year teacher need to write very specific lesson plans.
10. Do you have a question you would like to introduce for class discussion? How might the answer be found?

How Can I Individualize the Learning Experience for Students?

Learning is an individual experience. Unfortunately, teaching is one of the few professions where the practitioner is expected to effectively work with "clients" on something other than an individual basis—more likely thirty to one. Much has been written of the importance of dealing with the individual. We know of the individuality of the learning experience, we know of the differences in learning strengths of individuals (modality strengths) within a group, but we place the teacher in the difficult position of treating thirty students as individuals, all at the same time. It seems an impossible expectation indeed, and if occasionally you do fail, at least we will understand. This chapter is designed to help you to minimize your failures and enhance your successes.

Research evidence indicates that student achievement in learning is related to the time and attention being given to the learning task.[1] In 1968 Benjamin Bloom developed a concept of individualized instruction called "mastery learning," based on the idea that students need sufficient time-on-task to master content before moving on to new content.[2] Bloom was reinforcing a model developed earlier by John Carroll.[3]

A teaching strategy for the individualization and mastery of learning that is particularly successful is that of the use of self-instructional packages, a strategy about which the major portion of this chapter is devoted. But, before we address that strategy let us identify some of the other things a teacher can do to individualize learning, that is, addressing the needs of individual students.

---

[1] See Carl H. Rinne, *Attention: The Fundamentals of Classroom Control* (Columbus, OH: Merrill, 1984).
[2] Benjamin Bloom, *Human Characteristics and School Learning* (New York: McGraw-Hill, 1976).
[3] John Carroll, "A Model of School Learning," *Teachers College Record,* Vol. 64, No. 8 (May 1963), pp. 723-733.

A. IDENTIFYING THE STUDENTS' NEEDS IN YOUR CLASSROOM

We can learn more about how to individualize as we pay particular attention to the techniques used for attending to the learning of "mainstreamed" students (see Chapter 1). Each student identified as exceptional will have an individualized educational plan (IEP) which provides the regular classroom teacher with the overall goals and objectives for that student, based on an assessment of that student's performance. These goals and objectives are helpful in planning for both the strengths and weaknesses of this student. However, the recognized needs of exceptional students are further affected by the specific classrooms in which the student is placed. As a regular classroom teacher of a secondary single subject field, you will consider the student's performance as it relates to your class. Such a system of consideration is approached by asking the following:

1. Do I teach my class mostly through visual or auditory channels?
2. Do I require students to complete work most often in a visual or an auditory way?
3. Do I allow modifications of assignments, such as:
   a. amount of work (5 instead of 25 math facts)?
   b. way of responding (underlining answers rather than writing out)?
4. Do I have a system of peer tutoring established?
5. Do I provide a structured classroom schedule, so students know *what* to expect?
6. Do I provide clear assignments and requirements so that students know what *is expected* of them?
7. Do I teach in a step-by-step sequence from simple to more difficult?
8. Do I provide for overlearning of skills?
9. Do I teach observation and generalization skills in order to attend to skills that are not learned incidentally?
10. Do I positively attend to behaviors I want to continue or to increase?
11. Do I provide alternatives to paper/pencil tasks?
12. Do I pair less-preferred activities with more-preferred activities?

These questions are based on procedures that have been found to be useful in working with many types of students with special needs. As you respond to each of these questions, you should compare your answer to the unique needs of the exceptional student being considered. This will enable you to focus on specific adjustments that can be made in your particular classroom.

Teaching to Different Needs at the Same Time

Grouping for instruction is a widely used procedure in regular classrooms. Grouping arrangements[4] may vary as follows:

1. Monads—individual, student-directed settings, such as cubicles.
2. Dyads—one-to-one teacher-directed settings; includes peer teaching.
3. Personal groups—groups of 3-4 students in a teacher- or student-directed setting.
4. Small groups—5-15 students, in a teacher- or a student-directed setting.
5. Large groups—15-35 students, generally in a teacher-directed setting.

[4] G. R. Alley, "Grouping Secondary Learning Disabled Students," *Academic Therapy,* Vol. 13, No. 1 (1977), pp. 37-45.

Although monad- and dyad-grouping procedures are recognized as useful for individualized instruction, personal groups, small groups, and large groups are usually considered most practical for additional practice and repetition of newly learned skills, rather than for individualized instruction. However, in a regular classroom it is often necessary to provide instruction to groups of varying size and skill level during the same time period. A procedure that has been successfully used in providing individualized instruction to groups of varying size and skill levels is one known as multilevel teaching.[5] Multilevel teaching is accomplished through one of two ways:

1. Using the same materials to teach different objectives.
2. Using different materials to teach the same objectives.

Several students can be working on different levels using the same materials or the same objectives, whichever is more appropriate. The steps that should be used in implementing multilevel teaching are these:

1. Define the objective for each skill and the sequence of steps necessary to teach each of these objectives.
2. Pretest each student to determine his/her entry level for a particular objective.
3. Prepare data sheets for recording performance during the instructional session. These sheets should be prepared prior to the start of the session.
4. Select materials that are easy to manipulate and adapt.
5. Present instructional tasks, record responses and other relevant information.
6. Analyze the data after each session.

Teaching Students Who Do Not Receive Special Services

In addition to those students who are mainstreamed from the special education resource or special day classes, there will be students in the regular class who have special needs but do not qualify for special education services. These students are often referred for special education assessment, and are subsequently determined to be ineligible for these services. Most of these are working significantly below grade level, and continue to fall further and further behind. Often, they have been held back, especially by the time they reach the intermediate grades. Other typical characteristics include inattention, poor listening skills, difficulty following directions, and inconsistent academic performance. The majority of these students are those students who have had chronic middle-ear problems since early development. The language deprivation associated with chronic middle-ear problems during early development may be devastating later, during the school years, even if the middle-ear disorder no longer exists. The regular classroom teacher will usually be solely responsible for providing instruction for this group of students.[6] The best educational approach to be used will depend upon two factors: whether the middle-ear difficulties are still occurring and the current age of the student. In younger students, the goal would be to teach to "fill in the gaps," in the older student, to catch up. Specific attention should be given to overlearning skills and to developing strategies for learning.

[5] N. Peterson, *Multilevel Teaching* (Lawrence, KS: Bureau of Child Research, University of Kansas, 1979).

[6] R. R. Houchins and M. J. Pearson, "An Inservice Training Program to Assist Regular Classroom Teachers in Serving the Middle Hearing Impaired," *Journal of the Academy of Rehabilitative Audiology*, Vol. 12, No. 2 (1979), pp. 86-94.

TEACHING THE SLOW LEARNERS

1. Emphasize effective communication skills (speaking, listening, reading, and writing).
2. Help them to improve their reading skills (pronunciation, word meaning, and comprehension). Reading is a *skill* that every teacher must teach no matter what subject he/she teaches.
3. Teach subject-matter content in small sequential steps, with provision for lesson options.
4. Use a wide variety of audiovisual and game materials, as they tend to appeal to more than one sense at a time.
5. Through constructive discipline, teach positive attitudes toward self.
6. Do not depend on a single textbook. Use interesting supplementary materials of different reading levels.
7. Minimize homework assignments. Let them work in class with your assistance and under your supervision.
8. Review and reinforce the materials as frequently and as meaningfully as possible.
9. Compliment and reward for work well done.
10. Whenever and wherever appropriate, subdivide the class into several small groups of similar ability and interest.
11. Learn as much about each of your students as you can.
12. Cover the material *slowly* and methodically.
13. Help the students in the development of their reading skills.
14. Prepare self-instructional packets for individual students.

TEACHING THE MORE CAPABLE AND GIFTED STUDENTS

1. Find out as accurately as possible the present level of achievement of the student.
2. Enrich the student's reading skills (speed reading or enrichment reading program).
3. Provide self-instructional, independent learning opportunities. Try programmed texts, teaching machines, learning activity packets, self-instructional packages, or time waiver assignments.
4. Emphasize skills in critical thinking, problem solving, and research.
5. Provide as many alternatives as possible for projects, experiments, investigations, or assignment options.
6. Let the student plan and carry out with responsibility his/her own activities for learning.
7. Provide seminar situations for the students to discuss topics or problems under study.
8. Stress the quality of the process and product of learning rather than the quantity and duration of various activities.
9. Encourage your department to adopt "enrichment" classes and to pursue the development of an "alternative" curriculum.
10. Bring in effective guest speakers with whom the students can identify and relate.
11. Plan field trips.

B. DEVELOPING THE SELF-INSTRUCTIONAL PACKAGE

The self-instructional technique, or S.I.P., was developed by Rita and Stuart Johnson.[7] Although there are a number of devices designed to individualize teaching, the S.I.P. is one we have found to be quite popular with teachers of all grade levels, from kindergarten through college. We believe the reasons for this popularity are that:

1. *The S.I.P. allows the teacher to create an experience that assures learning.*
2. The S.I.P. *is truly individualized*, that is, it is a package written with an individual student in mind.
3. Although it takes time to prepare, the S.I.P. *requires little or no financial expenditure.*

What Is the Self-Instructional Package?

The S.I.P. is a learning package designed for an individual student and requires 15-50 minutes of learning time. The final package may be written, on tape, on video, on computer disc, or any combination of these. Teachers have found the S.I.P. useful in the following ways:

1. As an enrichment activity for a fast student.
2. As a strategy for make-up for the student who has been absent or is behind the rest of the class, or for the culturally different, or the "mainstreamed" learner.
3. As a means of allowing each student to work at his/her own pace, such as in "contract teaching."
4. As a strategy for introducing basic information, such as learning to use the microscope, thus freeing the teacher to work with individual students and so better utilize teacher time.
5. As a learning experience especially coordinated with manipulative materials, such as a microcomputer, tape recorder, film-loop projector, or materials for science experimentation.

The most important single characteristic of the S.I.P. is that it uses small sequential steps, along with immediate feedback to the learner. In this respect the S.I.P. resembles programmed learning.

A second important characteristic of the S.I.P. is the amount of learning contained in one package. Each package is designed to teach a relatively small amount of material, but to do it well. The S.I.P. may be written for any topic at any grade level, and for any of the three domains— cognitive, psychomotor, affective.

---

[7] Rita Johnson and Stuart Johnson, *Assuring Learning with Self-Instructional Packages* (Chapel Hill, NC: Self-Instructional Packages, Inc., 1971).

How Do I Develop the Self-Instructional Package?

As with any good lesson plan, it takes time to develop an effective S.I.P. Indeed, preparation of your first S.I.P. will test your writing skills. Nevertheless, we suspect you will be very pleased with your product. The process of developing your first S.I.P. will emphasize the importance of planning learning activities in small sequential steps, writing your objectives clearly, providing immediate feedback and assurance to the learner, and preparing test questions that measure the instructional objectives.

The following points should be kept in mind as you begin to prepare what may be the best lesson plan you will ever write:

1. Prepare your *first* S.I.P. so that it will take no more than 30 minutes of student time.
2. Write the package in the first person, as though you are talking directly to the learner.
3. Make your package attractive and fun for the student; use cartoons, puns, pictures, scratch-and-sniff stickers.
4. Use members of your class as resource persons, trying your ideas with one another as you proceed through each step of package preparation.
5. *The package should not read (or be heard) like a lecture.* It should involve small sequential steps with frequent practice and corrective feedback instruction to the learner.
6. The package should contain variety in activities involving visual, auditory, and kinesthetic experiences.
7. Vary your margins and indentations so that the final package does not look like the usual textbook or worksheet with which students are so familiar.
8. Review the model provided in this chapter to get an idea of the S.I.P. The model provided is one that we could fit into this text, but be advised that the S.I.P. may take many forms, i.e., it does not have to fit on 8½ x 11 pages. Br creative in your design.
9. Like any lesson plan, the S.I.P. is always open to revision for improvement.
10. The well-written S.I.P. *will* assure learning. What more can a teacher ask for?

Your first package will take many hours for you to produce, but it will be worth it. Begin by following carefully the steps of Exercise 9.1.

EXERCISE 9.1: DEVELOPING MY FIRST SELF-INSTRUCTIONAL PACKAGE

Instructions: It is most important that you follow this exercise step-by-step. One of the things you will notice is that immediately after writing your objectives you will write your test questions; both steps precede the preparation of the learning activities. That is not the usual order that a teacher follows when preparing lesson plans, but it does help assure that the test items match the objectives. Now, here we go! Remember to check the model that follows.

1. *Prepare the cover sheet.* This is the cover page and includes the title, author, intended students, and estimated working time.
2. *Prepare the instructional objectives.* These should be written in specific performance terms, with conditions. Later, when putting these into your final package, you can phrase them in more general terms if you like, perhaps in an introduction or overview. We recommend that you include at least one attitudinal objective, if nothing more than: "Tell me how you felt about this package."
3. *Share what you have done so far with the members of your class,* to solicit their suggestions.
4. *Rework Steps 1 and 2* if necessary.
5. *Prepare a pretest.* If the learner does well on the pretest, there may be no need for him/her to continue with the package. Some packages may not include a pretest, although most will and we think you should include one with your first S.I.P. writing experience.
6. *Prepare a posttest.* The pretest and the posttest *could* be identical, but usually the posttest is longer. It is important that the posttest items test the objectives of Step 2. Avoid, as much as possible, subjective test items (refer to Chapter 16, Section G if you need help here), keeping the test as objective as possible. We do recommend at least one test item in the affective domain.
7. *Share the pretest and posttest with your classmates* for their evaluation and feedback to you for improvement before continuing to the next step.
8. *Prepare the text of your S.I.P.* This is the "meat" of your package, that which goes between the pretest and the posttest, the learning activities. Remember: the learner must be able to work through the package with little or preferably no help from you.

   An important ingredient is the *directions.* S.I.P.'s are intended to be self-directed and therefore each step of the package should be spelled out for the student.

   Use small sequential steps with frequent practice and corrective feedback for the learner. Make it fun and interesting with a variety of activities for students to do that provide for learning in many ways from writing to reading, from viewing a filmstrip to drawing, from listening to a tape recording to a "hands-on" activity. A word of caution: make sure your activities correlate with your objectives.
9. *Test your package.* Test it on some of your classmates as they look for errors, clarity, and make suggestions for improvement.
10. *Revision if necessary.* Make any necessary changes. Then you are ready to give your S.I.P. its first real test—try it on the student for whom it is intended, perhaps during your practice teaching.

C. THE SELF-INSTRUCTIONAL PACKAGE MODEL

SELF-INSTRUCTIONAL PACKAGE—Model

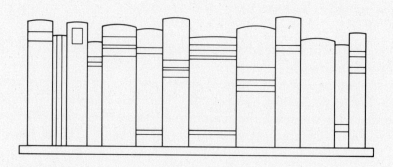

Instructor: ___Suzie Plecas[8]___

School: ___Independence High School___

Course: ___English___

Intended Students: ___8th, 9th, and 10th Grades___

Topic: ___Basic Library Skills___

Estimated Working Time: ___45 minutes___

    This self-instructional package is designed to help you find books in the library. You will learn some very basic skills and information that will show you how to use the library card catalog and how to find books on the library shelves.

Objectives

    Upon completion of this self-instructional package, you will be able to:

1. Identify how fiction and nonfiction books are arranged on library shelves.
2. Identify fiction and nonfiction books by looking at book spines.
3. Use a library card catalog.
4. Identify three ways nonfiction books are filed in the library card catalog.
5. Feel confident and comfortable in using the library—both in finding books listed in the card catalog and in locating the books on the library shelves.

---

[8] Suzie Plecas, unpublished material. Reprinted by permission.

SELF-INSTRUCTIONAL PACKAGE—Model *(Continued)*

Pretest

1. Library books are divided into two main groups on the shelves. What are they?
2. How are nonfiction books arranged in the library?
3. How are fiction books arranged in the library?
4. Nonfiction books are filed in the library card catalog in three places. What are these three places?
5. Fiction books are filed in the library card catalog in two places. What are these two places?

5. By author and title
4. By author, title, and subject
3. Alphabetically by author
2. According to topics
1. Fiction and Nonfiction

If you have answered all of these questions correctly, please see me for another package.

If you have missed any of these answers, complete this package.

Have you ever wondered how a librarian keeps track of all of the books in a library?

The arrangement system of books in a library is really quite simple. Let's take a look.

Books are divided into two main categories: *NONFICTION* books (dealing with true, not imaginary, topics or experiences) and *FICTION* books.

FICTION books are easy to find—especially if you already know the author's name. These books are arranged *alphabetically* by the *last names* of the authors.

'Hm . . . no numbers; these must be miscellaneous."

SELF-INSTRUCTIONAL PACKAGE—Model *(Continued)*

If a library has more than one fiction book by the same author, the books are arranged first by the author, and next alphabetically by title. (If the first work of the title is "a," "an," or "the," the second word of the title is used for alphabetizing.)

1. Books in the library are arranged into two main categories. What are these two categories?

ANSWER: Fiction and Nonfiction

2. Which of the following books would you find first in the fiction section of the library?
   a. *Curtain,* by Agatha Christie
   b. *Crooked House,* by Agatha Christie
   c. *The Incredible Journey,* by Sheila Burnford

ANSWER: c. is correct. Books in the fiction section are arranged first by author's name—Burnford comes before Christie.

3. Which of the following fiction books would you find first on the library shelves?
   a. *The Light in the Forest,* by Conrad Richter
   b. *Rough Road to Glory,* by William Campbell Gault
   c. *Dirt Track Summer,* by William Campbell Gault

ANSWER: c. is correct. Once you find which author's name comes first alphabetically, look to see which titles comes first alphabetically.

4. Which of these books would you find first on the fiction book shelves?
   a. *Jane Eyre,* by Charlotte Bronte
   b. *Wuthering Heights,* by Emile Bronte

ANSWER: a. is correct. But do you know why? Right! Look first at the authors' names. FIRST names count, too. Charlotte comes before Emily. Kind of tricky!

Now that you know how fiction books are arranged on library shelves (by authors' names), let's look at the second group of books, NONFICTION, and see how they are arranged.

In most libraries NONFICTION books are grouped by the books' *subjects,* not authors' names.

SELF-INSTRUCTIONAL PACKAGE—Model (Continued)

NONFICTION books are arranged into a numerical plan called the Dewey Decimal System. In 1876 Melvil Dewey created ten major groups of subjects into which all nonfiction books could be filed. You don't need to memorize the groups! With some practice using the library, you will probably learn some of the categories by heart; but for now, let's just learn that these ten categories exist. Their purpose is to group together books of similar topics.

NONFICTION books are given numbers according to Dewey's list. The numbers appear on a nonfiction book's spine.

000-099	*General Works*	(encyclopedias, almanacs)
100-199	*Philosophy*	(conduct, psychology)
200-299	*Religion*	(the Bible, mythology)
300-399	*Social Science*	(economics, law, education, government)
400-499	*Language*	(languages, grammar, dictionaries)
500-599	*Science*	(math, biology, chemistry)
600-699	*Useful Arts*	(farming, cooking, sewing, business)
700-799	*Fine Arts*	(music, photography, games, sports)
800-899	*Literature*	(poetry, plays)
900-999	*History*	(biography, travel, geography)

On the spine of each nonfiction book is a *call number*. This number includes the Dewey Decimal number, as well as other information that identifies a book and author.

This is what a nonfiction book spine resembles:

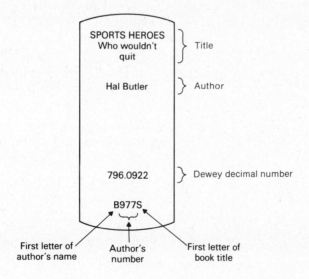

SELF-INSTRUCTIONAL PACKAGE—Model *(Continued)*

1. Under what main category of books would *Sports Heroes Who Wouldn't Quit* (in the book spine illustration) be filed? Use the Dewey Decimal list on the previous page.

ANSWER: Fine Arts. The call number, 796.0992, falls into the 700-799 category. (As you can see, decimal points are used with the Dewey system.)

2. Using the Dewey Decimal System list on the previous page, decide under which number range you would find *The Story of My Life,* by Helen Keller.

ANSWER: If you answered 900-999 (the History category), you are correct! Biographies are real experiences, not fiction.

"These must tell the number of pages in the book."

Now you can browse through a library and see how fiction and nonfiction books are arranged on the shelves.

But suppose you know only the *title* of a book. Do you think you could locate it on the library shelves? Well—if you knew it was a fiction book and knew the author, you could find it. Or, if it were a nonfiction book and you knew the Dewey category, you could go through the whole category of numbers on the shelves to find it (whew!).

But there's a better way to find a book by its title—by using the library *card catalog.*

SELF-INSTRUCTIONAL PACKAGE—Model *(Continued)*

"Hm . . . This must be where they keep the records
of the pupils in the school!"

The card catalog is the key to finding books in a library. Usually, when you want to find a book, you first use the card catalog. It is a series of small drawers arranged *alphabetically*. *Each card* lists the author and title of one book in the library.

For each nonfiction book in the library, three cards are filed in the card catalog. Nonfiction books have a card by author, book title, and subject:

FILED BY AUTHOR

```
793.8   Rydell, Wendy
R972g      The great book of magic:   including 150
           mystifying tricks you can perform/by
           Wendy Rydell, with George Gilbert.
           New York:   H. N. Abrams, c. 1976
             271 p.: ill. (some col.); 28 cm.
             Bibliography: p. 264
```

FILED BY TITLE

```
793.8   The greatest book of magic
R972g      The great book of magic:   including 150
           mystifying tricks you can perform/by
           Wendy Rydell, with George Gilbert.
           New York:   H. N. Abrams, c. 1976
             271 p.: ill. (some col.); 28 cm.
             Bibliography: p. 264
```

SELF-INSTRUCTIONAL PACKAGE—Model *(Continued)*

FILED BY SUBJECT

> 793.8   MAGIC
> R972g   The great book of magic: including 150
>   mystifying tricks you can perform/by
>   Wendy Rydell, with George Gilbert.
>   New York: H. N. Abrams, c. 1976
>   271 p.: ill. (some col.); 28 cm.
>   Bibliography: p. 264

Notice that each card has the same call number in the left-hand corner. This is the number you would write down from the card and use to find the book on the shelf.

A fiction book would have *two* cards filed in the card catalog. Fiction books are filed by author and title.

> 796.34   RACQUETBALL
> B63r   Boccaccio, Tony.
>   Racquetball basics/by Tony Boccaccio;
>   illustrated by Bill Gow; photos by Paul
>   Jacobs; created and produced by Arvid
>   Knudsen.—Englewood Cliffs, N. J.:
>   Prentice-Hall, 1979.
>   48 p.: ill.; 24 cm.
>   Includes index.
>   SUMMARY: Discusses the equipment and
>   fundamentals of racquetball.

1. Using the above card, decide what kind of card this is—author, title, or subject? _____

ANSWER: This is a Subject card. Cards are filed by the information appearing on the first line.

2. What is the title of the book? _____

ANSWER: *Racquetball Basics*

SELF-INSTRUCTIONAL PACKAGE—Model *(Continued)*

3. Who is the author of the book? _____

_____

ANSWER: Tony Boccaccio

4. How many pages are in the book? _____

_____

ANSWER: 48 pages—you need to read the whole card for this information.

5. Is this book fiction or nonfiction? How do you know? _____

_____

ANSWER: Nonfiction. This book has a Dewey number, 796.34. This means that it belongs within the nonfiction category of Fine Arts.

Posttest

Now you are ready to take the posttest. Good luck!

Under what letter on the library shelves would you find these fiction books?

_____ *Roller Skates,* by Ruth Sawyer

_____ *Homer Price,* by Robert McClosky

_____ *Thimble Summer,* by Elizabeth Enright

_____ *Brighty of the Grand Canyon,* by Marguerite Henry

_____ *The Runaway Robot,* by Lester Del Rey

ANSWERS: S. M. E. H. D

SELF-INSTRUCTIONAL PACKAGE—Model *(Continued)*

000-099	*General Works*	(encyclopedias, almanacs)
100-199	*Philosophy*	(conduct, psychology)
200-299	*Religion*	(the Bible, mythology)
300-399	*Social Science*	(economics, law, education, government)
400-499	*Language*	(languages, grammar, dictionaries)
500-599	*Science*	(math, biology, chemistry)
600-699	*Useful Arts*	(farming, cooking, sewing, business)
700-799	*Fine Arts*	(music, photography, games, sports)
800-899	*Literature*	(poetry, plays)
900-999	*History*	(biography, travel, geography)

Using the list above, in which category would each of the following nonfiction books be found? Write the number range.

_____ *A Book of Nature Poems*, selected by William Cole

_____ *Let's Travel in Canada*, ed. by Joan Downing and Frances Dyra

_____ *Understanding Congress*, by Joe L. Evans

_____ *Musical Instruments*, by Robina Beckles Willson

_____ *Science Experiments with Water*, by Sam Rosenfield

ANSWERS: 800-899, 900-999, 300-399, 700-799, 500-599

SELF-INSTRUCTIONAL PACKAGE—Model *(Continued)*

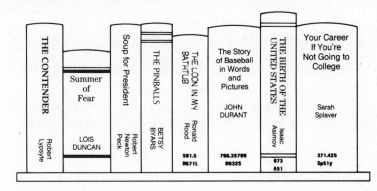

1. Which of the above books are fiction? _____

    _____

    ANSWERS: *The Contender; Summer of Fear; Soup for President;
    and The Pinballs*

2. Which of the above books are nonfiction? _____

    _____

    ANSWERS: *The Loon in My Bathtub; The Story of Baseball in Words
    and Pictures; The Birth of the United States; and Your
    Career If You're Not Going to College*
    (These have Dewey numbers on the spines.)

3. Using the list above, what kind of a book is *The Loon in My Bathtub*? _____

    _____

    ANSWER: The Science category

4. How many cards will be listed in the card catalog for *The Loon in My Bathtub*? What are

    these cards listed under? _____

    _____

    ANSWERS: 3 cards: Subject card, Author card, and Title card

QUESTIONS FOR CLASS DISCUSSION

1. Which psychology of learning theory does the self-instructional package concept most closely follow?
2. Would your school district make your self-instructional packages available to other teachers in the district?
3. How are self-instructional packages different from unit-activity packages?
4. Have you seen any computer programs that follow the technique prescribed for writing self-instructional packages?
5. Do you think you could write a self-instructional package to be programmed for microcomputer use? Investigate to see if any software companies are interested. If they are, they likely will do the programming for you.
6. Earlier in this chapter we stated that the self-instructional package will represent the most perfect lesson plan you will ever write. Now that you have written an S.I.P., how do you feel about that statement? Agree or disagree? Why?
7. We would not wish a teacher to teach solely via the use of the self-instructional package any more than we would wish the teacher to teach solely by lecturing. Do you agree or disagree with this opinion? Why?
8. How could you prepare a self-instructional package for nonreaders of the English language?
9. Since the use of video playback equipment is popular in today's secondary school classrooms, can you think of an imaginative combination of that equipment with the self-instructional package concept for your own teaching? Share your idea with your classmates.
10. Do you have a question for class discussion?

SELECTED READINGS AND REFERENCES FOR CHAPTERS 5 THROUGH 9

Catania, A. C. *Learning.* Englewood Cliffs, NJ: Prentice-Hall, 1982.
Charles, C. M. *Individualizing Instruction.* St. Louis, MO: C. V. Mosby Co., 1980.
Gronlund, Norman E. *Stating Objectives for Classroom Instruction,* 3rd ed. New York: Macmillan Publishing Company, 1985.
Jenkinson, Edward B. *The Schoolbook Protest Movement: 40 Questions and Answers.* Bloomington, IN: Phi Delta Kappa Educational Foundation, 1986.
Simpson, E. J. *The Classification of Educational Objectives in the Psychomotor Domain,* Vol. 3. Washington, DC: Gryphon House, 1972.

Part III

Choosing and Implementing Instructional Strategies in the Secondary Classroom

Tell me, I forget;
show me, I remember;
involve me, I understand.
—Elaine Haglund

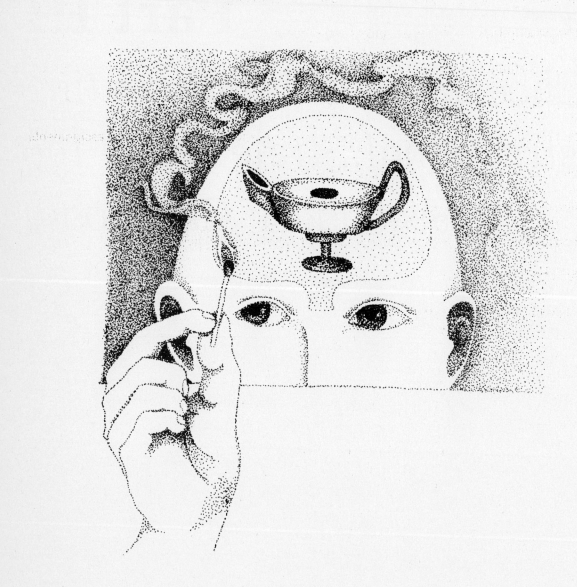

Drawing by Carol Wilson, unpublished material. Reprinted by permission.

Part III helps you choose and implement a particular instructional strategy by:

- Providing guidelines for your use of facilitating behaviors.

- Providing skill development exercises for the use of questioning.

- Providing descriptions of the access and delivery modes.

- Providing guidelines for the use of the lecture.

- Providing descriptions of inquiry and discovery methods.

- Providing guidelines for your use of discussions, demonstrations, the textbook, and assignments.

- Providing descriptive educational games and sources of games.

- Providing guidelines for the use of audiovisual aids.

- Providing an annotated list of motivational ideas for various subject fields.

- Identifying professional journals.

- Helping you to begin your resource file.

What Are the Basic Teacher Behaviors that Facilitate Student Learning?

During your career as a teacher you will continue to build your strategy repertoire and to develop your teaching skills. The competent teacher has a large repertoire from which to select a specific strategy for a particular goal. In addition, that teacher has developed skill in using that strategy. This part of our resource guide is designed to assist your building of that repertoire and to begin developing your skill in the use of particular strategies.

It is important that the teacher know why he/she has selected a particular strategy. The unskilled teacher is likely to be inclined to use the strategy that was most commonly used in his/her college classes—the lecture—but, except for 15-minute minilectures, the pure lecture is seldom an effective way to instruct junior and senior high school students, and even then it needs to be supplemented with other important teacher behaviors. As discussed in Chapter 3, today's secondary teacher needs to be eclectic in strategy implementation, choosing the most appropriate combination of strategies to achieve specific goals with particular groups of students.

While there is a seemingly endless list of strategies from which to choose (see next chapter), there are ten basic teacher behaviors that the secondary teacher uses to facilitate student learning, almost without regard to strategy used. These facilitating teacher behaviors are those that produce the following results:

- The students are actively involved in the learning activities.
- Instructional time is efficiently used—student and teacher times are used to complete quality tasks.
- There is a minimum of classroom interruption.

The effectiveness with which a teacher implements these facilitating behaviors can be measured, and the bottom-line result of effective implementation is that *the students learn*. Let us now describe the ten specific teacher behaviors that create the basic conditions that enable a student to learn anything, whether that learning be a further understanding of concepts, the internalization of attitudes and values, or the development of cognitive processes and psychomotor skills.

A. TEN BASIC TEACHER BEHAVIORS

The Behavior	Description	How the Teacher Does It
1. *Structuring*	The teacher provides the climate in which students productively act and react.	1.1.0 Plans lessons in detail and uses advance organizers. 1.2.0 Defines roles, tasks, and expectations. 1.3.0 Establishes ground rules. 1.4.0 Provides a clear definition. 1.5.0 Identifies limitations of time and circumstances. 1.6.0 Organizes the students. 1.7.0 Clearly communicates objectives to the students. 1.8.0 Clearly communicates to the students his/her tolerance levels.
2. *Accountability*	The teacher indicates a willingness to be accountable for what is expected of him/her, and holds the students accountable for learning.	2.1.0 Is attentive to a student's recitation. 2.2.0 Requires students to demonstrate their work. 2.3.0 Signals students that they may be called upon. 2.4.0 Plans activities that engage the learners, with objectives they clearly understand. 2.4.1 Communicates 2.4.0 to parents and administration. 2.5.0 Provides continuous cues for desired behavior. 2.6.0 Provides incentives contingent upon acceptable performance (e.g., grades, points, rewards, privileges).
3. *Overlapping*	The teacher gives attention to several matters at the same time.	3.1.0 Attentive to entire class while working with one student or a small group of students. 3.1.1 Communicates this awareness by gestures or verbal cues. 3.1.2 Refocuses or shifts activities when attention begins to wane. 3.1.3 Dwells on one thing only as long as necessary for the students' understanding.
4. *Varied and Challenging*	The teacher provides a variety of activities to motivate and challenge the students to work at the optimum of their abilities and to reach the modality strengths of more students more of the time.	4.1.0 Demonstrates enthusiasm for what is going on and being learned. 4.2.0 Demonstrates optimism toward each student's ability. 4.3.0 Uses interval shifts in kinds of activity and intellectual challenges. 4.3.1 Carefully plans transitional shifts designed to be interest-boosting. 4.4.0 Demonstrates a pride in the profession.

The Behavior	*Description*	*How the Teacher Does It*
5. *Modeling*	Teacher behavior is consistent with the behavior expected of his/her students.	5.1.0 Exhibits behaviors the teacher expects from the students. 5.1.1 Turns off the classroom lights upon leaving the room for lunch in response to a just finished lesson on energy conservation. 5.1.2 When the development of rational problem-solving is a major learning goal, and a classroom problem arises, teacher collects data, weighs decisions, explores options, and tries tentative solutions. 5.2.0 Really involves the students in discussion. 5.3.0 Uses "I" when he/she means "I," and "We" when he/she means "We." 5.4.0 Readily admits when he/she makes a mistake. 5.5.0 Spells correctly because he/she expects students to learn to spell. 5.6.0 Writes legibly and expects students to communicate clearly.
6. *Facilitating the acquisition of data*	Makes data accessible to the students as input they can process.	6.1.0 Creates a responsive classroom environment. 6.1.1 Creates a classroom that is a pleasant place to be. 6.1.2 Provides manipulative materials for learners to work with. 6.1.3 Acts as a resource person. 6.1.4 Regards the students as potential resources, too. 6.1.5 Makes sources of information readily available. 6.1.6 Utilizes resource persons from the community.
7. *Acceptance*	Nonevaluative and nonjudgmental responses that provide a psychologically safe learning environment.	7.1.0 Conservatively uses strong praise for specific reasons, such as acceptance of a student's correct answer. 7.2.0 Uses paraphrasing or reflective listening for actively accepting students' interpretation of concepts and original ideas. 7.3.0 Uses minimal reinforcement (passive acceptance) frequently (i.e., comments such as "uh-huh," "right," and "okay"). 7.4.0 Demonstrates empathic acceptance when the teacher accepts a student's mood or feelings.

The Behavior	Description	How the Teacher Does It
8. *Clarifying*	A teacher's responding behavior whereby the teacher seeks elaboration on a student's idea or behavior.	8.1.0 Invites the student to be more specific. 8.2.0 Asks the student to elaborate on or rephrase the student's idea. 8.3.0 Asks the student to provide a concrete illustration of the idea.
9. *Silence*	Periods of quiet in the classroom.	9.1.0 Pauses for longer than 2 seconds (perhaps 7-9 seconds, to allow students to think and to respond) after asking a question or posing a problem. 9.2.0 Provides planned quiet time.
10. *Questioning*	A behavior used by the teacher to elicit cognitive learning or thinking development.	10.1.0 Uses questions that require divergent as well as convergent thinking. 10.2.0 Helps students develop their own questioning skills. 10.3.0 Plans the questioning sequence so as to elicit a variety of thinking skills, and to move the learners into higher levels of cognitive operations. 10.4.0 Listens carefully to students' questions and responds, building upon their content.

B. ABOUT QUESTIONING

Questioning is one of the most important and frequently used teaching strategies. Questions are used for a variety of purposes. The teacher might use a rhetorical question for the purpose of giving directions, e.g., "Why don't we all come around the terrarium to watch the salamander?" Or, the purpose might be to control behavior, e.g., "I think we should all get quiet now, don't you?" Questions are used to gather information about the class, e.g., "How many of you have finished doing the worksheet?" And, questions are used by the teacher to help students to develop their cognitive thinking skills, and that is what we would like to focus your attention on now.

The nature of questions asked by the teacher has a significant impact upon the progression of student thinking, as the teacher's questions are cues for the level of thinking expected of the students. The level of questioning may range from the lowest, requiring only simple recall, to the highest, requiring application of divergent thinking. The levels of questioning may be thought of as analogous to the three basic thought clusters of intellectual functioning, as (1) an *INPUT* of data from the senses and from memory; (2) the *PROCESSING* of those data into meaningful relationships; and (3) the *OUTPUT* or *application* of those relationships to novel situations.[1]

---

[1] Arthur L. Costa, *The Enabling Behaviors* (San Anselmo, CA: Search Models Unlimited, 1983), p. 3. Copyright by Arthur Costa.

Recognizing Levels of Classroom Questions

What is expected in the use of questioning is for you to guide the students from simple cognitive levels of recall to highest levels of application. The material that follows will identify the three levels of questioning and provide exercises designed to assist you in recognizing and developing your questioning skills.

I. Gathering and Recalling Information (INPUT)[2]

To cause the student to INPUT data, questions and statements are designed to draw from the student the concepts, information, feelings, or experiences acquired in the past and stored in long- or short-term memory. They can also be designed to activate the senses to gather data which the student can then process at the next higher level. There are several cognitive processes included at the INPUT level of thinking. Some verbs that may serve as the predicate of a behavioral objective statement are:

completing	describing	matching	reciting
counting	identifying	naming	selecting
defining	listing	observing	scanning

Examples of questions and statements designed to elicit these cognitive objectives are:

Question/Statement	*Desired Cognitive Behavior*
"Name the states that bound California."	Listing
"How does the picture make you feel?"	Describing
"What word does this picture go with?"	Matching
"Define the word 'haggard.'"	Defining
"What were the names of the children in the story?"	Naming
"What did you see the man doing in the film?"	Observing
"Which ball is the blue one?"	Identifying
"How does the Gettysburg Address begin?"	Reciting
"How many coins are there in the stack?"	Counting
"Which words in this list are rhyming words?"	Selecting
"The Mexican houses were made of mud bricks called . . . what?"	Completing
"Watch what color the litmus paper turns when I put it in the liquid."	Observing

II. Making Sense Out of the Information Gathered (PROCESSING)

To cause the student to PROCESS the data gathered through the senses and retrieved from long- and short-term memory, questions and statements are designed to draw some relationships of cause and effect, to synthesize, analyze, summarize, compare, contrast, or classify the data that

---

[2] Costa, op. cit., pp. 7-9. Reprinted by permission.

he/she has acquired or observed. Following are verbs that may serve as the predicate of a behavioral objective statement if the desired cognitive behavior of students is at the level of processing.

synthesizing	contrasting	explaining	making analogies
analyzing	distinguishing	grouping	organizing
classifying	experimenting	inferring	sequencing
comparing	planning		

Examples of questions designed to elicit these cognitive objectives are:

Question/Statement	Desired Cognitive Behavior
"Compare the strength of steel to the strength of copper."	Comparing
"Why did Columbus believe he could get to the East by sailing West?"	Explaining
"From our experiments with food coloring in different water temperatures, what can you infer about the movement of molecules?"	Inferring
"How can you arrange the rocks in the order of their size?"	Sequencing
"How can you arrange the leaves so that all those that are alike are in groups?"	Classifying
"What do you think caused the liquid to turn blue?"	Explaining cause and effect
"Arrange in groups the things that a magnet will and will not pick up."	Grouping
"What other machines can you think of that work in the same way that this one does?"	Making Analogies
"What are some characteristics of Van Gogh's work that makes you think this painting is his?"	Distinguishing
"What can you do to test your idea?"	Experimenting
"How are pine needles different from redwood needles?"	Contrasting
"How can you arrange the blocks to give a crowded feeling?"	Organizing
"How can we go about solving this problem of the lost playground equipment?"	Planning
"What data are we going to need in order to solve this problem?"	Analyzing

III. Applying and Evaluating Actions in Novel Situations (OUTPUT)

Questions and statements that cause OUTPUT are designed to have the student go beyond the concept or principle that he/she has developed and to use this relationship in a novel or hypothetical situation. Application invites the student to think creatively and hypothetically, to use imagination, to expose a value system, or to make a judgment. Verbs that may serve as the predicate of a behavioral objective statement if your desired cognitive behaviors of students is at the level of application include:

applying a principle	forecasting	imagining	predicting
evaluating	generalizing	judging	speculating
extrapolating	hypothesizing	model building	

Examples of questions designed to elicit these cognitive objectives are:

Question/Statement	*Desired Cognitive Behavior*
"What will happen to our weather if a high-pressure area moves in?"	Forecasting
"If our population continues to grow as it does, what will life be like in the twenty-first century?"	Speculating
"Since the amount of heat does affect the speed of movement of the molecules, what will happen when we put the liquid in the refrigerator?"	Predicting
"Imagine what life would be like if there were no laws to govern us."	Imagining
"What can you say about all countries' economies that are dependent upon only one crop?"	Generalizing
"Is there a way you can think of to use this bimetal strip to make a fire alarm?"	Applying
"With this clay make a model of a plant cell."	Model building
"What would be a fair solution to this problem?"	Evaluating
"Which of the two paintings do you think is more interesting?"	Judging
"From what we have learned, what other examples of romantic music can you cite?"	Applying a principle
"What do you think might happen if we placed the saltwater fish in the tank of fresh water?"	Hypothesizing

Exercises 10.1-10.6, which follow, will assist your understanding and use of questioning as a valuable teaching strategy.

EXERCISE 10.1: IDENTIFYING COGNITIVE LEVELS OF CLASSROOM QUESTIONS[3]

Instructions: Mark each question with
        1 if it asks the student to input data.
        2 if it asks the student to process data.
        3 if it asks the student to apply.

_____ 1. Who was the author of the poem we read yesterday?

_____ 2. How is the poem we read yesterday like the poem we are reading today?

_____ 3. For what reasons do you think the author of this poem repeated the last line of every verse?

_____ 4. Why do you think salmon always return to spawn in the same river in which they were born?

_____ 5. What do you think would happen if the Rocky Mountains were to disappear?

_____ 6. Mary, which states bound California?

_____ 7. How do you account for the fact that some Mexican Indian tribes actually helped Cortes conquer the Aztecs?

_____ 8. Who discovered San Francisco Bay?

_____ 9. Who can summarize some of the things we learned about the nomads of the desert?

_____ 10. How did the life style of the nomads differ from ours?

_____ 11. How do you think their lives would be different if they had all the water they could use?

_____ 12. Why did the tribes have to fight each other for the land?

_____ 13. What would happen if we held the test tube upside-down?

_____ 14. From what you have read, what are three laws that both governments have in common?

_____ 15. What are some similarities between our concept of law and the concept held by an authoritarian form of government?

_____ 16. What would life be like if there were no laws?

_____ 17. What are the three levels of thinking?

_____ 18. How does Guilford's structure of the intellect compare with Bloom's taxonomy?

_____ 19. In what ways are spoken and written questions similar and different?

_____ 20. How would classroom dialogue be affected if students understood the questioning strategy the teacher was using?

Now check your responses to this exercise with those of other members of your class and discuss until you concur and understand.

---

[3] Costa, op. cit., p. 11. Reprinted by permission.

EXERCISE 10.2: OBSERVING THE COGNITIVE LEVELS OF CLASSROOM VERBAL INTERACTION

Instructions: Make the proper arrangements to visit a secondary classroom. In the spaces provided, tally the number of times you hear questions or statements that cause students to gather or recall information, to process that information, and to apply or evaluate. Try to capture a few key words to remind you of the cognitive levels used. (Refer to section preceding Exercise 10.1.) After your observation, compare and discuss with your classmates.

Teacher _____ Date _____

Grade level _____ School _____

BEHAVIORS OBSERVED

Questions/Statements at Recall Level	
Questions/Statements at Process Level	
Questions/Statements at Application Level	

EXERCISE 10.3: RAISING QUESTIONS TO HIGHER LEVELS[4]

Complete the blanks and share your responses with other members of the class.

Recall	Processing	Application
1. How many of you are buying milk today?	Why are you buying milk today? Are there more students in Mrs. Smith's room than ours who are buying milk?	What do you think would happen if nobody bought milk anymore? What do you think would happen if all the children of the world had all the milk they needed?
2. What was our weather like yesterday?	How does the weather today compare to the weather yesterday? Why is our weather so different today? How does our weather compare with that of Moscow?	What do you think the weather will be like tomorrow? What do you think would happen if the weather was uniform all over the world?
3. What is the capital of Maryland?		
4. What are the names of the primary colors?		
5. Create your own question.		

[4] Costa, op. cit., p. 10. Adapted and used by permission.

EXERCISE 10.4: CREATING COGNITIVE QUESTIONS

Read the following, then compose three questions that cause students to identify, list, and recall; three that cause students to analyze, compare, and explain; and, three that cause the students to predict, apply, and hypothesize. Then check your responses with those of other members of your class.

A Short Course in Human Relations

The SIX most important words:
  "I admit I made a mistake."
The FIVE most important words:
  "You did a good job."
The FOUR most important words:
  "What is your opinion?"
The THREE most important words:
  "If you please."
The TWO most important words:
  "Thank you."
The ONE most important word:
  "We"
The LEAST important word:
  "I"

—Unknown

Recall Questions: 1. (to identify) _____

_____

_____

2. (to list) _____

_____

_____

3. (to recall) _____

_____

_____

Processing Questions: 1. (to analyze) _____

_____

_____

2. (to compare) _____

_____

_____

3. (to explain) _____

_____

_____

Application Questions: 1. (to predict) _____

_____

_____

2. (to apply) _____

_____

_____

3. (to hypothesize) _____

_____

_____

EXERCISE 10.5: ANALYZING THE LEVEL OF QUESTIONS IN TEXTBOOKS[5]

Examine questions posed in the student edition and the teacher's manual of any textbook. Also examine workbooks, evaluation materials, or discussion guides.

1. List examples of recall questions you found: _____

_____

_____

2. List examples of process questions you found: _____

_____

_____

3. List examples of application questions you found: _____

_____

_____

Rewrite an example of a recall question you found into a processing and an application question.

Recall question: _____

Rewritten into a processing question: _____

_____

Rewritten into an application question: _____

_____

Describe the sequence in which a series of questions appeared in the text. _____

_____

_____

Compare this text with another in the same grade/subject area. Which one would you select? Why?

_____

_____

_____

_____

_____

_____

_____

[5] Costa, op. cit., p. 16. Reprinted by permission.

EXERCISE 10.6: MINI PEER TEACHING LESSON FOR PRACTICING QUESTIONING

Before class each member should prepare a five-minute lesson for the purpose of posing different types of questions, and teaching the lesson to one student by guiding that student from the lowest level of thinking to the highest level of operation.

In class, form groups of four:

1. Sender
2. Receiver
3. Judge
4. Recorder

Some suggested topics for discussion:

1. Explaining to others what you learned so far.
2. The use of questions in teacher's manuals, courses of study, and textbooks.
3. Problems of translating the content of this exercise with others.
4. The evaluation of classroom teaching.

Your tasks—

1. The Sender: Pose input, processing, and application questions related to one of the above topics.
2. The Receiver: Respond to the questions of the sender.
3. The Judge: After the sender has asked a question and the receiver has responded, identify the level of question used by the sender and the level of thinking demonstrated by the receiver.
4. The Recorder: Tally the number of each level of question or statement used by the sender on the tally sheet and

Record any "hang ups" or problems which your group encounters or identifies.

Each member of the group will function in each role for about five minutes, then switch roles, so that each member has an opportunity to serve in each role.

This section on the use of questions as a teaching strategy has but touched the surface; indeed entire texts are devoted to the topic. Questioning is one of your more important tools and we hope we have helped your developing competency in the use of that tool. We conclude this section with these reminders about the use of questions for teaching.

TEN GUIDELINES FOR THE USE OF QUESTIONING

1. The questions you plan to use should be written out in advance in order to reduce ambiguity, to be specific, and to be sure you are using vocabulary suitable for the age and developmental level of your students.
2. Arrange your questions in order so that the learners are guided from low-input type questions through processing to application thinking, avoiding a steady dependency on low-level recall. Match the type of question with the purpose it is intended to serve.
3. Give the students time to think after you have asked the question. Wait in silence for at least seven seconds. If you have still not gotten a response, then you might ask it again slightly clarified. DO NOT ANSWER IT YOURSELF. Wait even longer, perhaps as long as nine seconds. You will be surprised how often you will then get a response and how often that will be a higher-level response than those that came after a wait time of only two seconds or so.
4. Avoid bombarding the students with "shotgun questioning." Rapid-fire questioning leaves no time for them to think, and it is unnerving. Too much teacher talk, and too little student think time is detrimental to quality learning.
5. Be sure you practice calling on *all* of the students.
6. Use strong praise sparingly, passive acceptance more frequently.
7. Ask the question first; pause; then you can call on an individual student.
8. Allow the students to ask questions. You should help them to formulate good questions, questions that they can try and find answers to.
9. If you are asked a question for which you do not know the answer, don't guess or bluff an answer. Look it up, or have the students help you find an answer.
10. Being able to ask good questions is perhaps more important than having the right answers.

The exercise that follows is designed to test your identification of certain of the basic teaching behaviors in a classroom interaction.

EXERCISE 10.7: IDENTIFYING BASIC TEACHER BEHAVIORS IN CLASSROOM INTERACTION[6]

The following is a sample classroom interaction. There are examples of various levels of questions and structuring and response behaviors. See if you can identify them. Your answers should be from this list: structuring; facilitating; acceptance-active; acceptance-passive; clarifying; questioning-input; questioning-processing; questioning-application. Compare your answers with those at the end of the exercise.

Interaction	*Teacher's Behavior*
John: Mr. Brown, here's a picture that shows how a magnet works.	
Teacher: O.K. John, would you please share this with the rest of the group? Tell us what you think is happening.	1. _____
John: Well, this boy is in the garage using a magnet to pick up things, and over here it shows all the things a magnet will pick up.	
Teacher: What kind of things are they, John?	2. _____
John: Nails, paper clips, spoons, screws, screwdri . . .	
Jim: It will not pick up spoons, John. I've tried it.	
John: It will too. It shows right here.	
Bill: I picked up a spoon with a magnet that my uncle gave me.	
John: Sure it will!	
Gregory: No it won't, 'cause . . .	
Teacher: Just a minute. We'd like to hear everyone's idea, but we can't if we all talk at once. If you'll raise your hand, then I'll know who to call on next.	3. _____
Teacher: Now, John says a magnet will pick up spoons. Bill says he has picked up one. Jim says that a magnet can't pick it up.	4. _____
Teacher: Yes, Cathy, what do you think?	5. _____
Cathy: I'm not sure, but I think it has to be metal.	
Maria: I think it depends upon the kind of spoon. Some spoons have metal and some are plastic and other stuff.	
Teacher: That's another possibility.	6. _____
Teacher: How can we solve this problem as to whether a magnet will pick up the spoons?	7. _____
Jim: We can get some spoons and try it with our magnet.	
Teacher: All right. Anybody know where we can get some spoons?	8. _____

(continued)

---

[6] Costa, op. cit., pp. 75-78. Reprinted by permission.

	Interaction	*Teacher's Behavior*

Shelly: There's a spoon in my lunch bag.

Bill: There are some spoons in the cafeteria. Can we go and get them?

Teacher: Yes. Shelly, would you get yours? Bill, would you get some from the cafeteria? John, would you get the magnet?

9. _____

Later

Teacher: Now, because this is Shelly's spoon, what do you think would be the fair thing to do?

10. _____

Cathy: Let her try it on her own spoon.

Teacher: All right, Shelly, what do you think will happen when we touch the magnet to the spoon?

11. _____

Shelly: It probably won't pick it up because it's not the right kind of stuff for a magnet to pick up.

Teacher: What do you mean, "the right kind of stuff?"

12. _____

Gregory: She means the right kind of metal.

Teacher: Shelly, would you try it. Let's all watch.

13. _____

Jim: See, I told you a magnet wouldn't pick up a spoon.

Rick: But it does pick up some spoons.

John: I don't mean all spoons, only those made of metal. The spoon in the book is made of metal.

Maria: Is this pin out of steel?

Teacher: No, Maria, it isn't.

14. _____

Maria: I thought it was steel or stuff like that—like a piece of car.

Teacher: I don't undersand what you mean, Maria. What do you mean, "a piece of car?"

15. _____

Maria: When mom banged up our fender, you could see the shining metal under the paint. Dad said it was steel.

Gregory: I think the most powerful magnet in the world might be able to pick it up.

Cathy: An electro-magnet, I think, is the strongest magnet that was ever invented by the earliest scientist.

Teacher: Are you saying, Cathy, that you think a stronger magnet would pick up the spoon?

16. _____

Cathy: Um—hm. I think so.

Teacher: What would you want to do to find out?

17. _____

Cathy: We could set up our electro-magnet and try it.

Teacher: O.K.

18. _____

1. Structuring
2. Question-Input (Listing)
3. Structuring
4. Accepting—Actively
5. Question—Processing (Explaining)
6. Accepting—Passively
7. Question—Processing (Problem solving)
8. Question—Input (Locating)
9. Facilitating Acquisition of Data—Note: This might also be interpreted as a structuring behavior since the teacher directs the students to perform a task.
10. Question—Application (Evaluation)
11. Question—Application (Predicting)
12. Clarifying
13. Facilitating the Acquisition of Data
14. Facilitating the Acquisition of Data
15. Clarifying
16. Clarifying
17. Question—Processing (Planning)
18. Accepting—Passively

Key: Identifying Basic Teacher Behaviors in Classroom Interaction

QUESTIONS FOR CLASS DISCUSSION

1. For one week, practice empathic acceptance behaviors. What did you learn from the experience?
2. For one week (perhaps not the same week as for number one), practice periods of controlled silence, i.e., pausing longer than normal in all your verbal communications. What did you learn from the experience?
3. For one day, ask *no* questions. What did you learn from this experience? Did you find yourself doing anything different in the absence of asking questions?
4. The next time you watch television, have Exercise 10.2 with you. Clarify the types of questions or statements you hear in a typical evening of television viewing. What did you learn?
5. Teachers usually communicate structuring to students by verbal structuring, written structuring, nonverbal structuring, and logistical structuring. What are examples of nonverbal structuring? Of logistical structuring?
6. Frequent discussion in education circles speaks of the needs of individual students. Is this true today? What has been its emphasis, historically?
7. Some would say that students are learning better in the schools today than they were ten years ago. Find evidence to support or reject this notion.
8. What "ground rules" (1.3.0) would you establish with your class during the first week of school? How would you do it?
9. What are your tolerance levels? (1.8.0) That is, how much noise can you tolerate? How much confusion?
10. How would you signal a student that you are about to call on him/her? (2.3.0)
11. What would you do to signify your attentiveness to a student's recitation? (2.1.0)
12. What specific ways can you communicate overlapping awareness to students? (3.1.1)
13. What other questions do you have about the content of this chapter? How might answers be found?

SELECTED READINGS AND REFERENCES FOR CHAPTER 10

Costa, Arthur L. (Editor). *Developing Minds: A Resource Book for Teaching Thinking.* Washington, DC: Association for Supervision and Curriculum Development, 1985.

Costa, Arthur L. *Enabling Behaviors.* San Anselmo, CA: Search Models Unlimited, 1985.

Moore, R. E. "Can Advance Organizers Influence Meaningful Learning?" *Review of Educational Research,* Vol. 42, No. 2 (1979), p. 371.

Reilly, Robert R., and Ernest L. Lewis. *Educational Psychology: Application for Classroom Learning and Instruction.* New York: Macmillan Publishing Company, 1983.

Rinne, Carl H. *Attention: The Fundamentals of Classroom Control.* Columbus, OH: Charles E. Merrill, 1984.

Seifert, Edward H., and John J. Beck, Jr. "Relationships between Task Time and Learning Gains in Secondary Schools." *Journal of Educational Research,* Vol. 78, No. 1 (September-October 1984), pp. 5-10.

Smith, Howard A. "The Marking of Transitions by More and Less Effective Teachers." *Theory into Practice,* Vol. 24, No. 1 (Winter 1985), pp. 57-62.

11

What Are the Guidelines for the Use of Specific Teaching Strategies?

As stated in the previous chapter, the secondary school teacher has a large repertoire from which to select a specific strategy to achieve a particular goal with his/her own class of students. Consider this list.

SOME INSTRUCTIONAL STRATEGIES

*Assignment
Audiovisual
Committee activity (small group work)
Computer-assisted instruction
Debate
*Demonstration
*Discovery
*Discussion
Drama
Drill
Expository
Field trip
*Games
Guest speaker
Independent study
Individualized instruction
*Inquiry
Laboratory investigation

Learning activity packages
*Lecture
Library/resource center
Panel discussion
Problem solving
Questioning
Review and practice
Role play
Self-instructional packages
*Simulations
Study guides
Supervised study
Symposium
Teaching machine
Team learning
Telephone teaching
*Textbook learning

Our experiences indicate that competent teachers in secondary schools are skillful in combining various strategies listed above into a total lesson plan package. In this chapter we elaborate on those strategies marked with an asterisk in the preceding list. Most of the remaining strategies are discussed elsewhere in this resource guide. (Consult the index for their locations).

A. YOUR FIRST DECISION IN STRATEGY SELECTION: THE DELIVERY OR THE ACCESS MODE?

Two distinct avenues exist for your consideration when selecting a strategy to teach content or processes. One avenue is the *delivery mode* where you, the teacher, see that information is delivered to the students. This is the "traditional" or didactic mode where knowledge is passed on to the learners via the teacher, or from content reading in a textbook, or both. The most time-honored strategies within the delivery mode are textbook reading and lecture-discussion.

The second avenue is the *access mode,* where the teacher's task is to provide to the students access to information and experiences whereby they develop knowledge and skills. The most popular teaching strategy here is pure inquiry.

In this chapter we will familiarize you with techniques from both modes so that as a teacher you will have a better idea regarding which mode might be best for a particular goal and your unique class of students. Since the delivery mode is that with which you are undoubtedly more experienced, and although we will provide guidelines for use of strategies within that mode, we wish to acquaint you well with use of access strategies. Our intent is *not* to imply a favorite, but to encourage your skill development with both. Let us explain.

The *strengths* of the delivery mode *are* these.

- Much content can be covered within a relatively short span of time—it is time-efficient.
- It is highly controllable—the teacher is in control.
- Student learning is predictable and manageable.

The *weaknesses* of the delivery mode *can be* these.

- The lack of intrinsic sources for student motivation.
- The students are not involved in as much decision-making.
- The stifling of creative thinking.
- The students' self concepts are not adequately attended.

The strengths and weaknesses of the access mode are just the reverse of those for the delivery mode. In the access mode students make more real decisions about what is to be learned, and how, and their source of motivation is more intrinsic in origin. As they learn to solve problems *they* feel important, they develop better feelings of self because they develop a sense of "can do." However, with the access mode, less content is "covered," there is less predictability about what will be learned, and the teacher constantly feels that he/she may at any moment lose control of the class.

The traditional mode of delivery is safer for the beginning teacher because the teacher is in control of content and time, and it is the mode with which you are most familiar. We believe, however, that it is important for children to have experiences in both modes and we encourage you to develop your skills in the use of each. We now provide specific guidelines for particular strategies.

B. USING THE LECTURE IN SECONDARY SCHOOL TEACHING

Lecturing to junior and senior high school students is inevitable for most teachers. A well-planned and executed lecture can be an exciting learning experience for the students. A poorly planned and delivered lecture can create more problems than the teacher ever imagined! It takes time to develop skill in lecturing; in the meantime use it cautiously, keeping in mind the guidelines we present here.

Guidelines for Lecturing

1. The short (15-20 minutes maximum) *informal lecture* is preferable for most secondary school classes. The more advanced students may be able to handle a twenty-minute lecture, but in other cases a brief five- or ten-minute minilecture may be better.

2. The *purposes* of a lecture might include the introducing of a unit, summarizing a problem, explaining an inquiry, providing information difficult for students to obtain elsewhere, motivating an inquiry, or sharing the teacher's experience with the class. A lecture can be designed to promote student inquiry and critical thinking. A lecture interspersed with well-designed questions (moving students into higher-order thinking) can help build student reasoning skills.

3. The students should know what the *objectives* of the lecture are, and there should not be too many for one lecture.

4. The lecture should be *rehearsed* by the teacher (preferably in front of a mirror), well planned, researched, and augmented by *multisensory stimulation,* and just plain interesting to watch and to listen to, complete with a little tasteful and appropriate humor.

5. The lecture should *enhance* the content already found in the student textbook, rather than to simply repeat it.

6. *Pacing* should be moderate (not too slow or too fast) and interspersed with feedback checks to see if students are understanding the material.

7. The lecturer's *voice* should be pleasant and interesting to listen to, not a monotone or a shrieking irritable high pitch, and the language used should be understood by the learners.

8. Lecturing should be used sparingly, and mixed with other strategies. Within a typical 50-minute class period you might do best to change your strategy two or three times, each time changing to a distinctly different modality in order to retain more of the student attention for a longer period of time. In other words, following teacher talk (lecture) with more teacher talk (discussion or question-and-answer) is not as productive as following teacher talk (lecture) with student doing (worksheet; small group discussion; student investigation). This is appropriate use of *stimulus variation.*

9. *Lecture only when appropriate.* Don't lecture when a student handout might be better. Most secondary students can read and understand faster than they can listen and understand. Keep that in mind as you plan your strategies.

10. As you plan your lecture, create an effective orientation set to "grab the students' attention." Prepare an *outline format* rather than reading your lecture. (Recall how awful it is when a lecturer reads notes verbatim!) If you use a formal lecture, students may benefit from an outline of the key points and words on an overhead transparency or in a handout. Part of your responsibility as a secondary teacher is to help the students learn *how to learn,* which includes helping them to organize thoughts, to take meaningful notes, and how to learn from those notes.

11. A *summary and followup* activity is important to the effective use of the lecture. Allowing students to question and discuss the material will enhance their learning. Because lecture learning is for students mostly passive learning, it should be followed by activities that engage them in more active learning. Better yet, five- or ten-minute minilectures can be designed that follow or precede activity-oriented learning within the same class period.

12. Keep in mind those students in your class with the "special needs"—the handicapped, the mainstreamed, the culturally and linguistically different—and design your lecture to *personalize* with the use of special analogies, examples, and appropriate student "name-dropping." Remember what we have said elsewhere, that the most beautiful sound in the whole world is the hearing of your own name, in a positive tone and in good taste, of course.

C. USING INQUIRY AND DISCOVERY IN SECONDARY SCHOOL TEACHING

There is a lot of confusion as to exactly what inquiry teaching really is; indeed, there may be as many definitions as there are people defining it. Sometimes (and understandably so) inquiry is confused with other strategies, such as discovery. Let us share with you our own interpretation of these two distinct, but related, strategies—inquiry and discovery.

First, and the major reason why they are confused with one another, is that in both strategies the students are *actively engaged in problem solving.* That is the major advantage of these two techniques, because it is vastly important that students gain skill in recognizing and solving real life problems. However, before we continue with the advantages and disadvantages of inquiry and discovery, let us identify the difference between them. To understand this difference it is helpful to study the following chart, which identifies *three levels of inquiry according to what it is the students do.*

LEVELS OF INQUIRY

	I	*II*	*III*
Problem Identification	Identified by teacher or textbook	Identified by teacher or textbook	Identified by student
Process of Solving the Problem	Decided by teacher or textbook	Decided by student	Decided by student
Identification of Tentative *Solution* to Problem	Resolved by student	Resolved by student	Resolved by student

It should be readily apparent from the chart that what we refer to as Level I Inquiry is in fact the traditional "cookbook" approach to teaching, where the problem is defined for the student, as is the process for working through the problem to the inevitable solution; if the "program" is well designed then the end result is inevitable as the students "discover" the intended "answers." This level of inquiry teaching can also be referred to as *guided inquiry* or guided *discovery*. The students are carefully guided through the process to "discovery."

The advantages of Level I Inquiry have been stated earlier. It is in reality didactic teaching and is highly manageable and predictable. It is probably best for teaching fundamental concepts and principles. However, students who never experience beyond Level I are missing the opportunity to engage their higher mental operations, they do not experience more motivating real-life problem solving, and they come away with the false notion that problem solving is a linear operation, which it is not!

It is our hope that by the time students are in high school they are permitted to experience real inquiry, which begins with Level II, where the students actually design the processes of their inquiry.

True inquiry is cyclic rather than linear! We diagram this cyclic process as follows.

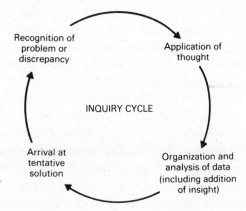

One enters this inquiry cycle whenever a discrepancy is observed. (Recall Piaget's "cognitive disequilibrium"?) *Discrepancy recognition can occur at any point in the cycle.* In the use of real inquiry we emphasize the tentative nature of the conclusions reached and that makes it more like real-life problem solving, where we make decisions based on data but recognize that those decisions may be altered when new data indicate that need.

In Level III Inquiry, the students actually identify the problem as well as decide the processes and reach the conclusion. Perhaps this is what graduate education should be about, rather than the more traditional study of what others have already done—an hypothesis we shall leave for other authors to pursue.

In inquiry learning the students generate ideas and then design ways to test their ideas. The processes are varied—some are concerned with generating and organizing data, others with building and using ideas. The following diagram illustrates processes in each of these operations.

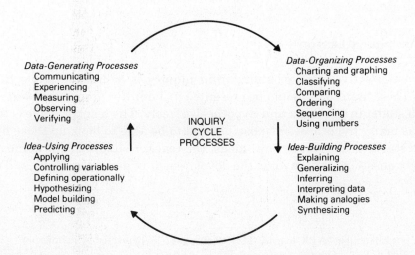

Some of the processes in the cycle are *discovery,* others are *inquiry*. Inquiry processes are more complex mental operations (all of those in the idea-using category); consequently, early grades usually concentrate on the discovery skills. *By the time children are adolescents, they are in the process of developing formal thought and should be provided experiences requiring the more complex, higher-level inquiry skills.*

At the beginning of this section we promised to give you our interpretation of how inquiry and discovery teaching are similar and how they differ. Have we made it clear, in a way that makes sense to you? Inquiry learning is a higher-level mental operation that introduces the concept of the *discrepant event,* a concept which helps learners develop skill in observing and watching for discrepancies and then providing opportunities for the students to investigate their own ideas regarding explanations. Inquiry, like discovery, is a problem-solving strategy; the difference is in the amount of decision making performed by the students. Inquiry also helps students to understand the nature and importance of suspension of judgment, the tentativeness of "answers or solutions," and perhaps to better deal with ambiguity.

Now that you understand the difference between discovery and inquiry, let's continue as we describe the kind of classroom environment that promotes inquiry. First let us emphasize that *dogmatic teaching is lethal* if a teacher wants to use a Level II Inquiry model; whereas freedom of thought enhances the class as if it were a "think tank," encouraging guessing and intuitive thought. Healthy skepticism and practice in suspending judgment are prized behaviors for inquiry, and the teacher's modeling of these behaviors counts! An *open classroom* environment is more conducive to effective inquiry teaching. Openness *does* require planning, conviction, self-control, cooperation, and trust. Openness allows for the suddenness of discovery—serendipity. It places value on mistakes and on diversity. Openness is *not* to be confused with permissiveness or sloppy teaching, and it does not imply that all students are to "rediscover fire" for themselves.

In a time in our society when we have been experiencing school reform with strong "back to basics" movements, an occasional shift to open inquiry may be welcomed by you and your students. We know that *the retention rate from inquiry learning is superior to the rate from most other teaching strategies,* and the highly personal involvement of the learners can be a positive contributor to their developing feelings of self-worth.

Inquiry teaching is a technique that will take time for you to develop skill and confidence in using. During practice teaching you may wish to gain the support and guidance of your supervisors and practice some inquiry-oriented lessons. These are especially important for student learning in science and social science. The lesson that follows is a good one for you to practice in a methods class, and one that you can perhaps modify for use in your own teaching.

Mystery Island: An Inquiry Lesson[1]

One of the most effective ways of stimulating inquiry is to use materials that provoke the students' interest. These materials should be presented in a nonthreatening context, such as a game or puzzle, in which students can think and hypothesize freely. The teacher's role is to encourage the students to form as many hypotheses as possible and to be able to back up these hypotheses with reasons. After the students suggest several ideas, the teacher should begin to move on to higher-order, more abstract questions that involve the development of generalizations and evaluations.

[1] Jack Zevin, "Today's Education," *NEA Journal* (May 1969), pp. 42-43. Reprinted by permission.

Inquiry lessons, such as the Mystery Island geography problem presented here, have a special advantage because they can be used with almost any group of students, regardless of ability. Members of each group approach the problem as an adventure in thinking and apply it to whatever background they can muster. Background experience may enrich a student's approach to the problem but is not crucial to the use or understanding of the evidence presented to him/her.

Mystery Island is presented as it is given to students. They receive information about the island in sequence. Map 1 includes data abour rivers, lakes, and size (scale). This map is followed by information about landforms (Map 2), vegetation (May 3), and climate (Map 4). Other data maps, showing mineral deposits or transportation networks, for example, could easily be added to this series.

All students are asked to solve the same problem after getting each new piece of information. The key problem is to locate "the biggest city." Students are asked, in effect, to accumulate geographic evidence about a place, to form hypotheses, to review these hypotheses in the light of new evidence, and to refine their notions about the reasons underlying the location of cities.

After introducing each new element of Mystery Island, the instructor could ask: "Now that you have this information about Mystery Island, what additional information would be most important to you in understanding the Island? Explain why." Other questions could include: "Where would most people live?" "Where would the least number of people live?" and "What would people do for a living on Mystery Island?"

All student hypotheses or predictions about the location of cities, population distribution, or the economy of Mystery Island should be backed by reasons. These hypotheses can then be analyzed, discussed, and evaluated by the class as a whole.

In addition to analytical problems concerning Mystery Island, value issues may also be proposed for solution. One such issue could center on the clash that occurs when a technologically advanced culture and a technologically undeveloped culture meet on the island. For example, what would happen if Mystery Island were inhabited by a group of hunters and gatherers and was then invaded by people of a different racial or ethnic origin who possessed superior skills?

Students could be asked such questions as: Should the original population be allowed to mix with the new people? What problems will each group face if they live separately? If they live together? What would be best for all concerned parties? Why?

The reader is invited to look at Mystery Island and try to solve the problem posed to the students—locating the biggest city on the island. Take into account all the evidence provided here and make a list of reasons to back up your decision.

D. USING DISCUSSIONS IN SECONDARY SCHOOL TEACHING

Discussion as a teaching strategy probably ranks right up there with lecture and questioning in frequency of use in junior and senior high school teaching, but because you have been a student for a number of years and are already knowledgeable about the advantages and disadvantages of this technique we will not bore you with a lengthy discussion of discussion as a strategy, but will "pick *your* brains" by letting you begin with responses to Exercise 11.1, which follows on page 209.

1. MYSTERY ISLAND
   SCALE: 1 INCH = 100 MILES
   ∿∿∿ Stands for sea water
   ──── Stands for rivers
   ⌒ Stands for lakes

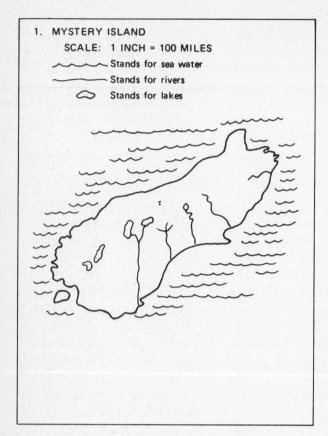

3. MYSTERY ISLAND: VEGETATION
   ▨▨▨ Stands for grassy areas or grasslands
   ⑴⑴⑴ Stands for needleleaf trees, such as pine
   ⋎⋎⋎⋎ Stands for broadleaf trees, such as oak or maple
   ∧∧∧∿ Stands for mountains and mountainous areas with little or no plant life

2. MYSTERY ISLAND: LANDFORM MAP
   ∧∧∧∿ Stands for mountains and mountainous areas
   ⌢⌢⌢ Stands for hills and hilly areas
   ▭ Stands for plains or flat areas

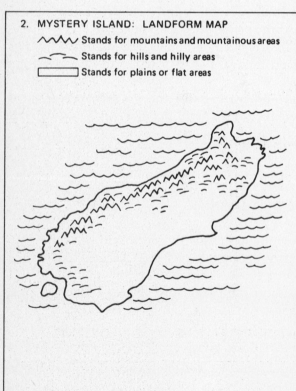

4. MYSTERY ISLAND: RAINFALL
   (Average yearly amount)
   ▨ Stands for areas getting between 20 and 40 in.
   ▨ Stands for areas getting between 40 and 60 in.
   ▭ Stands for areas getting between 60 and 80 in.
   ☰ Stands for areas getting more than 100 in.

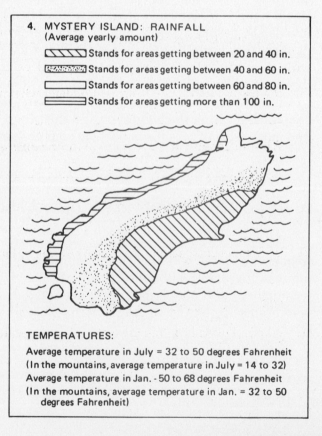

TEMPERATURES:

Average temperature in July = 32 to 50 degrees Fahrenheit
(In the mountains, average temperature in July = 14 to 32)
Average temperature in Jan. - 50 to 68 degrees Fahrenheit
(In the mountains, average temperature in Jan. = 32 to 50 degrees Fahrenheit)

EXERCISE 11.1: DISCUSSION AS A STRATEGY: WHAT DO I ALREADY KNOW?

Please answer these questions, then share your responses with other members of your class, perhaps in subject field discussion groups.

1. My subject field is _____

2. What would be the reasons I would hold class discussions? _____
    _____

3. How would I arrange the student seating? _____

4. What ground rules would I establish before starting the discussion? _____
    _____
    _____
    _____

5. Should participation be forced? _____
    How would I encourage participation? _____
    How would I discourage one or two students from dominating the discussion? _____
    _____

6. What preparation should the students and I make before the discussion session? _____
    _____

7. How would I handle digression? _____
    _____

8. If I use students as discussion leaders, what training should they receive? _____
    _____

9. What different roles are options for me during class discussions? _____
    _____
    When is each most appropriate? _____
    _____

10. Is a whole-class discussion (20 or more students) ever appropriate or effective? If so, when?
    _____
    How? _____

11. When, if ever, is a "class meeting" appropriate in junior or senior high school teaching?
    _____
    _____

12. Can "brainstorming" be a form of discussion? _____

13. What follow-up activities would be appropriate after a discussion session? _____
   _____
   _____

Share your group discussion results with your entire class. As a class, can you evolve some general guidelines for the use of the discussion as a strategy? How effective were the small group discussions you had? What allowed for or inhibited effectiveness? How effective was the whole class activity? What allowed for or stifled its effectiveness? You may wish to discuss those questions and others in small or large groups to complete your list of guidelines for the use of discussioon as a teaching strategy. Your instructor may wish to model the role of moderator for the closure of this activity, along with the following points for a successful discussion activity.

The Teacher Should:

1. Clearly identify the purposes/objectives for the discussion.
2. Suggest and guide the development of a topic to be discussed.
3. Provide background information and resources.
4. Assist students in a maximum participation in the discussion.
5. Assign responsibilities for the chairperson and others according to abilities and interests.
6. Accept student contributions as worthwhile, no matter how limited the value may be.
7. Suggest appropriate time schedules.
8. Monitor students closely during their discussion.
9. Provide summary remarks or conclusion based on what students have discussed.
10. Evaluate the discussion activity—what went well and what to improve.

E. USING THE DEMONSTRATION IN SECONDARY SCHOOL TEACHING

Like other strategies, the success of the demonstration will largely depend on how well you prepare before class. Remember, if anything can go wrong, it will!

The demonstration can be effective in many different subject fields, not only science, home economics, physical education, art, and shop. For example, the English teacher might demonstrate steps in paragraph writing; the mathematics teacher demonstrates steps in solving a quadratic equation. In any demonstration, the learners are motivated by the fact that the demonstrator is actually engaged in a learning activity rather than merely verbalizing it.

The following are guidelines for an effective use of the demonstration strategy.

1. Identify for yourself and the students the purpose of your demonstration. The purpose might be one of the following:
   a. To illustrate a particular concept.
   b. To set up a discrepancy or to establish problem recognition.
   c. To assist in the recognition of a solution to an existing problem.
   d. To serve as a means of review
   e. To serve as an unusual lesson closure.

2. Familiarize yourself with the advantages and disadvantages of the demonstration as a teaching strategy. Incorporate this awareness in your planning for the demonstration lesson. A potential disadvantage is a result of the fact that the students are not learning by doing but rather by watching, but this may be necessary because of time pressures, lack of sufficient

materials, or potential hazards involved. A good demonstration, however, can stimulate thinking and productive discussion. Use the following guidelines in planning your demonstration.

a.   Decide the best way to conduct the demonstration, i.e., talk or be silent; student or teacher; entire class or small groups.

b.   Ensure that the demonstration is visible to all students. The installation of overhead mirrors is sometimes worth the expenditure in classrooms where demonstrations are frequent.

c.   Be sure to familiarize your class with materials and procedures being used in demonstration.

d.   Carefully plan your pacing in the demonstration, allowing time for wait-see events.

e.   Take time to ensure the understanding of events.

f.   Keep your demonstration as simple as possible and keep it working towards its stated purpose.

g.   And, finally, plan for what could go wrong during the demonstration. Make a dry-run demonstration.

3.   If you want to create some special effects during your demonstration, you can spotlight them by turning off classroom lights and using a slide projector as the spotlight. Special prerecorded music can add an even greater dramatic effect.

4.   Follow the demonstration with a question and discussion closure.

F. USING THE TEXTBOOK IN SECONDARY SCHOOL TEACHING
(See also Chapters 6 and 10)

Secondary schools usually go through periodic textbook adoption procedures, then they use the adopted books for a number of years before the next adoption cycle begins. This means for you, the student teacher, or for the beginning first-year teacher, that most likely someone will tell you, "Here are the textbooks you will be using." That is why in Exercise 6.3 we hope that you became familiar with standard textbooks that you are likely to be using in your subject field. After you find out exactly what textbook you are to use comes your decision regarding *how to use it.*

There are many methods from which you may select your use of the student textbook, perhaps the *least* acceptable of which is for you to show a complete dependence on a single textbook and require the students to simply memorize content from that book. That is the lowest level of cognitive learning; furthermore, it implies that the teacher is unaware of other significant reading materials and has nothing more to contribute to the learning of the students.

Another problem brought about by the teacher's reliance upon a single textbook is that for many students that textbook may just not be at the appropriate reading level. In today's secondary school classes the reading range of a class may vary by as much as two thirds of the chronological age of the students in the class.[2] This means that if the chronological age is 15 years (typical for tenth-grade students) then the reading level range would be 10 years; that is to say, the class may have some students reading only at the fifth-grade level and others with post-high-school reading

[2] See H. Singer and D. Donlan, *Reading and Learning from Texts* (Boston: Little, Brown & Co., 1980), p. 35.

ability. And that is the reason why many teacher education programs today require a teaching-of-reading course for secondary credential candidates: teachers in most subject fields will need to devote time to helping students develop their reading skills.

With that introduction to this section, coupled with what you learned about textbooks in Chapter 6, let us now turn your attention to the following general guidelines about the use of the textbook in secondary school teaching.

1. Secondary school students should have a textbook (for most courses) and the textbook *should* be the current edition. If not a current edition, then you, the teacher, will need to supplement it with current material. That is not unusual; indeed, it is your professional license!

2. Maintain supplementary reading materials for student use in the classroom; your professional librarian will be most delighted to cooperate in the selection and provision of materials.

3. Some students in your class may benefit from drill, practice, and reinforcement as provided in accompanying workbooks, but this does not mean that all students necessarily benefit from identical activity.

4. Provide vocabulary lists to help your students learn meanings of important words and phrases.

5. Teach your students how to study from their textbook, perhaps by using the S4R method[3]: *surveying* the chapter first, then *reading* the chapter, then *reciting* what was in the chapter, *recording* important items from the chapter in their notebooks, then *reviewing* it all.

6. Encourage students to search in other sources for content that will update the textbook (particularly important in science, social studies, and certain other disciplines).

7. Encourage students to watch for errors in the textbook, errors in content or in publishing—perhaps giving them points when they discover an error. This encourages critical thinking, skill development, and healthy skepticism.

8. In certain classes, particularly in college preparatory studies, the textbook should serve more as a reference; students should be encouraged to utilize a variety of resources to enhance their learning. Going from one cover of the textbook to the other in nine months is not necessarily "teaching."

9. Individualize the learning as much as possible to try to teach students of varying reading and learning abilities. Consider differentiated reading assignments, both in the textbook and in the supplementary resources.

10. Encourage your students to respect their books, perhaps by covering and protecting them and by not marking in them. In many secondary schools this is a rule, and at the end of the semester students are charged for damaged or lost books.

Within the span of your teaching career you may witness and be a part of a revolution in the design of school textbooks. The prediction has been made that with the revolution going on in microcomputer chip technology student textbooks will take on a whole new appearance. Along with this, we are told, will come dramatic changes in the importance and use of student texts and new problems for the teacher, some of which are predictable. Student "texts" may become credit card size—increasing, of course, the probability of students "losing" their books. On the positive side, it would seem likely that a classroom teacher will have available a variety of "textbooks" to better address the reading levels and interests of individual students in the class. Distribution and maintenance of reading materials might create a new demand on the teacher's time. In any case, we expect that dramatic and exciting events will occur to a teaching tool that has not changed a whole lot throughout the history of education in this country.

---

[3] See E. G. Stetson, "Improving Textbook Learning with S4R: A Strategy for Teachers, not Students," *Reading Horizons,* Vol. 22, No. 2 (1982), p. 129.

G. USING ASSIGNMENTS IN SECONDARY SCHOOL TEACHING
(See Also Chapter 16, Section G)

Whether completed in class or as homework, assignments help students learn new content, practice what has already been taught, and develop their personal learning. For use of this important teaching strategy, consider the following guidelines.

1. *Plan early* the types of assignments you will give (daily and long-range, minor and major), and prepare assignment specifications. Assignments must *correlate with the specific instructional objectives,* and should never be given as "busy work" or for punishment!
2. Provide *differentiated assignments,* different assignments, or with variations to be selected by the students on the basis of their individual interests and abilities.
3. Determine in advance the *resources* that will be needed by the students in order to complete their assignments; check the availability of those resources. Again, your librarian is an excellent source of help.
4. *Follow-up* of assignments is important. If it is important for the student to do, then it is important for you to give your full attention to the product of the student's efforts. *Read everything that the student writes!*
5. Provide your *written or verbal comments* about the student's work, and try to be *positive* in your comments. Think carefully about your own written comments, to be relatively certain that they will convey your meaning to the student.
6. Use *positive reward reinforcers* as frequently as possible, in order to continue to encourage, rather than discourage, the student.
7. *When giving assignments,* it is best to write them on the board or in written form with clear specifications, so that the students understand your expectations.
8. Be prepared when the students' parents complain that you do not assign any homework.
9. *Maintain assignment due dates,* allowing, of course, for legitimate excuses, but also consider allowing students to select their own due dates from teacher-provided options.
10. Allow *time in class* for students to begin work on homework assignments, so you can give individual attention to students who need your help.
11. Also consider asking teacher colleagues to work with students who may benefit from their help on certain assignments.
12. Use *caution* when giving assignments that may be controversial or that may pose a safety hazard to the student. In such cases, before giving the assignment you may wish to talk it over with your departmental chairperson, and/or have students obtain parental permission to do the assignment.
13. One final guideline regarding the use of assignments: when writing your comments on student papers, *use a color other than traditional red.* Red brings with it a host of negative connotations—blood, hurt, danger, stop. We admit that this is our own prejudice, and merely ask that you consider it and form your own opinion about it.

Let us now take a break from our discussion of particular teaching strategies, and give *you* an assignment where you will gather what you have learned into an analysis of a real teaching episode. That is the nature of Exercise 11.2, which follows.

EXERCISE 11.2: ANALYSIS OF A TEACHING EPISODE

Instructions: The following scenario describes an actual teaching episode. Read it carefully, then answer the questions that follow and prepare to discuss in class.

Background Information: A high school government class
                               30 students present on this day
                               A Monday in March
                               Period 1, 8:30-9:20 a.m.

The Episode:

8:25-8:30 —The students are arriving, teacher is in room chatting with some of the early arriving students.

8:30   —Bell rings, all stand for Pledge of Allegiance.

8:31   —Teacher: "Open your books to p. 49 and read for about 10 minutes the background material for today's lesson, to. p. 55."

8:31-8:41 —Students read quietly, one or two arrive (tardy) during this time; teacher takes attendance, places attendance slip on door hook; teacher writes on board a list of words to remember and the word "SAVE."

8:41   —A quiet buzz session involving three students begins in one area of room, teacher moves there and quietly asks if they are finished reading, students answer "yes"—the three students quiet now, teacher moves and stands in rear of room.

8:45   —Teacher: "Is everybody finished?" No response tells teacher it is time to begin lecture.
            Teacher: "From the reading, what problems faced the organization of labor?" (pause) "Anyone?"
            1st Student: "Leadership!"
               Teacher writes "leadership" on board.
            2nd Student: "Money!"
               Teacher writes "financial" on board.
            3rd Student: "Time!"
               Teacher writes "time" on board.
            1st Student again: "Criminal infiltration!"
               Teacher writes "criminal infiltration" on board.

8:58   —Teacher lectures for next 20 minutes on "problems of organizing," mentioning the problems the Indians of South Dakota must be facing today in organization.
            Although no student response was solicited, one boy says, "Yeh! Let's go on strike against the school."
            Another says, "Yeh, man, let's go sit in the Principal's office."
            Another student adds, "Let's get the Principal!"
            A fourth student comments, "Right on, man. Teachers' strike!"
            The teacher does not respond to these comments, other than with an occasional smile.

9:18   —Teacher completes the lecture and adds, "Tomorrow we will look at the way in which labor solved these problems."

9:19   —Students begin to meander toward exit in anticipation of class change bell.

End of scenario

Questions to Answer for Exercise 11.2

1. *Identify* the teaching strategies used by this teacher. Consider specifically orientation set induction, closure, methods and materials used, and specific teacher behaviors such as acceptance, silence, etc.
2. How effective was each strategy during this lesson?
3. What were the good points of the instruction?
4. How might the instruction have been improved?

H. USING GAMES IN SECONDARY SCHOOL TEACHING

The use of games in the secondary classroom is a common practice and can be of real value in enriching the effectiveness of your instruction. We encourage you to add games to your repertoire of instructional strategies. Just as with the use of any other teaching strategy, your use of games should follow a clear purpose, careful planning, and be related to the instructional objectives. Frequently in secondary school classrooms, the "game" is used simply as an instructional "time out," perhaps as a teacher reward to the students for "good" behavior or a job well done, and as a time-filler just before a holiday or vacation begins, and that is perfectly all right; but there are other reasons for using games in teaching. Consider the following list.

Why Are Games Used?

Educational games may have one or several functions, depending upon their nature. They can serve as any of the following:

- Devices to socialize the class.
- Devices to motivate students.
- Devices to add variety and a change of pace to your instruction.
- Strategies for teaching content and/or process.
- Opportunities for simulation and/or role-playing.
- Devices to stimulate creativity.
- Devices to stimulate inductive thinking.
- Devices to stimulate critical thinking.
- Devices to evaluate a student's progress.
- Strategies for reaching effective objectives.
- Devices to stimulate interest and skill in microcomputer usage.
- A simple "time out" from the usual rigors of learning.
- Devices to review content.

What Are Educational Games?: A Classification

There are seven categories or types of games under the general heading of "educational games."

Type	Characteristic	Example
*1. *pure game*	promotes laughter and is fun	*New Games*
2. *pure contest*	stimulates competition	political contests
*3. *pure simulation*	models reality	toddler play
4. *contest game*	fun and competition	golf
*5. *simulation game*	fun, and models reality	*Redwood Controversy*
6. *contest simulation*	competition, models reality	boxcar derby
7. *simulation game contest*	models reality, fun, competition	*Life, Careers, Monopoly*

It is beyond the scope of this text to present the advantages and disadvantages for instructional use of each of the seven types. Certain types have greater educational benefits, particularly types 1, 3, and 5.* We specially recommend these because they do not accentuate the competitive aspect of contest-type games. The psychology of this is something you may wish to explore in further detail, using references cited at the end of the chapter.

What Are Some "Homemade" Games?—Samples

There is no question but that teachers can create games useful in their own teaching. Exercise 11.3 will guide you through the process.

Generally, teacher-made games follow one of several formats: board games, paper and pencil games, card games, mental games, role-play and simulation games, and materials-manipulation games. Each of these might fit any of the purposes and be of any of the types. Here are a few examples of teacher-made games that can be applied to almost any subject-matter:

GAME 1: LIVING TIC TAC TOE

Grade level: any
Type: contest game
Number of players: class
Area: any
Suggested purpose: review of content
Materials: none

Instructions: Place nine chairs in the center of the room, to represent the Tic Tac Toe diagram. Divide class into two teams. You ask Side 1 a question; if a student gets the right answer, he/she takes a position as desired to represent an "X." If he/she answers incorrectly, the teacher then asks Side 2 a question. Alternate sides until one has made three in a row, or until the diagram is filled with student bodies.

GAME 2: ORAL COMMUNICATION

Have all students pair off and stand shoulder to shoulder but facing opposite directions. Student 1 is to talk for two minutes *without looking* at Student 2. Student 2 is not to interrupt. Then Student 2 talks for two minutes under the same rules. (All the class does this together.) Then ask the students to write their reactions to the exercise. Collect and discuss these orally. In addition to saying that the exercise is stupid and dumb, students of all ages will usually discover for themselves the need for eye contact, the pleasure of talking uninterrupted, the need for feedback, and so on.

Have each student write a sentence of ten words or so containing an abstract idea, such as, "Love is the most important thing in the world to me." The student then tries to get his idea across to others, without words. This exercise helps students discover why we study words and methods of verbal expression. (They have to know and feel comfortable with each other before they will do this one.)

GAME 3: COOPERATION SQUARE GAME: AN EXPERIMENT IN COOPERATION[4]

Grade level: any
Type: pure game
Number of players: five or more in multiples of three
Suggested purpose: to learn about cooperation

Materials: Before class, prepare a set of squares and an instruction sheet for each five students. A set consists of five envelopes containing pieces of stiff paper cut into patterns that will form five 6 x 6-inch squares, as shown in the diagram. Several individual combinations will be possible, but only one total combination. Cut each square into parts *a* through *j* and lightly pencil in the letters. Then mark the envelopes *A* through *E* and distribute the pieces thus: Envelope *A*, pieces *i, h, e; B*, pieces *a, a, a, c; C*, pieces *a, j; D*, pieces *d, f;* and *E*, pieces *g, b, f, c*. Erase the small letters from the pieces and write instead the envelope letters *A* through *E*, so that the pieces can be easily returned for reuse.

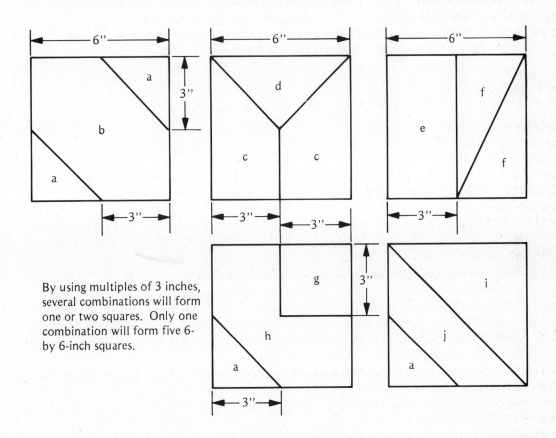

By using multiples of 3 inches, several combinations will form one or two squares. Only one combination will form five 6-by 6-inch squares.

Instructions: Divide the class into groups of five and seat each group at a table equipped with a set of envelopes and an instruction sheet. Ask that the envelopes be opened only on signal. Begin the exercise by asking what *cooperation* means. List on the board the behaviors required in cooperation. For example: Everyone has to understand the problem. Everyone needs to believe that he can help. Instructions must be clear. Everyone needs to think of the other person as well as himself.

---

[4] "Today's Education," *NEA Journal* (October 1969), p. 57. Reprinted by permission; also reproduced with permission from *The Handbook of Staff Development and Human Relations Training: Material Developed for Use in Africa*, by D. Nylen, J. R. Mitchell, and A. Stout. Copyright 1967, NTL Institute.

Describe the experiment as a puzzle that requires cooperation. Read the instructions aloud, point out that each table has a reference copy of them, then give the signal to open the envelopes. The instructions are as follows: Each person should have an envelope containing pieces for forming squares. At the signal, the task of the group is to form five squares of equal size. The task is not completed until everyone has formed a perfect square and all the squares are of the same size.

These are the rules: No member may speak. No member may ask for a card or in any way signal that he/she wants one. Members may give cards to others.

When all or most of the groups have finished, call "time," then discuss the experience. Ask such questions as: How did you feel when someone held a piece and did not see the solution? What was your reaction when someone finished a square and then sat back without seeing whether his/her solution prevented others from solving the problem?

What were your feelings if you finished your square and then began to realize that you would have to break it up and give away a piece? How did you feel about the person who was slow at seeing the solution? If you were that person, how did you feel? Was there a climate that helped or hindered? If students have helped to monitor, they may have observations to share.

In summarizing the discussion, the teacher may wish to review behaviors listed at the beginning and ask whether the game relates to the way the class works from day to day.

GAME 4: LUNAR SURVIVAL GAME: LOST ON THE MOON

Grade Level: Three and up
Type: simulation game
Number of players: class
Area: science, social studies
Suggested purpose: to encourage inductive reasoning
Materials: paper and pencil
Instructions: The following is placed on a ditto and distributed to class members, perhaps divided into small groups.

You are in a space crew scheduled to rendezvous with a mother ship on the lighted surface of the moon. Mechanical difficulties, however, have forced your ship to crash-land at a spot some two hundred miles from the rendezvous point. The rough landing damaged much of the equipment aboard. Survival depends on reaching the mother ship, so the most critical items available must be chosen for the two hundred-mile trip. Below are listed the fifteen items left intact after landing. Your task is to rank them in terms of their importance to your crew, in its attempt to reach the rendezvous point. Place a number *1* by the most important item, a number *2* by the second must important, and so on through number *15*, the least important.

_____ Box of matches
_____ Food concentrate
_____ Fifty feet of nylon rope
_____ Parachute silk
_____ Portable heating unit
_____ Two .45-caliber pistols
_____ One case of dehydrated milk
_____ Two 100-pound tanks of oxygen
_____ Star map of the moon's constellations
_____ Life raft
_____ Magnetic compass
_____ Five gallons of water
_____ Signal flares
_____ First-aid kit containing injection needles
_____ Solar-powered FM receiver-transmitter

SCORING KEY—Lost on the Moon

Listed below are the correct rankings for the "Lost on the Moon" items, along with the reasons for the rankings.

- 15   Box of matches   (little or no use on the moon)
- 4   Food concentrate   (supplies daily food)
- 6   Fifty feet of nylon rope   (useful in tying the injured; helps when climbing)
- 8   Parachute silk   (shelter against sun's rays)
- 13   Portable heating unit   (useful only if party landed on dark side of moon)
- 11   Two .45-caliber pistols   (self propulsion devices could be made from them)
- 12   One case of dehydrated milk   (food; mixed with water for drinking)
- 1   Two 100-pound tanks of oxygen   (filled respiration requirement)
- 3   Star map of the moon's constellations   (one of the principal means of finding directions)
- 9   Life raft   (its carbon dioxide bottles could assist in self-propulsion across chasms and the like)
- 14   Magnetic compass   (probably no magnetized poles, thus useless)
- 2   Five gallons of water   (replenishes water loss, e.g., from sweating)
- 10   Signal flares   (distress call within line of sight)
- 7   First-aid kit containing injection needles   (oral pills or injection medicine valuable)
- 5   Solar-powered FM receiver-transmitter   (distress signal transmitter, possible communication with mother ship)

GAME 5: MUSICAL BINGO (ADAPTABLE TO ANY SUBJECT)

Five categories are chosen. In the sample music game, the categories are: rock groups; solo artists; songs; solo or band artists from the 1950s; and, instruments.

The bingo caller will draw a category with a corresponding column on it and the student will cover the subject that relates to the particular category. For example: the caller would say "G song" and if the student has a song title in the "G" column he/she will cover it with his/her marker. The game continues until there is a winner.

Different varieties of bingo may be played, e.g., blackout, four corners, across, up and down, and diagonal.

Blank bingo cards are given to the students before the game begins and the students fill in the squares with subjects pertaining to the five categories chosen.

B I N G O

Eagles	piano	tambourine	trumpet	The Four Seasons
Chuck Berry	Fats Domino	America	Cher	guitar
Drums	Paul Simon	Free Spot	Rhinestone Cowboy	Neil Sedaka
Elton John	Let Your Love Flow	Barry Manilow	Chicago	Oh What A Night
Silly Love Song	Spinners	Elvis Presley	Platters	Bill Haley

Commercially Produced Games

This is a sample of the many educational games that are available and that can be used to teach, in a fun-filled and interesting way, the understanding of various concepts. This list is by no means exhaustive. Please add to this list successful games that you have used.

All games listed here are suitable for use with persons of junior high school through adult age. The game titles sometimes imply that the game is worthwhile only in a specific subject field, but this is not always the case, as the list will indicate. The games are listed alphabetically according to their titles.

Subject Area	Title	Approximate Cost	Publisher	Address
Biology	*Biology Bingo*	$12.75	Nova Scientific	5
	Blood Flow	16.95	Carolina	13
	Cell Game	17.95	Carolina	13
	Dirty Water	10.00	Urban Systems	10
	Ecology	10.00	Nova Scientific	5
	Endangered Species	9.95	Nova Scientific	5
	Extinction	12.00	Sinauer	7
	Evolution: Geologic Time Chart	17.50	Nova Scientific	5
	Food Chains	20.00	Nova Scientific	5
	Food Web	15.00	Nova Scientific	5
	Metric Bingo	12.75	Nova Scientific	5
	Mouse in the Maze	6.00	Houghton Mifflin	1
	Monarch: Game of B & M	6.75	Carolina	13
	Pollution	19.95	Carolina	13
	Population	10.00	Urban Systems	10
	Predator-Prey Ecology Kit	6.00	Urban Systems	10
	Predator: The Food Chain Game	4.50	Carolina	13
	Redwood Controversy	7.50	Houghton Mifflin	1
	Smog	10.00	Urban Systems	10
	The Pollination Game	6.60	Nova Scientific	5
	110 Animals	7.00	Carolina	13
Business	*Ecology*	10.00	Urban Systems	10
Chemistry	*Elements*	5.60	Union Printing Company	11
	Metric Bingo	12.75	Nova Scientific	5
Civics	(see Government)			
Computer Programming	(see Mathematics)			
Consumer Education	(see Home Economics)			
Earth Science	(see Science)			
Ecology	(see Environmental Education)			
Economics	*Inflation*	23.00	Social Studies School Service	8
	Planet Management	12.00	Houghton Mifflin	1
	Pollution	19.00	Carolina	13
	Star Power	3.00	Social Studies School Service	8
	(see also Social Studies)			

Subject	Title	Approximate Cost	Publisher	Address
Energy Education	Energy Bingo	12.50	Nova Scientific	5
	Energy Management	38.50	Nova Scientific	5
	Energy Quest	9.95	Carolina	13
English	Modern Logic	13.00	Wiff'n Proof	12
	Phlounder	7.95	3M Company	4
	Propaganda Game	11.00	Wiff'n Proof	12
	Redwood Controversy	7.50	Houghton Mifflin	1
	Science & Language	13.00	Wiff'n Proof	12
	Word Structures	10.00	Wiff'n Proof	12
Environmental Education	Anyone Can	29.50	Nova Scientific	5
	Blacks & Whites	6.95	Psychology Today	6
	The Cities Game	6.95	Psychology Today	6
	Commercial Land Use Game	75.00	IHERS	2
	Dirty Water	10.00	Urban Systems	10
	Ecology	10.00	Urban Systems	10
	Energy Management	38.50	Nova Scientific	5
	Environmental Planning	12.60	Nova Scientific	5
	Endangered Species	9.95	Nova Scientific	5
	Food Chains	20.00	Nova Scientific	5
	Food Web	15.00	Nova Scientific	5
	Predator: Food Chain Game	4.50	Carolina	13
	The Dead River	15.00	Nova Scientific	5
Health Science	Health Science Bingo	12.75	Nova Scientific	5
	Super Sandwich	14.95	Nova Scientific	5
General Science	110 Animals	7.00	Carolina	13
	AC/DC: The Electric Circuit Game	5.75	Nova Scientific	5
	Constellation: Card Game of the Stars	3.50	Nova Scientific	5
	Elements	5.60	Union Printing	11
	General Science Bingo	12.75	Nova Scientific	5
	Metric Bingo	12.75	Nova Scientific	5
	Mouse in the Maze	6.00	Houghton Mifflin	1
	Nautilus: Game of Seashells	6.75	Carolina	13
	Science and Language	13.00	Wiff'n Proof	12
	Space Hop	13.95	Nova Scientific	5
Government	Acquire	7.95	3M Company	4
	Election U.S.A.	16.95	Social Studies School Service	8
	Metropolis	3.00	Social Studies School Service	8
	Redwood Controversy	7.50	Houghton Mifflin	1
	Smog	10.00	Urban Systems	10
	(see also Environmental Education)			
History	American History Game	210.00	Science Research Associates	9
	North vs. South	10.00	Social Studies School Service	8
	Redwood Controversy	7.50	Houghton Mifflin	1
Home Economics	Cost of Living Game	3.00	Social Studies School Service	8
	Decimeter	14.00	Nova Scientific	5
	Go and Grow	26.00	Nova Scientific	5
	Inflation	23.00	Social Studies School Service	8
	Metric Bingo	12.75	Nova Scientific	5
	Super Sandwich	14.95	Nova Scientific	5

Subject Area	Title	Approxi-mate Cost	Publisher	Address
Industrial Arts	AC/DC: The Electric Circuit Game	5.75	Nova Scientific	5
Mathematics	Creative Mathematics	10.00	Wiff'n Proof	12
	Decimeter	14.00	Nova Scientific	5
	Metric Bingo	12.75	Nova Scientific	5
	Set Theory	10.00	Wiff'n Proof	12
Psychology	Ghetto	24.00	Social Studies School Service	8
	Propaganda Game	6.00	Social Studies School Service	8
	Society Today	7.95	Psychology Today	6
Social Studies	Acquire	7.95	3M Company	4
	Blacks & Whites	6.95	Psychology Today	6
	The Cities Game	6.95	Psychology Today	6
	Community Land Use Game	75.00	IHERS	2
	Cost of Living Game	3.00	Social Studies School Service	8
	Dirty Water	10.00	Urban Systems	10
	Ecology	10.00	Urban Systems	10
	Extinction	12.00	Sinauer	7
	Ghetto	24.00	Social Studies School Service	8
	Indian Reservation Life	12.00	IHERS	2
	Mouse in the Maze	6.00	Houghton Mifflin	1
	Planet Management	12.00	Houghton Mifflin	1
	Pollution	9.00	Urban Systems	10
	Population	10.00	Urban Systems	10
	Propaganda Game	11.00	Wiff'n Proof	12
	Redwood Controversy	7.50	Houghton Mifflin	1
	Science and Language	13.00	Wiff'n Proof	12
	SIMSOC	20.00	Macmillan	3
	Slave Auction	12.95	Social Studies School Service	8
	Society Today	7.95	Psychology Today	6
	Star Power	3.00	Social Studies School Service	8
	The End of the Line	75.00	IHERS	2
	The Union Divider	10.00	Social Studies School Service	8
	They Shoot Marbles Don't They	45.00	IHERS	2
	Urban Dynamics	75.00	IHERS	2

PUBLISHERS' ADDRESSES

1. Houghton Mifflin Company, 110 Tremont Street, Boston, MA 02107
2. Institute of Higher Education Research and Services, P.O. Box 6293, University, AL 35486
3. Macmillan Publishing Company, 866 Third Avenue, New York, NY 10022
4. 3M Company (Minnesota Mining and Manufacturing Company), St. Paul, MN 55119
5. Nova Scientific Corporation, 111 Tucker Street, P.O. Box 500, Burlington, NC 27215
6. Psychology Today, P.O. Box 4523, Des Moines, IA 50336
7. Sinauer Associates, 20 Second Street, Stanford, CT 06905
8. Social Studies School Service, 10,000 Culver Blvd., Culver City, CA 90230
9. Science Research Associates, Inc., 259 East Erie Street, Chicago, IL 60611
10. Urban Systems, 1033 Massachusetts Avenue, Cambridge, MA 02138
11. Union Printing Co., 17 W. Washington Street, Athens, OH 45701
12. Wiff'n Proof Games, 1490-Yx South Blvd., Ann Arbor, MI 48104
13. Carolina Biological Supply Company, 2700 York Road, Burlington, NC 27215

ADDITIONAL SOURCES OF GAME IDEAS AND MATERIALS
(see also Chapter 12, Section D)

The following is a listing of but a few of the publishers of educational games and game ideas. You should write to them for their current listings and prices.

Abt Associates Inc., 140 Concord Lane, Cambridge, MA 02138
Allied Educational Council, P.O. Box 78, Galien, MI 49113
Brain Teaser Games, Cresline Manufacturing Co., 1502 Santa Fe Street, Santa Ana, CA
Creative Publications, Inc., P.O. Box 10328, Palo Alto, CA
Dannon Educational Division, 80 Wilson Way, Westwood, MA 02090
Educational Activities Inc., 164 E. Dane Street, Mountain View, CA 94040
Entelek, Inc., 42 Pleasant Street, Newburyport, MA 01950
Hounshell, P. B., and I. R. Trolinger. *Games for the Science Classroom: An Annotated Bibliography.* Washington, DC: NSTA, 1977.
Interact, P.O. Box 1023, Lakeside, CA 92040
Marie's Educational Materials, Inc., 193 S. Murphy Avenue, Sunnyvale, CA 94086
Systems Gaming Associates, Triphammer Road, Ithaca, NY 14850
Western Publishing Co., Inc., School and Library Department, 850 Third Avenue, New York, NY 10022
World Law Fund, 11 West 42nd Street, New York, NY 10036

EXERCISE 11.3: CREATING MY OWN GAME FOR TEACHING

Instructions: Follow the general steps below in designing your own educational game. Try the game out on your classmates, for their criticisms.

Step 1. Decide what the function(s) of your game will be.
Step 2. Outline (if relevant) specifically what you want your game to teach.
Step 3. Decide the best format for your game.
Step 4. Design the materials for your game.
Step 5. Write the rules for your game.
Step 6. Test and revise where necessary.

_____

_____

_____

_____

_____

_____

_____

_____

_____

_____

_____

_____

_____

_____

_____

_____

_____

_____

_____

_____

_____

_____

EXERCISE 11.4: SUPPORTING MY INSTRUCTION: SELECTING GUIDELINES FOR TEACHING STRATEGIES

We have reviewed basic guidelines for teaching strategies in the use of questioning, lecturing, inquiry, discussion, demonstration, textbook, assignments, and games. Select guidelines from one of these strategy areas and discuss them with members of your class. How will you use these guidelines? Do they fill an educational need in your classroom teaching? Ask yourself: How do the guidelines help me?

Guidelines I have selected: _____

Reasons why I have an interest in these guidelines: _____

_____

_____

_____

_____

_____

_____

_____

_____

_____

_____

_____

Other helpful information I obtained from discussion with others: _____

_____

_____

_____

_____

_____

_____

_____

_____

_____

_____

_____

QUESTIONS FOR CLASS DISCUSSION

1. Would you like to teach by inquiry? Why or why not?
2. What new strategies have you learned about that you are now anxious to try in your own teaching?
3. What is your opinion regarding homogeneous grouping in the subjects you are preparing to teach?
4. In Exercise 11.2, did you consider the "Background Information"? Does it have a significance for the scenario?
5. Have you found any good games for secondary teaching in your field, and that you can share with members of your class?
6. In your town, have you found a source of game materials, e.g., blank game boards, blank cards, tokens?
7. Are there cautions teachers need to be aware of in the use of games in the classroom?
8. What is your favorite parlor game? Why do you like it? What characteristics make it enjoyable to you?
9. What is your opinion about the use in the classroom of computer games specific to your subject field?
10. What other questions do you have regarding content of this chapter? How might answers be found?

SELECTED READINGS AND REFERENCES FOR CHAPTER 11

Ames, Carole. "Competitive Versus Cooperative Structures: The Influence of Individual and Group Performance Factors on Achievement Attributions and Affect." *American Educational Research Journal,* Vol. 18 (1981), pp. 273-287.

Bernstein, Harriet T. "The New Politics of Textbook Adoption." *Phi Delta Kappan,* Vol. 66, No. 7 (March 1985), pp. 463-466.

Cruickshank, D. R., and Ross Tefler. "Classroom Games and Simulations." *Theory Into Practice,* Vol. 19 (Winter 1980), pp. 75-80.

Ellington, Henry, Eric Addinall, and Fred Percival. *A Handbook of Game Design.* New York: Nichols Publishing Co., 1982.

Horn, Robert E., and Anne Cleaves. *The Guide to Simulation Games for Education and Training,* 4th ed. Beverly Hills, CA: Sage Publications, Inc., 1980.

Horton, Lowell. *Mastery Learning.* Bloomington, IN: Phi Delta Kappa, 1981.

Hyman, Ronald T. "Fielding Student Questions." *Theory Into Practice,* Vol. 19 (Spring 1980), pp. 38-44.

Kemp, Jerold E. *Planning and Producing Audio-Visual Materials,* 4th ed. New York: Thomas Y. Crowell Publishing Co., 1980.

Paschal, Rosanne A., Thomas Weinstein, and Herbert J. Walberg. "The Effects of Homework on Learning: A Quantitative Synthesis." *Journal of Educational Research,* Vol. 78, No. 2 (November-December 1984), pp. 97-104.

Seifert, Edward H., and John J. Beck, Jr. "Relationships between Task Time and Learning Gains in Secondary Schools." *Journal of Educational Research,* Vol. 78, No. 1 (September-October 1984), pp. 5-10.

Sharon, S. "Cooperative Learning in Small Groups: Recent Methods and Effects on Achievement, Attitudes, and Ethnic Relations." *Review of Educational Research,* Vol. 50, No. 2 (Summer 1980), pp. 241-271.

Slavin, R. E. "Cooperative Learning." *Review of Educational Research,* Vol. 50, No. 2 (Summer 1980), pp. 315-342.

Vacca, R. T. *Content Area Reading.* Boston: Little, Brown & Co., 1981.

Webb, Patricia K. "Piaget: Implications for Teaching." *Theory Into Practice,* Vol. 19 (Spring 1980), pp. 93-97.

12

What Other Aids and Resources Are Available to the Secondary School Teacher?

You will be pleased to know that there is a vast amount of material from which to draw, as you plan instructional experiences. You might not be pleased to learn that you will be spending a lot of time sorting and selecting the materials most appropriate for your use. Nobody will know your students better than you, so, although we cannot tell you specifically what you should use, we can provide some guidelines and sources. And someday you may thank us for this recommendation: *Begin your resource file early—now.* Exercise 12.3 will get you started with this project, an activity you will continue throughout your teaching career.

A. GENERAL GUIDELINES FOR SELECTION OF AIDS AND RESOURCES: THE LEARNING-EXPERIENCES LADDER

An important general rule in planning is to select learning experiences that are as direct as possible. That is, have them do that which you are teaching them to do. When students are involved in experiences that are direct, they are utilizing all of their senses; and when all of the senses are engaged, learning is the most effective and the longest lasting. This is "learning by doing."

Conversely, at the other end of the spectrum are abstract experiences where students are exposed only to symbolization (i.e., words and numbers) using only one or two senses. Visual and verbal symbolic experiences, although impossible to avoid when teaching, are generally least effective in assuring that planned learning occurs. So, when planning experiences and selecting materials, we urge you to select activities that engage learners in the most direct experiences possible. The triangle that follows depicts this range of experiences from direct to abstract.

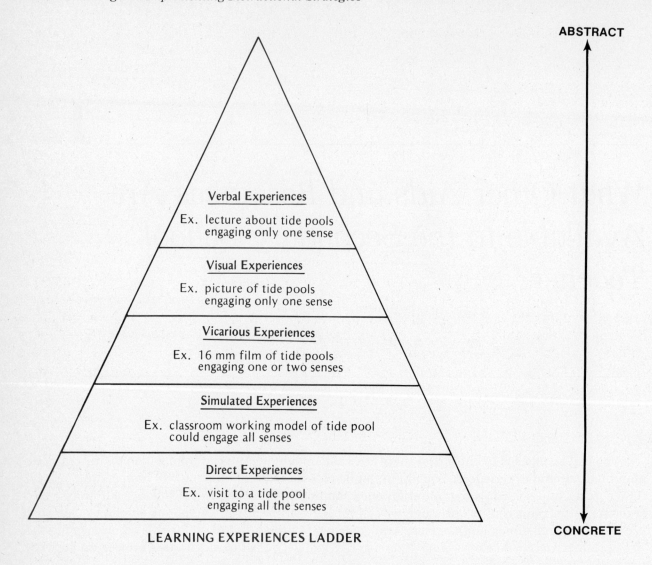

ABSTRACT

Verbal Experiences

Ex. lecture about tide pools
engaging only one sense

Visual Experiences

Ex. picture of tide pools
engaging only one sense

Vicarious Experiences

Ex. 16 mm film of tide pools
engaging one or two senses

Simulated Experiences

Ex. classroom working model of tide pool
could engage all senses

Direct Experiences

Ex. visit to a tide pool
engaging all the senses

CONCRETE

LEARNING EXPERIENCES LADDER

As you can see, when teaching about tide pools, the *most* effective mode is to actually take students to a tide pool (bottom of ladder, most direct experience) where they can see, hear, touch, smell, and perhaps even taste the tide pool. The *least* effective mode is for the teacher to simply lecture (top of ladder, most abstract experience) about the tide pool, engaging only one sense—hearing.

Of course, for various reasons—safety, lack of field-trip money, location of your school—you may not be able to take the students to a tide pool. We cannot, nor should we, always use the most direct experience, so sometimes we settle for an experience higher on the ladder. Self-discovery teaching is *not always best.* Sometimes it is more appropriate to build upon what others have learned. Learners do not need to reinvent the wheel, but the most effective learning *is* that which clearly engages many of their senses.

B. AIDS AND RESOURCES FOR DIRECT AND SIMULATED EXPERIENCES

Among the most likely sources of ideas for direct and simulated experiences related to specific content are the curriculum guides. Textbooks used in secondary school are usually accompanied by a teacher's edition, where you will find many useful ideas. Special methods books used in your teacher education program provide ideas for learning in a particular subject.

Another advantage of direct and simulated experiences is that they are often multidisciplined, that is, they cross subject boundaries. This is more like real life, and therefore provides an important benefit in the students' learning. Simulated experiences include such techniques as role-playing, experimenting, play production, skits, games, and the mock-up (e.g., the in-class tide pool).

C. AIDS AND RESOURCES FOR VICARIOUS EXPERIENCES

Vicarious experiences are those where the learner is indirectly involved in "the doing," where two or three senses usually are involved. Vicarious experiences include still pictures (slides and filmstrips), motion pictures, computer programs, models, maps, and globes. As with all materials, these should be carefully reviewed by the teacher prior to presentation to the class. One of the authors recalls a teaching experience in which he showed a filmstrip that he had not previewed since the year before. In the interim, someone had written an obscene word on one of the frames. How embarrassing!

D. AIDS AND RESOURCES FOR COMPUTER EXPERIENCES

How will you be able to use a computer in your classroom? You'll be able to use a computer to assist instruction and learning, and to help maintain records, collect data, or project information. A computer will help you create files, store information, compile records of students' progress, devise accounts of your library books, provide audiovisual material, list additional resources, and help you keep an up-to-date inventory. This computer use is referred to as Computer-Assisted Management or CAM. In addition, there are programs for learning enrichment, reinforcement, or supplement. This computer use is labeled Computer-Assisted Learning or CAL. Certain programs instruct your students in a particular skill or in a specific concept and this is labeled Computer-Assisted Instruction or CAI. What can you look for? Look for programs that provide tutoring (remedial instruction material), practice and drill, as well as for simulation programs appropriate to business, social science, mathematics, and science. Other programs give students an opportunity to write original materials as they explore word processing and authoring systems. Still other programs support the individualized needs of your students, and, with your authoring, will produce games, puzzles, or tests, based on your students' interests, the reading material, or other classroom information.

Why Use Computers?

What, in general, can computers do for you and your students?

1. *Computers Can Motivate.* Look for colorful, interesting, and animated programs. Does the program show what is expected of the student before the student is asked to respond? A

computer model supports a student's interest, and thus a student's motivation. Does the program provide a response or feedback to the student's responses? Is the correct response displayed? Is there a colorful graphic, such as hands that applaud, a familiar "smiley" face, or a winner's cheer? Or does a personalized statement, with the student's name, appear on the screen?

2. *Computers Can Activate.* Look for a program that can be controlled for rate-of-pacing by the student. Can the student move the program forward for rapidity, move it backward for review purposes, or skip the program and move ahead to the next level of difficulty? Does the program detect and then correct the inaccurate responses by the student? Does the program explain inaccurate responses and then provide a similar item for another learning experience? Does the program summarize the total of correct student responses and then provide an analysis of the errors as a basis for the teacher's diagnosis?

What Books Could I Select for My Computer Library?

For the teacher, *Instructional Computing for Today's Teachers* by Edward L. Vockell and Robert H. Rivers (Macmillan, 1984).

For the principal, *Microcomputers and Educational Administration* by Thomas Gustafson (Prentice-Hall, 1985).

What Software Could I Preview?

Computer journals, such as *Electronic Learning,* provide periodic information about available software. Software, like textbooks and workbooks, are subject to revision, so always look for the current edition of the programs.[1] Here is a sample list of educator-recommended programs:[2]

Arcademic Skill Builders. Developmental Learning Materials, One DLM Park, Allen TX 75002. High quality graphics for math drill and practice.

Gertrude's Puzzles. The Learning Company, 4270 Alpine Road, Portola Valley, CA 94025. Student interacts to make choices and solve problems.

The Bank Street Writer. Scholastic Inc., 730 Broadway, New York, NY 10003. Word processor with prompts for students age eight and up.

Paint. Reston Publishing Company, 11480 Sunset Hills Road, Reston, VA 22090. Creative art program for the electronic canvas.

Survival Math. Sunburst Communications, 39 Washington Avenue, Pleasantville, NY 10570. Students learn about consumer math as they assume roles as shoppers, travel agents, or businesspersons in simulations.

---

[1] For a list of reviewed computer software, see the *1986 Educational Software Preview Guide* published by CALIFORNIA TECC SOFTWARE LIBRARY AND CLEARINGHOUSE, Professional Library and Microcomputer Center, San Mateo County Office of Education, 333 Main Street, Redwood City, CA 94063. Also, for a list of "highly rated educational-software programs," see *Education Week*, April 16, 1986, p. 44.

[2] "Notable Software—1982-83," *Electronic Learning,* Vol. 2, No. 8 (May-June 1983), pp. 45-46. Copyright 1983 by Scholastic, Inc. Used by permission.

What Computer Periodicals Could I Review?

Classroom Computer News. (bimonthly) International Education, 51 Spring Street, Watertown, MA 02172. How to use microcomputers in the classroom.

Compute! The Journal of Progressive Computing. (monthly) Small Systems Services, Inc., Box 5406, Greensboro, NC 27401. Educational and recreational programs, sections for Apple, Atari, PET, and other systems.

Computers In the Schools. (quarterly) The Haworth Press, 28 East 22nd Street, New York, NY 10010. Assists educators in developing theory to guide practical application.

Creative Computing.(monthly) Box 789-M, Morristown, NJ 07960. "How-to" articles; personal, recreational, and educational purposes.

CRLA: Computers, Reading and Language Arts. (quarterly) P.O. Box 13039, Oakland, CA 94661. Pragmatic articles with clear classroom teaching implication. Focus on reading and language arts.

Educational Technology. (monthly) 140 Sylvan Avenue, Englewood Cliffs, NJ 07632. Theory and application of computers along with other reviewed technologies.

Electronic Learning. (bimonthly) Scholastic Inc., 50 West 44th Street, New York, NY 10036. Developments in education, educational applications, products.

Family Computing. (monthly) Scholastic Inc., P.O. Box 2512, Boulder, CO 80321. Focuses on "how-tos and what-tos," buying information, programming help.

Teaching and Computers. (monthly during school year) Scholastic Inc., 730 Broadway, New York, NY 10003. Information about the computer, and about teaching with use of tips, posters, and reproducible student activity pages.

The Computer Teacher. (monthly) Department of Computer and Information Science, University of Oregon, Eugene, OR 97403. Educational applications of computers; techniques, reviews, sample programs, professional organizations for teachers.

What Issues Should I Consider?

About Computers: Some Educators Say "YES" and Others Say "NO"

During the past few years, suggestions for using computers in the classroom have been made by a number of interested educators who emphasize that the microcomputer is a highly effective educational tool. Those educators interested in applying computers to classroom-assisted management and to classroom-assisted instruction have many points of agreement:

1. They emphasize that the microcomputer is a patient teaching system; a never-tiring reteaching tool; an uncritical classroom aide; and an able management assistant.
2. They seem to be united in advocating that students compose with microcomputers. Students can write, delete words, lines, paragraphs, and can rearrange their written materials by pressing selected keys. They point out that more students seem to be willing to revise their written work when using a microcomputer, because the system does not require a student to recopy an entire paper.
3. Those favoring the idea that all students should learn to program a microcomputer mention that for programming, the student uses logic, language facility, and mathematical skills, and that higher-thinking skills are developed as a student responds to a computer-simulated selection, such as participating in a simulated national election procedure or in a simulated business environment.

Those are some of the points on which some educators say "Yes!" to computer assistance in the classroom. Now consider the points of the educators who say "No!"

1. Not all believe that there is adequate classroom time or adequate quality software for computer use in the classroom. These critics believe that much of the available software is of questionable value, and is often boring. Some refer to some software as "fancy flash cards," an "electronic workbook page," or "high-tech tedium." Some believe there is too much emphasis on repetition and drill and too little emphasis on independent thinking skills. Others believe that the teacher's time is wasted if the teacher has to adjust a commercial program for the classroom and for student needs.

2. Not all believe that the microcomputer is cost-effective. They ask pertinent questions:
   - Will the dollar output be equivalent to the quality of student learning?
   - Will the hardware and software costs widen still further the financial gap between solvent school districts and struggling school districts?
   - Is it true that software programs are poorly produced because a high demand has accelerated companies' responses, resulting in poor-quality items?
   - Is it true that you may have to buy software programs without a preview because of the companies' fears that someone will copy their material?
   - If you purchase a program without a preview, how will you be able to tell if the software meets your students' needs?

3. Not all believe that the physical effects of a microcomputer on students have been adequately researched. Some questions are:
   - What are the effects of prolonged microcomputer use on a student's eyes, blood pressure, and skeletal structure?
   - Is there a possibility that the radiation from the microcomputer could have deleterious effects over a long period of time? If so, what are those effects?
   - Do students who use microcomputers experience blurred vision, burning eyes, eye irritation, eye strain, or eye muscle pains more often than students who do not use microcomputers?

4. Not all believe that the microcomputer's influence in the classroom will be benign. There is concern about the long-term effect the microcomputer may have on a student's social skills, and its emerging effect on the changing role of the classroom teacher.

5. Not all believe that teaching every student to use a computer is a high priority. As stated in *High School*, "The great urgency is not 'computer literacy' but 'technology literacy,' the need for students to see how society is being reshaped by our inventions . . . the challenge is not learning *how* to use the latest piece of hardware but asking when and why it should be used."[3]

E. AIDS AND RESOURCES FOR VISUAL AND VERBAL EXPERIENCES

The materials for the visual and verbal category of learning include the chalkboard, graphs, charts, and the overhead projector. Material of this category is usually only symbolic. Only one or two senses are involved, and because the experience is symbolic we cannot be absolutely certain the learner's concept of the symbol is clearly that which is intended.

This category is one frequently used by the classroom teacher; indeed, we would be most unlikely to find a classroom without the chalkboard, graphs and charts, an overhead projector, and teacher talk. Teacher talk is discussed in other chapters; here we provide guidelines for the other aids mentioned.

---

[3] Ernest L. Boyer, *High School* (New York: Harper, 1983), p. 111.

The Chalkboard

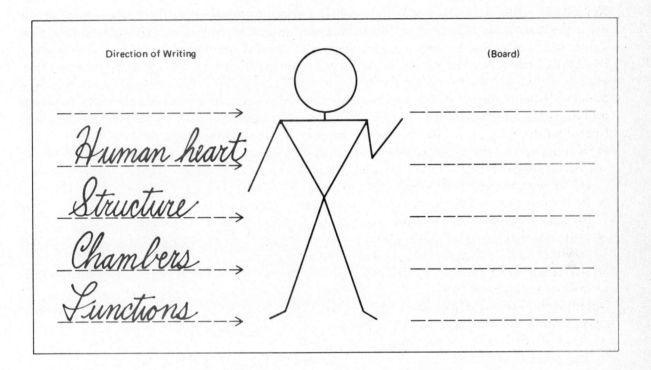

We call it the chalkboard, rather than the blackboard, because you will most likely have a board that is painted plywood, rather than the old slate blackboard. Here are guidelines for effective use of the chalkboard.

1. Do not wash it too often (paint comes off). Colored chalk is difficult to remove without washing unless you use colored chalk especially designed for your board. Please get yourself a supply of colored chalk; it helps to emphasize your "board talk!"
2. Start each day (and each class period) with a clean board! And leave a clean board when you leave a classroom—that is good professional manners!
3. Write on the board neatly, clearly, and orderly, beginning your writing at the far left. Practice writing on a chalkboard so your writing is plainly legible to all students, even those at farthest distance from the board.
4. Be sure nothing is obstructing the view of any student, including yourself!
5. Use the chalkboard to record what students contribute. When a student sees his/her name on the board for a positive contribution, that is a strong positive reinforcer to that student.
6. Use the chalkboard to write instructions, directions, and assignments (unless on ditto instead), rather than giving verbal instructions that will be missed or misunderstood by about half of your students.
7. Use the clips above your chalkboard (if there are any) to hang posters, maps, charts, student work, and so forth.
8. When using a chalkboard that is new, or that has been freshly painted (or washed), wipe it lightly with a chalky eraser to add a chalk base for better writing.

9. Keep your own personal supply of chalk handy at all times, as nothing can be more frustrating than having begun class and not being able to find the chalk (or eraser).

10. If you are fortunate enough to have in your classroom a slate blackboard, you will discover that the following hint might be useful: light pencil marks on the board can be visible to you but not to students as close as your first row. The pencil marks can serve as guides to you for that spectacular drawing you want to create "during" class (using colored chalk, of course), and the pencil marks will remain (for use during a subsequent class) long after you have erased that "artistic drawing."

11. Another useful hint: now is perhaps the time of year when you might want to begin accumulation of a "wish list" to give to those who may have you on their Christmas list. Instead of the usual gifts of perfume, cologne, toys, clothes, and so forth, you might prefer those items you will need in your teaching, several of which are hinted at in this section of the resource guide.

Overhead Projection

What did we do prior to the invention of the overhead projector? You have seen it used many times. In many respects, the overhead projector is more useful than the chalkboard, particularly for a novice teacher who is nervous: Use of the overhead projector rather than the chalkboard can help reduce some of the nervousness by decreasing the need to pace back and forth.

You can do a lot with the overhead projector. Here are guidelines:

1. Select a good transparency pen—as assortment of colors, preferably. Do not use an ordinary felt-tip pen; it is too messy and not likely to adhere to the transparency paper. We like to use Vis-a-Vis pens.[4]
2. Obtain a stack of clean transparencies from the office. If this is not possible, you can purchase them yourself. Try your college or university bookstore.
3. Find the best place in your classroom to set the projector. Use white butcher paper or a sheet, if you do not have a screen available.
4. When using the projector, face your class. You do not need to turn around to look at the screen. Practice alone, first! Also, you do *not* need to turn off the room lights.
5. Practice making and using overlays. Commercially produced transparencies are available for your use. Check catalogs. Some are free.
6. You can use on the projector any material that is transparent, such as rulers, protractor, Petri dishes, and even those which are not transparent, if you simply wish to show shapes.
7. You can use the projector as a source of light for demonstrations, too.
8. Be sure your projected light hits the screen at a 90° angle, to avoid distortion.
9. You can even obtain an "overhead calculator" that has been modified so that light passes through the display area to project the readout from the overhead projector onto a screen.[5]
10. Tracing charts or drawings, on construction paper or on the chalkboard, can be easily done by simply projecting the original transparency or transparent object onto the paper or chalkboard.
11. *Note:* Overhead projection is *not the same* as OPAQUE projection. You need to make the room totally dark for opaque projection.

SOURCES OF TRANSPARENCY MATERIALS

AeVac Educational Publishers, 1604 Park Avenue, South Plainsfield, NJ 07060
Encyclopedia Britannica Film Inc., 1150 Wilmette Avenue, Wilmette, IL 60091
Instructo Products Company, 1635 N. 55th Street, Philadelphia, PA 19131
3M Company, Visual Products, 2501 Hudson Road, St. Paul, MN 55119

---

[4] *Vis-a-Vis Visual Aid Pen,* from Sanford's, Bellwood, IL 60104.
[5] The "overhead calculator" may be purchased from Stokes Publishing Company, P.O. Box 415, Palo Alto, CA 94302. Write to them for current price.

**EXERCISE 12.1: USING THE CHALKBOARD AND THE OVERHEAD PROJECTOR
                 CREATIVELY**

Instructions: Think of some other uses for these teaching aids and share them with your
              classmates. Demonstrate!

1. _____

2. _____

3. _____

4. _____

5. _____

6. _____

Maps and Globes

Appropriate maps or globes should be used whenever referring to places or when teaching about the use of maps and/or globes. And, as with the use of all visual aids, the map or globe should be readily visible to each student. You should also equip yourself with a good-quality pointer to use when pointing to places on a map, globe, or wall chart. A student may be willing to make a pointer for you at cost in his/her woodshop class.

Charts, Graphs, and Pictures

These can also help students visualize important points, thus facilitating learning. A visual chart illustrating the effects of smoking from one-half pack to more than two packs of cigarettes a day, for instance, can really drive home the concept of the effects of smoking upon the human body.

Again, these visuals should be clearly visible to all students. The use of the *opaque* projector is recommended when showing relatively small (8½ x 11 or smaller) pictures, charts, or graphs to the entire class. A drawback to the use of the opaque projector is that the room must be darkened during its use, but it is useful in showing pictures, charts, or graphs, from a textbook for example. The interior of the projector can heat up, so don't leave your object in it too long.

Another way to show a single picture to the entire class is to slowly walk around the room with it, but that is sometimes a sure way to encourage discipline problems, too, so we do not encourage it, nor do we recommend passing the picture around allowing students to look at it while you, the teacher, continue the lesson. That, too, is asking for trouble in many classes. As a last resort you can always place the picture on the bulletin board for all to view later.

Library/Media Resource Center

Work closely with your school librarian and resource center specialists. Learn about the materials and resources available before you assign students to do work in the center. When assigning students to library work they should clearly understand what is expected of them and how it is related to course work. If you take your entire class to the library be sure you stay with them and supervise their library work.

Audio and Video Tapes

If you can remember the first time you ever heard your voice on tape, or saw yourself on video, you appreciate the usefulness of these devices in teaching. Perhaps you will learn from the exercise in Chapter 17 more about the teaching power of videotape. Find out what audio and video equipment are available in your school and plan ways of using this material effectively and creatively in your own teaching. Many teachers today are using VCRs in their classrooms.

Films, Filmstrips, and Slides

Carefully selected films, filmstrips, loop films, and slides can help students see concepts, events, and issues in a more concrete way. Examine your school's audiovisual catalog carefully, then preview your material before showing to class. *Always have your projectors set up and ready to go before class begins.* Learn how to operate the equipment, what to do if there is a breakdown, where extra bulbs are available.

Community Resources and Field Trips

Community resources can be one of your most valuable sources of help. You will want to build your own community resource file and plan field trips, perhaps with the help of parents. The local community is a rich resource, often with agencies and locations anxious to be of help.

Field trips to these places can be exciting and educational for students for most of secondary school subjects. When planning for a field trip, you need to keep the following in mind.

1. Secure the sanction of the school.
2. Coordinate with on-site personnel.
3. Explain the goals and objectives of the trip to both supervisors and students.
4. Develop necessary background information, including safety precautions.
5. Secure permission from parents.
6. Secure adult supervision.
7. Define your behavior expectations to students.

The Spirit Duplicator

Although most secondary schools have replaced the spirit duplicator, some of the schools in rural areas are still using them. The spirit duplicator, otherwise known as a ditto machine, is another device we have difficulty understanding how teachers of the past could do without. Most of you are familiar with the machine and its product. We provide these guidelines for use of the ditto.

1. If the ditto machine has broken down (as they are known to do occasionally), be certain *you* can still function. School should not be canceled because the ditto machine is not working!
2. Prepare your copies well in advance of the day you intend to use them.
3. Don't forget to remove the slip sheet from the ditto master before preparing the ditto.
4. Prepare the ditto so it is legible; proofread it before running it off. Dittos often are sent home to parents; therefore they should represent your best effort in spelling, grammar, and clarity.
5. Learn to operate the ditto machine.
6. Ditto masters come in purple (standard), blue, black, red, and green. Multicolored dittos are arresting and interesting, if not overused.
7. Up to 200 copies can be made from one master.
8. When using copyrighted material for use on a ditto, cite the source, and obtain written or oral permission to reprint. You should not have to pay a fee, as your purpose is educational and you are not planning to sell your dittos. Note at the end of your material that you have been given permission to reprint.

Objects

Sometimes referred to as "realia," objects are props that you (or your students) have provided to enhance the curriculum content by giving the students visual identification with what is being taught. The objects may be real, or may be models of the real thing. We heard of a history teacher who for several decades made a hobby of collecting history realia—election campaign buttons, posters from the past, war artifacts, and so forth. Display of his collected items during appropriate history lessons helped to bring history alive.

Not only does a visual prop help to enhance the learning, but it can also reduce some of the nervous tensions of a beginning teacher who may be inclined toward a heavy reliance upon verbal learning.

The use of a variety of strategies and media, indeed the use of multimedia presentations, can help the teacher reach more of the students more of the time. Secondary teachers are challenged to meet the needs and to teach content to a large variety of students within the "regular" classroom—mainstreamed, linguistically and culturally different, nonreaders and good readers. And you are expected to maintain classroom control as well as your sanity! We only hope the material in this and in previous chapters will be of help. Perhaps in the near future we will see new technological innovations that will be helpful to teachers; microcomputers may be the beginning of a new industrial revolution. But historically, about the only devices that have had staying power are those described in this chapter.

A BIBLIOGRAPHY OF FREE AND INEXPENSIVE RESOURCE MATERIALS FOR SECONDARY SCHOOL TEACHING

An Annotated Bibliography of Audiovisual Materials Related to Understanding and Teaching the Culturally Disadvantaged. Washington, DC: National Education Association.

Educational Film Guide. New York: H. W. Wilson Co.

Educator's Guide to Free Films. Randolph, WI: Educators Progress Service.

Educator's Guide to Free Film-Strips. Randolph, WI: Educators Progress Service.

Educator's Guide to Free and Inexpensive Teaching Materials. Randolph, WI: Educators Progress Service.

Educator's Guide to Free Science Materials. Randolph, WI: Educators Progress Service.

Educator's Guide to Free Social Studies Materials. Randolph, WI: Educators Progress Service.

QUESTIONS FOR CLASS DISCUSSION

1. What do you predict for the future of computers in the classroom during your teaching career? What is the basis for your prediction?
2. Have you found computer software that should be shared with your classmates?
3. Some people believe schools should proceed slowly in purchasing computer equipment that may be obsolete before students even leave the school. What do you think?
4. Have you found a good source of free or inexpensive materials you can use in teaching? Share with your classmates.
5. In classrooms you have visited, have you seen computers being used? How were they being used?
6. What other questions do you have regarding the content of this chapter? How might answers be found?

SELECTED READINGS AND REFERENCES FOR CHAPTER 12

Caissy, Gail A. "Evaluating Educational Software: A Practitioner's Guide." *Phi Delta Kappan,* Vol. 66, No. 4 (December 1984), pp. 249-250.

Kepner, Henry S., Jr., ed. *Computers in the Classroom.* Washington, DC: National Education Association, 1982.

Levin, Henry M., and Gail Meister. "Is CAI Cost-Effective?" *Phi Delta Kappan,* Vol. 67, No. 10 (June 1986), pp. 745-749.

Minor, Edward O. *Handbook for Preparing Visual Media,* 2nd ed. New York: McGraw-Hill Book Co., 1978.

Papert, S. *Mindstorms: Children, Computers and Powerful Ideas.* New York: Basic Books, 1980.

Satterthwaite, Les. *Graphics: Skills, Media, and Materials.* Dubuque, IA: Kendall/Hunt Publishing Co., 1977.

Woodbury, Marda. *Selecting Materials for Instruction: Subject Areas and Implementation.* Littleton, CO: Libraries Unlimited, 1980.

13

What Are Some Motivational Strategies? An Annotated List of 210 Possibilities— An Idea Bank

What causes you to read this chapter? What makes the "punk-rocks" cut their hair "weird" and dye it with psychedelic colors? What made you "tick" when you were going to junior and senior high school? What forces drive our behavior, what motivates us to behave in a particular way? When we ask questions such as these, we are talking about *d*rives, *i*ncentives, *n*eeds, *m*otivations, and *a*spirations. We shall refer to this as DINMA.

The word *motive* is derived from the Latin *motivum*, meaning moving or impulse, and the psychologist's study of DINMA is analogous to the physicist's study of the phenomenon of motion: What starts the movement, what keeps it going, what stops it, and what decides the direction of the motion?

In this chapter, our intent is to identify salient features of DINMA as they relate to today's secondary school students and to suggest possible applications for secondary school teaching. As teachers, we must be cognizant of the significance of motivation:

- Motivation is a concept of major importance in American society.
- DINMA plays a major role in the sucess of a student's learning.
- Motivation in the secondary school sets the initial tone for career choices.

The teenagers of today are used to multimillion-dollar productions on television and the movie screen, but when they come into a classroom and are subjected each day to something short of a high-budget production, it is no wonder that they sometimes react in a less than highly motivated fashion. There is no doubt that our youth are growing up in a highly stimulated instant-action society, a society that has learned to expect instant headache relief, instant turn-on television sets, instant dinners, and perhaps even instant high-payment employment. In light of this we are on the side of you, the teacher, who is on the firing line each day, and who is expected to perform, perhaps instantly and entertainingly, but most certainly in a highly competent and professional manner, and in situations not even close to ideal. But in any case,

YOU MUST GAIN YOUR STUDENTS' ATTENTION BEFORE YOU CAN TEACH!

In this chapter we provide a long list of potential motivators, first those general to all fields, then those more specific to particular subjects. We suggest that you read all of the entries for each field, for although one entry might be identified as specific to one field it may also be useful in other areas or it might stimulate a creative idea for your own stock of motivational techniques.

A. GENERAL IDEAS FOR MOTIVATION

1. Your students should clearly understand the objectives of your class actvities and assignments.
2. Show enthusiasm and interest in what you have planned and are doing.
3. Present the proper quantity of content at the proper pace.
4. Vary the teaching procedures and the activities. Let students follow the activities of their choice with responsibility for change.
5. Use familiar examples in presenting your materials. Don't just teach definitions, principles, theorems, or rules. Be certain to explicate these with concrete examples that can be understood by students.
6. Use audiovisual materials—but do not assume that films or filmstrips have "built-in motivation." Select those that would be relevant and interesting to the students on the topic or subject matter that is under consideration.
7. Use objects for the lesson—foreign stamps, coins, models, antiques, toys, and so on.
8. Plan your orientation set induction (what you do the first few minutes of a class period) with care.
9. Keep students informed of their progress. Don't keep them in the dark as to where they stand.
10. Remember that students need to be recognized by you, by their parents, and by their peers.
11. Remember that students need steady awareness of progress being made, of "How am I doing?", "What can I do better next time?"
12. Talk with individual students about their problems and their interests.
13. Go down your roll book periodically and ask yourself what you know about each individual in the class.
14. Students are sometimes motivated by extrinsic devices such as tests. Use this technique judiciously, not as a weapon for punishment.
15. Give praise or rewards for jobs well done. But in groups, use strong praise sparingly.
16. Utilize a modified version of the elementary show-and-tell activity.
17. Have the students make a movie or slide show of class activities (e.g., a role-playing lesson). Let them plan and write the narration.
18. Word naming in various categories—such as synonyms, same initial letters, various uses of a term—becomes an indicator of ideational fluency.
19. Invite guest speakers when and where appropriate. Perhaps some of the parents can be resource persons. (See also number 22)
20. Hold small-group discussions in class. These often are more beneficial than are large-group or all-class discussions.
21. Utilize Mondays or days following holidays to share with your class an exciting or enjoyable experience.

22. Have students prepare a potential guest speaker resource file.
23. Try playing music in your classroom for mood setting, to relieve anxieties and tensions.
24. Use educational games in your teaching. Many are being made available all the time. (Refer to Chapter 11 for sources.)
25. Try role playing to enhance the reality of material being learned.
26. Try Unit Contract or contract teaching.
27. Write individual and personalized notes to students on their papers, rather than merely letter grades or point scores.
28. Try videotaping an activity and replaying to the entire class.
29. Invent a useful educational game with class help.
30. Have students plan with you the "open house" and/or "back-to-school-night" activities. This helps in getting parents out, too.
31. Let the class help plan a field trip.
32. Have the students create and design a simulation game for a specific subject area or controversial issue in your field.
33. Create student mailboxes out of ice cream cartons for distribution of papers. Be sure to have one for yourself. Everyone likes to receive mail. You may wish to limit mail delivery time to the first few minutes of the class period.
34. Recycle old textbooks by removing all text material but leaving pictures and diagrams, then have students create their own texts.
35. Get permission from the administration to redecorate your classroom with colorful walls, drapes, and stuffed furniture.

B. EXPRESSING ENCOURAGEMENT AS A MOTIVATOR

Parents and teachers often express words of encouragement as a motivator. Words and expressions have many different shades and connotations, and therefore it would be very useful for teachers to know what kind of messages the student is receiving: Does the expression truly convey acceptance, trust, confidence and praise, or does it imply impatience, disappointment, and preaching? Consider the expressions that follow:

36. *"You have improved in . . ."* Improvement may not be where we would like it to be, but if there is progress, there is better chance for success. Students will usually continue to try if they can see some improvement.
37. *"You do a good job of . . ."* Point out some useful act or contribution in each student. Even a comment about something small and insignificant to the teacher may have great importance to a student.
38. *"We like (enjoy) you, but, we don't like what you do."* The student should never think he/she is not liked. It is important to distinguish between the student and his/her behavior, between the act and the actor.
39. *"You can help me (us, the others, etc.) by . . ."* To feel useful and helpful is important to everyone. Students want to be helpful; we have only to give them the opportunity.
40. *"Let's try it together."* Students who think they have to do things perfectly are often afraid to attempt something new for fear of making a mistake or failing.
41. *"You would like us to think you can't do it, but we think you can."* The student says or conveys that something is too difficult for him/her, and hesitates to even try it. If he/she tries and fails, he/she has at least had the courage to try.

42. *"I'm sure you can straighten this out [solve this problem] but if you need any help, you know where to find me."* Adults need to express confidence that students are able to and will resolve their own conflicts, if given a chance.
43. *"I can understand how you feel [not sympathy, but empathy] but I'm sure you'll be able to handle it."* Sympathizing with another person seldom helps him/her, but understanding the situation and believing in the person's ability to adjust to it is of much greater motivation to the student.

C. MOTIVATIONAL IDEAS SPECIFIC TO SUBJECT AREAS

Art

44. Use lyrics from popular music to influence class work, such as by putting the lyrics into pictures.
45. Bring in examples of the instructor's work, both current and beginning. This would enable students to relate more easily their own beginning frustrations with instructors.
46. Go outside into the schoolyard for free drawing experience.
47. Have them draw with the hand they never use.
48. Do a class mural on a piece of quarter-inch plywood.
49. Let them make their own kites and paint them. Demonstrate.
50. Arrange a field trip for class to dig up natural clay. In class, sift and refine it, soak in water, and work it into usable clay. Follow with hand-built clay project.
51. As part of a unit on the creative process, have each student draw on a piece of paper, then pass it on to the person next to him/her, and that person will make additions to the paper. Instructions could include "improve the drawing," "make the drawing ugly," "add what you think would be necessary to complete the composition."
52. As part of a unit on design or creativity, have students construct, design, and decorate their own kite. When the projects are complete, designate a time to fly them. Make necessary arrangements.
53. Listen to a musical recording and try to illustrate it.
54. Imagine that you're a bird flying over the largest city you have visited. What do you see, hear, smell, feel, taste? Draw a "sensory" map.
55. Assign a different color to each student. Have them arrange themselves into warm and cool colors and explain their decision (why blue is cool, etc.). (Include emotional responses to the color.)
56. Make a class visit to local galleries to observe works of contemporary artists.

Business Education

57. Choose a sentence or paragraph everyone has typed several times already. The instructions are for the students to type until they make an error, whether it be not capitalizing a word, typing a wrong letter, or whatever. The last one typing is the winner.
58. For production work, such as typing letters in a second-semester typing class, you, the teacher, take on the role of the "boss." Therefore, when a letter is typed the "boss" will receive it for signing. In this way the students are not just typing a letter for a grade, but typing it for the "boss," which will mean the letter will be set up according to his/her instructions.

59. Make a field trip to the front office to observe and talk to the office workers. Those included in the interviews would be the principal's and vice-principal's secretary, the registrar, and attendance clerks. This field trip would interest some students to seek student jobs in the office. In addition, there are other jobs on campus that they can find out about and investigate for possible employment. Back in the classroom, have each student report his/her findings to the rest of the class.

60. Have office (administration) personnel come into class and dictate some "real" letters and have students experience office-style dictation.

61. Compose crossword puzzles and newspaper cartoon strips in shorthand.

62. Arrange the students (on a rotational basis) to be "aides" to administration or to free teachers in order to take, transcribe, and type dictation.

63. Flash cards with account titles. Depending on the lesson, students could tell which type of statement the account would be found on or you could use such cards to reinforce debits and credits. They could be used also as a few-minute drill with the whole class. They are more useful, though, to use as a game between two pupils who need to review. The one who gets most right wins.

64. In typing, on a designated day each week everyone could bring anything they wished to type, e.g., a page from a book, a friendly letter, a magazine article, a term paper, anything they wished.

65. In teaching T-accounts, divide the room into teams; the number on a team depending upon class size. There are four teams usually, so teams will be small. First have one team make up transactions and the other try to answer, then reverse. The team to get the most right out of 20 transactions would win.

66. In typing, by use of letters and following specific directions, students can type pictures.

67. In choosing "practice sets" for accounting, as a teacher try to choose from the sets available several different ones, trying to match student interest.

68. In accounting or shorthand, be specific about amount of work to be done during the week, the work to be collected the following Monday. If the work is all done by Friday at the end of class, there would be no homework over the weekend.

69. Use computer programs, if available, as another activity to stimulate interest.

English (Including ESL, Speech, Drama, Journalism)

70. For a unit such as Elizabethan English, a wall-to-wall mural depicting a village of the times may be a total class project. Students can research customs, costumes, and architecture. Others may paint or draw.

71. For the holidays students can design their own holiday cards, creating their own poems for their cards.

72. To enhance understanding of parts of speech, set up this problem: Provide several boxes containing different parts of speech. Each student is to form one sentence from the fragments chosen from each box, being allowed to discard only at a penalty. The students then nonverbally make trades with other students to make coherent, and perhaps meaningfully amusing sentences. A student may trade a noun for a verb but will have to keep in mind what parts of speech are essential for a sentence. Results may be read aloud as a culmination to this activity.

73. Try this for an exercise in objective versus subjective writing: After a lesson on descriptive writing, bring to the class a nondescript object, such as a potato, and place it before the class. Ask them to write a paragraph either describing the potato in detail, that is, its color, size, markings, and other characteristics, or describing how the potato feels about them.

74. Set up a special communications board somewhere in the room where students may write anonymously or post sealed comments addressed to particular individuals, including the teacher.

75. Read to the class a story without an ending, then ask the students to write their own endings or conclusions.

76. Ask the students to create an advertisement using a propaganda device of their choice.

77. Ask the students to each create and design an invention and then to write a "patent description" for the invention.

78. Establish a "mini-library" in a corner of your room.

79. Ask students to write a physical description of some well-known public figure, such as a movie star, politician, athlete, or musician. Other class members may enjoy trying to identify the "mystery" personality from the written descriptions.

80. A bulletin board may be designated for current events and news in the world of writers. Included may be new books and record releases as well as reviews. News of poets and authors may also be displayed.

81. Start a paperback book library in your classroom. Set aside some time each week for reading. Perhaps one of your students would volunteer to serve as your "librarian."

82. Ask your students to maintain a daily "journal," with emphasis on expressing their feelings and unedited thoughts. Journals should be accepted as personal statements, which are to remain unjudged.

83. Provide students a choice as to which novel they will read next.

84. Design a "game" where students give original names to stories or captions to cartoons.

85. Remove the text from a Sunday newspaper comic strip and have the students create the story line.

86. Use popular recordings to introduce vocabulary words. Use for analysis of antonyms, synonyms, listening, writing, comprehension, and other skill development.

87. Use newspaper want ads to locate jobs as a base for completing job application forms and creating letters of inquiry.

88. Use videotape equipment to record employer-employee role-play situations, interviews for jobs, or child-parent situations, to develop language and listening skills.

89. Have students choose a short story from a text and write it into a play.

90. Use a round robin type of oral exercise to practice different kinds of sentence development.

91. Design an antonym game such as: have one student write a word on the board, then a student who correctly guesses the antonym goes to the board.

92. Have students look in newspapers and magazines for examples of the type of writing being studied in class. Give points for correct examples brought in.

93. When beginning a poetry unit ask students to bring in the words to their favorite songs. Show how these fit into the genre of poetry.

94. Once in a while dress yourself in costume and makeup and role-play the character your class is studying.

95. Have your students look for commercial examples of advertisements that might be classed as "eco-pornographic," i.e., ads that push a product that is potentially damaging to our environment.

96. Change the environment and ask students to write poetry to see if the change in surroundings stimulates or discourages their creativeness. For example, take your class to a large supermarket to write (you are advised to make arrangements first).
97. Bring a television set to class and have your students analyze advertisements for the emotions they appeal to, techniques used, and their integrity. Try the same thing with radio, teen magazines, and other media.

Foreign Languages

98. Draw a large outline of France on cardboard and have students fill in the major cities, rivers, and mountains. They can illustrate products of different regions, costumes, and other significant characteristics of the country.
99. Translate the school menu into French each day. This could be the daily project of selected groups from within the class.
100. Perhaps your class could earn money and go to a French restaurant as an end-of-the-year activity. You could obtain copies of the menu in advance so that students could select and practice ordering in French.
101. Organize a spelling bee in French, using the French alphabet.
102. Play "Password" in French.
103. Begin a game by saying "I went to France and took a radio" in French. The next person repeats the sentence adding another item, e.g., "I went to France and took a radio, a raincoat." If a student misses an item he/she is out; this continues until only one person remains.
104. Show the students a tray containing several or many items they know how to say in French. Allow them a few minutes to study it, then remove it and ask them to list all of the items on the tray.
105. Provide puppets in native costume for students to use in practicing dialogue.
106. Invite an exchange student from Germany [Austria, Switzerland] to talk with the class. He/She could discuss what he/she liked and disliked about America and funny experiences he/she might have had. The students would have an opportunity to ask about the guest's culture.
107. Once a month take the students on a "trip" to a German-speaking city through the use of slides, pictures, and music.
108. Have a mini "Oktoberfest" with dancing, singing, and German food.
109. Set up a pen-pal exchange with a beginning English class in Germany.
110. Teach a dialog with *puppets*. Depending on the age of the students, they might make puppets too and follow the dialog with their puppets. Older students can take turns manipulating the puppets in front of the class.
111. "Fill-in-the-word" game. Each student has a card with one word on it and must find other students with other parts of the sentence. Each sentence must be complete and *the students can only speak the target language.*
112. Conduct a spelling bee in the target language.
113. Take a field trip to a foreign language movie.

Home Economics

114. Take still photos of class members at special events such as dinners, fashion shows, field trips, and special projects. Build a scrapbook or bulletin board with these and display on campus or at Open House.

115. Encourage students to enter their projects in outside contests such as county fairs.
116. Collect cartoons related to food costs, consumer problems, and family relationships.
117. Instruct students on the means of obtaining and completing consumer complaint forms.
118. Set up authentic food tasting booths; set up campus tasting contests.
119. Establish a play school or nursery in conjunction with a child development class.
120. Use a large box wrapped as a gift to open a lesson on toy safety or toy purchasing.
121. Allow the students to plan and do the shopping for a food lab assignment.
122. Plan a unit on cultural foods, using the traditions, costumes, and music of a particular culture. Have the students decorate the room. Invite the principal for a meal and visit.
123. Take a trip to Small Claims Court. (Plan ahead and obtain permission from the Court.)
124. Plan a color and grooming unit. Ask students to match their personal colors closely to magazine photos. Match to color schemes to determine the most complimentary colors to wear or to use in household furnishings.
125. Try these nutrition-related games:
    a. Bring a bag full of all types of foods. Ask students to group them into the four basic food types. Let them eat the food as a reward for correct classifications.
    b. Pin the name of a food on a student's back. The student must ask another student questions until he/she guesses which food he/she is. Only "yes" or "no" response questions may be asked.
126. Plan a bulletin board displaying pictures of 100-calorie portions of basic nutritional foods and popular fad foods that contain only empty calories. The display can motivate a discussion on foods with calories and nutrients versus foods with empty calories.
127. Try this for motivation toward a unit on laundry: Pin the names of different garments on the back of students. The students are then to sort themselves into different wash loads. This is a fun game that motivates and involves an entire class.
128. For a clothing unit hold an "idea day." Ask each student to bring in an idea of something that can be done to give clothes a new look, a fun touch, or an extended wearing life. Ideas they may come with include: appliques, embroidery, tie-dye, batik, colorful patches, and restyling old clothes into current or creative fashions.
129. Have the students write, practice, and present skits, perhaps for videotape presentation, on consumer fraud.
130. Take the class on a field trip to the school cafeteria, a nearby supermarket, or a large restaurant. (Make necessary arrangements.)
131. Students should become familiar with shelving practices in stores and supermarkets.

Mathematics

132. Plan an in-class mathematical debate.
133. Try a game of mathematical baseball. Divide the class into two teams. Arrange the room as a baseball field. The "pitcher" fires content questions to the "hitter." This can be a fun way to review for an examination.
134. Arrange mathematical tournaments with other schools.
135. Do a mathematical survey of your school campus.
136. Plan with your class a role-play unit where members role-play the solar system. Students calculate their weights, set up a proportion system, find a large field, and on the final day actually simulate the solar system using their own bodies to represent the sun, planets, and moons. Arrange to have it photographed.

137. Have your students build mathematical models. Pyramids can be of special interest to the students.

138. Encourage your students to look for evidence of Fibonacci number series* in nature and in man-made objects. Here are some examples of where evidence may be found: piano keyboard, petals on flowers, spermatogenesis and oogenesis, and many places in mathematics. Perhaps your students might like to organize a Fibonacci Club.

139. Become familiar with the many games available for teaching mathematics.

140. Divide the class into two teams—the metric team and the nonmetric team. Have each team solve a series of measurement conversion problems. One team would convert nonmetric to metric, the other would convert metric to nonmetric. The team with the most problems correct wins.

141. Join with a physical science class and visit a science museum.

142. Invite an engineer, physical scientist, or computer program writer to speak to the class on how mathematics applies to their profession.

Music

143. Hang a cloth bag on the wall. Buy a sack of potatoes. For every song that students learn to sing, get a potato, write a date and a title of the song learned, and put the potato in the bag. At the end of the semester, buy a MacDonald's certificate for each potato and divide them among the students.

144. Take the class to a concert. They can observe others playing their instruments.

145. Have students find ways in which music is used around them, i.e., for television.

146. Periodically during the school year, after the students are very familiar with a certain piece (have memorized it or can play it perfectly) switch the band or orchestra around by not putting any two of the same instruments together. For example, put no flutes next to each other, put a cello by a trumpet, a violin beside a drummer, or a saxophone next to a viola and bass. This ensures that each person knows his own part and can carry his own weight in terms of performance. This can also be done in chorus, mixing sopranos with altos, tenors, and basses, etc.

147. Find a popular song on the radio the students like. Transpose the melody into unfamiliar keys for each instrument. This makes the student want to learn the song, but in the process he/she will have to become more familiar with his/her instrument.

148. Set aside one weekend morning a month and hold small informal recitals (workshops) allowing students to participate/observe the performance situation(s) among their peers and themselves. (Students might be told previously about these "special days" and encouraged to prepare a selection of their own choosing.)

149. Listen to current popular musical recordings and discuss them as to musical content and performance techniques.

150. As an extra credit project, have students prepare brief oral reports on past composers and give an example of their music by recording, performance. (The student may even enjoy dressing the part of the composer.)

151. Trumpet Clinics: A. With trumpet teachers; B. With trumpet performers (all styles of music); C. With other students from other schools.

152. Plan different money-making projects such as singing telegrams.

---

* Fibonacci numbers are a series of numbers, each of which is the sum of the preceding two, i.e., 1, 1, 2, 3, 5, 8 . . .

153. Play a group-activity rhythm game, one such as the "Dutch Shoe Game" to get students to cooperate, work together, and enjoy themselves using rhythm. If students are willing to sit on the floor, it can be adaptable to any age level. Participants sit in a circle, and as the song is sung, each person passes one of his/her shoes to the person on the right in rhythm to the music. Shoes continue to be passed as long as verses are sung. Those with poor rhythm will end up with a pile of shoes in front of them!

154. Choose a rhythmical, humorous poem or verse to conduct. The students read the poem in chorus, while the teacher stands before them and conducts the poem as if it were a musical work. Students must be sensitive to the intonation, speed, inflection, mood, and dynamics that the teacher wants them to convey in their reading.

155. Play the game "Name that Tune" using works by composers the students have been studying, or take various styles of music and ask them to identify them with composers.

156. Do a series of studies of non-Western music. As a break from studying just Western music, once a week or once every two weeks prepare a program to expose students to the music of a different country, for example, Japan or India or the Polynesian Islands. Records can be used to introduce the sound of the music, slides can be used to view the country and its people, and instruments can be found from different countries. Guest speakers may be available to lecture or perform.

157. A field trip to the Opera or a concert can be scheduled. Group rates are usually available, with half price for students as a rule.

158. To motivate a marching band and to let them know how much work goes into making a half-time show, have students form groups and let each group design a portion of a half-time show. For example, one group can put together what tunes should be played and another group could put together the entrance movements of the show.

159. Pick students at random to be the drum major (student band leader) and lead the band in a tune or a given portion of a half-time show; this will not only stimulate interest, but also help students to be able to organize musical patterns.

160. Have the students bring in some of their favorite recordings of popular present-day bands. Play the recordings for the entire class while analyzing each band's style. Give a contest by dividing the class and having the students attempt to classify each band by the style of each recording.

161. To improve marching band skills and to motivate precision marching, let each section of the band (brass, woodwinds, and percussion) demonstrate its marching ability before the rest of the band. At the end of the semester the best marching section can be rewarded.

162. Give students the opportunity to write their own original composition which can be performed in public.

Physical Education

163. Students will choose the famous athlete whom they most admire. A short report will be written about the athlete. The student will then discuss the attributes and/or characteristics that they admire in the athlete, and how they feel they can emulate those qualities.

164. Students will make up an exercise routine to their favorite record and share it with the class.

165. Have class divide into groups. Given the basic nonlocomotive skills, have each group come up with a "people machine." Each student within the group is hooked up to another demonstrating a nonlocomotive skill and adding some sort of noise to it. Have a contest for the most creative people machine.

166. Have a special talent day—where students may demonstrate an individual talent or group talent, relating it to physical education. (Might have them keep this in mind, practice on rainy days, and present it on a rainy day)

167. Have a mini-Olympic day where students help create the various events to be used and give honors to winners.

168. Students are given a chance to design a balance beam routine that has two passes on the beam and that must include: front support mount, forward roll, leap, low or high turn, visit, chasse, and cross support dismount. These routines will be posted to show the variety of ways the different maneuvers can be put together.

169. Divide the class into groups. Have them create a new game or activity for the class, using only the equipment they are given. Let the class play these newly created games.

170. Use Friday as a game day—do not introduce anything new. Review what was taught earlier in the week. Have some kind of competitive games or relays related to the skills previously learned.

171. Videotaping is a good device to show students their errors and their improvements in a skill such as batting. It helps them see what they are doing and helps them develop a kinesthetic awareness of their movement.

172. Organize and make available to your students a trip to a professional, collegiate or any highly skilled team's game. This usually will motivate them if they are at all interested in the sport.

173. Engage a guest speaker, preferably a professional athlete or coach in the sport you are teaching, to talk or demonstrate specific skills.

174. Exercises done to popular music. Let students take turns bringing in music and leading the exercises. The teacher will furnish a general outline to follow.

Science

175. Have your students create microscopes with bamboo rods and drops of water at each end.

176. Have your students make litmus indicators from petals of flowers.

177. Assign themes or problems that require students to predict or hypothesize decision making in a critical incident.

178. Use Polaroid cameras for students to record and immediately share observations.

179. Use cassette-tape recorders to record sounds of the environment. Compare day and night sounds. (This can also be helpful in poetry writing.)

180. If you are a life science teacher, make sure your classroom looks like a place for studying life rather than death.

181. The technique of "show and tell" is an excellent motivator and can be modified to be useful to the secondary school teacher. Do not allow students to "rip off" the environment of such things as flowers or beneficial insects or tide-pool life.

182. Encourage students to hypothesize, then to collect data, using their own environment.

183. Use your imagination. If you want, for example, to study predator-prey relationships but you are located in an inner-city school, then your class might use landlord-tenant situations for the study.

184. Have your students make their own cosmetics. Share what you are doing with the Home Economics teachers—perhaps you can combine your efforts.

185. Divide your class into groups and ask each group to create an environment for an imaginary animal, using discarded items from the environment. By asking questions each group will try and learn about other groups' "mystery" animals.

186. Be aware of relevant programs being shown on local television stations. Perhaps you can let students observe one during class time, by pretaping if necessary.

187. If your students have never seen an ocean, a forest, or mountains, and you cannot take them on an appropriate field trip, then do the next best thing and go yourself (perhaps during vacations) and take slides or moving pictures to show them. (Become aware of any income-tax advantages available to you as a teacher.)

188. Become familiar with the many educational games available for teaching science.

189. Students can summarize the steps in a process (for example, setting up a distillation) by *taking photos* of each step to illustrate an instruction book for other students.

190. Let each student "adopt" a chemical element. The student then researches that element and becomes the class expert whenever that particular substance comes up in discussion. There could be a special bulletin board for putting up questions on interesting or little-known facts about the elements.

191. Have the students bring to class current newspaper clippings on environmental problems having to do with chemistry (toxic waste spills, pesticide application, etc.). Have students form discussion groups to try to find practical ways to deal with the problem. This could become a longer-term project, with library research and letter-writing for more information.

192. Milk can be precipitated, separated, and the solid product dried to form a very hard substance that was, in the days before plastic, used to make buttons. Let students make their own buttons from milk.

193. Spray paint molecular models gold. Give the "golden molecule" award for exceptional lab projects, etc. Or give the award for the most disastrous failure (*if the student has a good sense of humor*). The award could be given to a lab group each week to encourage working as a group.

194. Have your students build a model of a molecule using gumdrops and toothpicks. Different colored gumdrops are to represent different elemental atoms. When they show the teacher that they have correctly named and constructed their models, they can eat the gumdrops.

195. Blow a balloon up in class and hold it between your thumb and forefinger. Let it go. Explain that *you* have just demonstrated potential energy and rocket propulsion. Go into the lecture on potential energy.

196. Have your students make their own useful items as related to science, things such as the following:
    a. Library paste: one-half cup cornstarch to three-fourths cup cold water, stir to paste, then add six cups of boiling water and stir until translucent, then cool to room temperature.
    b. Baby oil: two tablespoons of almond oil, eight tablespoons of olive oil, and a few drops of perfume, stir all ingredients together—keep out of reach of children.
    c. Concrete cleaner: dry mix these—sodium metasilicate, three and one-quarter cups; trisodium phosphate, three-quarters cup; soda ash, one-half cup.

Social Science

197. Establish a special "people and things" bulletin board.
198. Have your class play charades to learn geography.
199. Set up a classroom broadcast studio where students prepare and present news broadcasts.
200. Take your class on an imaginary trip around the world. Students can role-play countries.

201. Let your class plan how they would improve their living environment, beginning with the classroom, then moving out to the school, home, and community.

202. Become familiar with the many games available for teaching social studies. Refer to Chapter 11 for sources.

203. Start a pictorial essay on the development and/or changes of a given area in your community, e.g., a major corner or block adjacent to the school. This is a study that would continue for years and that has many social, political, and economic implications.

204. Start a folk hero study. Each year ask "What prominent human being who has lived during the twentieth century do you most admire?" Collect individual responses to the question, tally, and discuss. After you have done this for several years you may wish to share with your class for discussion purposes the results of your surveys of previous years.

205. Play the *Redwood Controversy* game. (See Chapter 11.) Perhaps you and your class can design a simulation game on a controversial social issue.

206. Role-play a simulated family movement West in the 1800s. What items would they take? What would they throw out of the wagon to lighten the load?

207. Have students collect music, art, or athletic records from a particular period of history. Compare with today. Predict the future.

208. Using play money, establish a capitalistic economic system within your classroom. Salaries may be paid for attendance and bonus income for work well done, taxes may be collected for poor work, and a welfare section established in a corner of the room.

209. Divide your class into small groups and ask that each group make predictions as to what world governments, world geography, world social issues, or some other related topic will be like some time in the future. Let each group give its report, followed by debate and discussion.

210. "Alphabet Geography": A place is given by the teacher, such as a state, city, river, etc. The next person must name a place starting with the same letter as the last in that previously mentioned. Students are eliminated or given points. This game can be used as a drill to acquaint students with place names and where these places are. The class can be divided into groups such as boys vs. girls, row vs. row, or students can stand individually.

With the preceding suggestions we have only scratched the surface in providing ideas. The total possibilities are limited only by the courage and imagination of the teacher.

A source of valuable information, including ideas for motivation, can be the professional journal(s) for your field. We provide here a list for many fields. Check for their availability in your school library.

D. PROFESSIONAL PERIODICALS USEFUL TO SECONDARY SCHOOL TEACHERS

Art

Art Education
School Arts
Studies in Art Education
The Art Teacher

Bilingual Education

Bilingual Review
TESOL Quarterly (Teaching English for
    Speakers of Other Languages)

Business Education

American Business Education
Business Education Forum
Business Education World
Business Teacher
Journal of Business Education

English and Language Arts

English
English Journal
English Language Teaching Journal
Educational Theatre Journal
Journal of Reading
Research in the Teaching of English
TESOL Quarterly

Foreign Languages

Classic Journal
Hispania
Language Learning
Modern Language Forum
Modern Language Journal
The French Review
The German Quarterly

Home Economics

Forecast for Home Economics
Journal of Home Economics

Industrial Arts

Industrial Arts and Vocational Education
Industrial Arts Teacher
Industrial Education
School Shop

Mathematics

Arithmetic Teacher
Mathematics Teacher
School Science and Mathematics

Music

The American Music Teacher
Educational Music Magazine
Journal of Research in Music Education
Music Educators Journal
The School Musician

Physical Education

Athletic Journal
Journal of Physical Education
Journal of Physical Education and Recreation
Physical Education

Science

Journal of Chemistry Education
Journal of Geological Education
School Science and Mathematics
Science and Children
Science Education
The American Biology Teacher
The Chemistry Teacher
The Physics Teacher
The Science Teacher

Social Studies

Social Education
Social Studies
Integrated Education

EXERCISE 13.1: SELECTING AND EXPERIMENTING WITH A MOTIVATIONAL TECHNIQUE

From the list of motivational ideas select one (yes, only one!) and try it out during your practice teaching. Yes, you may modify it however you wish. After you have tried it, report back to this class and share the results.

My name _____ My subject field _____

Grade and school _____

The motivational idea I used: _____

_____

_____

_____

_____

The results: _____

_____

_____

_____

_____

_____

Would I use it again? _____

_____

_____

_____

_____

_____

Modifications I would make: _____

_____

_____

_____

_____

_____

EXERCISE 13.2: DEVELOPING MY OWN BANK OF MOTIVATIONAL TECHNIQUES

We leave this exercise somewhat open and to be designed by your class, but what we do suggest is that you build—perhaps by a card file—your own inventory of ideas you might sometime use as motivational strategies. Share your ideas with other members of your class. You might start by completing the following task: List four ideas on motivation that you might try and that are not included in the suggestions in this chapter.

_____

_____

_____

_____

EXERCISE 13.3: IDENTIFYING PROFESSIONAL JOURNALS

Your purpose for this exercise is to become familiar with the professional journals applicable to secondary teaching and which are available in your nearest professional library. Visit your college or university library and review the periodical reference book to locate the journals that interest you.

Select one journal and begin browsing through the current issues. Identify the title of the journal, the publication date, and, if available, the professional organization that supports or is affiliated with the journal.

Select one current article that reflects your interest.

Identify the title of the article, the author, and the bibliographical information. Identify which subject area the article has impact on. Take notes on the article and share your notes with others in your class.

Hand your bibliographical information and your notes to your instructor or a class volunteer. If your class members decide they want to develop a current bibliography of interesting journal articles, then the list should be alphabetized by the author's last name: show all of the needed bibliographical information, along with the annotation compiled from each reader's notes.

. . . .

Hand to class volunteer for current bibliography.

_____   _____
Author   Article title

_____   _____   _____   _____
Journal title   Volume   Number   Year/pps.

Annotation: _____

_____

_____

EXERCISE 13.4: BEGINNING MY RESOURCE FILE

Begin your own aids and resources file on 3x5 cards, listing (a) the name, (b) how and when available, (c) how to use, and (d) some evaluative comments. This file can build throughout your career.

You may wish to cross reference your filing system to accommodate the following categories of items:

1. Pictures, posters, and other visuals.
2. Articles for you and your students to use.
3. Dittos and worksheets.
4. Film catalogues.
5. Resources to order.
6. Games.

QUESTIONS FOR CLASS DISCUSSION

1. Did you find in our list any ideas that were particularly objectionable to you? Which and why?
2. Do you know the difference between extrinsic and intrinsic sources of motivation? Explain.
3. Did you "discover" a professional journal that is of particular interest to you? Which and why does it interest you?
4. What kinds of teaching/learning activities motivate junior high school students today? High school students? Any difference?
5. How long is the attention span of a typical secondary-school student today? Does it differ from that of the past? How do you know?
6. Has student viewing of television been beneficial or detrimental to the efforts of a secondary-school classroom teacher? What evidence can you find to support or reject your opinion?
7. Does the motivation of a secondary-school student vary from one period of the day to the next, simply because of the time of the day? Can you find any research evidence to support your opinion?
8. What effect does the blood sugar level of a secondary-school student have upon his/her motivation level? What research can you find regarding this?
9. Do certain subjects lend themselves to easier student motivation? Which and why? What could a teacher of a "low-motivation course" learn from this?
10. Is there a particular period of the day you would prefer to teach a particular subject to a particular group of students? Why or why not?
11. What other questions do you have regarding the general topic of motivation? How might answers be found?

SELECTED READINGS AND REFERENCES FOR CHAPTER 13

Ames, Carole. "Competitive Versus Cooperative Structures: The Influence of Individual and Group Performance Factors on Achievement Attributions and Affect." *American Educational Research Journal,* Vol. 18 (1981), pp. 273-287.

Moore, R. E. "Can Advance Organizers Influence Meaningful Learning?" *Review of Educational Research,* Vol. 42, No. 2 (1979), p. 371.

Reilly, Robert R., and Ernest L. Lewis. *Educational Psychology: Application for Classroom Learning and Instruction.* New York: Macmillan Publishing Company, 1983.

Rinne, Carl H. *Attention: The Fundamentals of Classroom Control.* Columbus, OH: Charles E. Merrill, 1984.

Part IV

Classroom Management, Discipline, and Legal Guidelines

A TEACHER'S CONTRACT IN 1923[1]

Your pay will be $5.00 a month, providing you meet these conditions:

1. *Don't get married, and don't keep company with men.*
2. *Don't be away from home between the hours of 8 p.m. and 6 a.m.*
3. *Don't loiter in ice cream parlors.*
4. *Don't smoke cigarettes, don't drink beer, wine, or whiskey.*
5. *Don't leave town without permission.*
6. *Don't ride in a carriage or automobile with any man except your father or brother.*
7. *Don't dress in bright colors, dye your hair, or use face powder, mascara, or lipstick.*

[1] Original source unknown, but thought to have been in an Idaho teacher's contract dated 1923.

Part IV assists you in coping with

- Daily challenges of teaching.

- Classroom environment.

- Clerical responsibilities.

- Classroom management.

- Discipline.

14

What Do I Need to Know to Cope With the Daily Challenge of Secondary Teaching?

Wet spit balls are flying. Some wads are sticking to the classroom ceiling. Aerodynamic paper shapes spin through the educational sky. Faces are made by creative students. Giggles and whispers are heard. Squirming students are seen. Some students are rude and others refuse to do their lessons as one teacher pleads, "Please be quiet" in Harry Allard's *Miss Nelsen is Missing* (Houghton, 1977). How Miss Nelsen solves her problem of class management (sending in a witchy substitute) may be entirely different from how you plan to solve your problems during the daily challenge of teaching. However, resolving your concerns about class management is one step—a giant step—in building your competency as a secondary school teacher.

When classroom management techniques are effective, the students learn, and those effective techniques result from careful thought and planning. Classroom management should not be left for the student teacher to learn on the job! As you develop your management skills, consider these general guidelines:

1. Your *voice* should be natural and relaxed. Never scream and shout at the students, or try to talk over the class. If the students are beginning to get too noisy, then change the lesson strategy (such as a silent board lesson) and/or use your best kinesic variation technique.
2. Know what to *expect* of each student. Clarify so each student knows what is expected of him/her. Remember, in both one and two your modeling behavior counts!
3. Match the *pacing* of the lessons to the capabilities of the students. Going too fast with slow students will bring trouble just as will going too slow with the more capable students.
4. Use *humor* when appropriate. It relaxes the tension and can facilitate learning. Laughing *with* the class is important in making the learning environment pleasant and productive.
5. There will be unexpected *class interruptions,* some of which will be out of your control. Prepare so that you can keep the class busy when such interruptions do occur.

6. Teach students your *classroom rules* early. The list of rules will perhaps be a bit longer for early junior high school grades than for later high school years. State your classroom behavior rules in positive, rather than negative, terms. In early junior high years you may wish to post the rules above the chalkboard. For all students, give positive verbal reinforcers to a student who "follows the rules." For students who "break" the rules, the following generalization might be well to keep in mind: one break gets a reminder; second break—note or call to parents; third break—trip to office; fourth break—suspension.

It is an aphorism in teaching that prevention of problems is easier than resolving them. From that standpoint we provide this list called "If I Do Any of These, Please Let Me Know."[2] This list provides an exhaustive number of things we as teachers like not to do. Of course, none of us is perfect and at times certain "violations" are unavoidable, but still the list provides an important set of standards that, when followed, should aid in our efforts toward attaining an ideal.

A. "IF I DO ANY OF THESE, PLEASE LET ME KNOW!"

RUGGED BEGINNING

Rushes in late to class.
Gives a ridiculous excuse for being late.
Asks, "What are we supposed to do today?"
Flips pages in the book looking for suitable material.
Has no chalk and goes out hunting for it, blaming the custodians.

LACK OF PREPARATION AND PLANNING

States definitions and content incorrectly.
Has no examples planned in advance.
Attempts to make up examples on the spot, which turn out to be overly complicated, very difficult, trivial, or inappropriate to the idea at hand.
Loses lines of reasoning and has to keep referring to the book.
Assigns homework thoughtlessly (e.g., to solve the odd-numbered problems from 1 to 200).

INEFFECTIVE STYLE OF PRESENTATION

Proceeds with maddening slowness.
Speaks in a monotonous, dull, pedantic, or inarticulate manner.
Rushes through the material, talking much too fast.
Does not write down enough of what is said.
Does not bother writing down definitions.
Uses terms without defining them.
Indicates diagrams only by handwaving.
Presents no overview, summary, or relationships among ideas.
Does not attempt to motivate students to study the material.

[2] Original source unknown.

Assumes that students already know the basic material and humiliates them when they do
    not.
Goes off on tangents involving overly advanced material.
Simply reads the book to the students.
Makes numerous errors in computations, logic, and grammar.

LACK OF RAPPORT WITH STUDENTS

Makes no eye contact with the class; talks to the board, walls, floor, or ceiling.
Loses everyone's attention and goes on anyway.
Makes disparaging comments about the low level of the course material.
Insults the students: tells them they are stupid or unprepared.
Keeps saying "trivial" or "obvious."
Shows no enthusiasm.
Keeps looking at the time.
Displays irritating mannerisms.
Does not know students' names.
Has no positive comments for anyone.

POOR HANDLING OF QUESTIONS

Does not permit questions or embarrasses students who ask them.
Does not answer questions adequately.
Tells students to look up the answers to their questions in the book.
Misunderstands the student and answers a question that has not been asked.
Spends excessive class time answering questions of little general interest.
Asks almost no questions of the students.
Ask questions that are vague, confusing, impossible, or extremely simple.
Calls on the first person to raise a hand, without giving others time to think.
Harshly criticizes student responses to teacher questions.

POOR BLACKBOARD TECHNIQUE

Makes messy, indistinct drawings.
Labels diagrams unclearly or inadequately.
Reverses coordinates.
Places figures too high or too low so that key portions run off the board.
Crowds items together.
Mixes distinct problem solutions together on the board.
Leaves insufficient space for important items.
Writes illegibly (too small, too large, or on a slant).
Blocks students' vision by standing in front of the board work.
Skips steps or combines too many steps at once.
Keeps changing the same statement by erasure or addition, rather than rewriting it on another
    line.
Erases too quickly, thereby preventing comprehension or questions.

To cope with the daily challenge of teaching, you should be able to maintain the physical environment of your classroom(s), be efficient in your handling of routines, and have an effective and efficient plan for the management of the classroom; and, you need to realize the legal guidelines that exist for you in your state's education code to protect and ensure your teaching rights as well as the rights of your secondary students.

B. SURVEYING THE PHYSICAL ENVIRONMENT OF THE CLASSROOM

As a beginning junior or senior high school teacher you will most likely share your classrooms with other teachers during the school day. Perhaps eventually you will be fortunate to have your own classroom. Whichever the case, consider the ever-present challenge of maintaining the physical environment for your learners as you check yourself on each item of the following exercise, and share your responses with other teacher candidates.

EXERCISE 14.1: WHAT SHOULD I DO TO MAINTAIN THE PHYSICAL ENVIRONMENT OF MY CLASSROOM?

	Needs Attention	*Satisfactory*
1. Am I always aware of the physical environment of my classroom?	_____	_____
2. Do I take the time to check the room temperature daily?	_____	_____
3. Do I ventilate the room properly?	_____	_____
4. Do I adjust the window shades to control any glare or bright light that enters the room as the sun changes position during the school day?	_____	_____
5. Am I concerned with the room's overall appearance?	_____	_____
6. Is my classroom neat and organized?	_____	_____
7. Do the bulletin boards contribute to the appearance of the classroom?	_____	_____
8. Have I included classroom decorations about approaching events, holidays, or information about units, topics, or themes the students are studying?	_____	_____
9. Are the classroom storage spaces organized?	_____	_____
10. Are the classroom shelves arranged in a neat and orderly manner?	_____	_____
11. Is classroom equipment accessible but out of the students' traffic patterns?	_____	_____
12. Have I considered a functional seating arrangement for the students and provided space for such activities as independent work, construction projects, and computer-assisted instruction?	_____	_____
13. Will this functional arrangement allow the students to quickly re-arrange the seating if needed for team-learning activities, or for a skit?	_____	_____
14. Have I considered the seating arrangements to meet the individual needs of left-handed students or those with hearing or vision difficulties?	_____	_____
15. Have I carefully planned the ways I will organize the materials I need for the lessons each day?	_____	_____
16. Have I systematically prepared and collected all of the supplies I will need and placed or stored them in a convenient location?	_____	_____
17. Have I considered the most efficient way to distribute these materials and/or supplies to the students?	_____	_____
18. Have I considered an effective collection method?	_____	_____
19. Have I considered hiring a private classroom-cleaning service?	_____	_____

Review your responses. What are some items that need your careful attention? Now, share your responses with other teacher candidates. After your discussion, turn your attention to the following statements for maintaining your efficiency, and respond to the suggestions about school routines and your clerical responsibilities.

C. ACHIEVING ROUTINE MAINTENANCE

Consider the routine maintenance procedures that you have observed in a junior high classroom. Did the teacher have a routine procedure for the start of the school day? What were the attendance procedures? the lunch count procedures? the tardy procedures?

Record your observations here and discuss with your classmates.

_____

_____

_____

_____

The normal routines of the classroom may be interrupted on certain days or at certain times during a day. For instance, not all days are equal in terms of the energy level of the students in the classroom. Your anticipation and careful planning for these days of high energy level will undoubtedly help preserve your own mental health. Times of high energy level for some students are:

- The beginning of each day, especially on Mondays and minimum days.
- The end of each school day.
- The ending of each Friday afternoon.
- The before-lunch period.
- The pre-holiday time.
- The pre-field trip time.
- The pre-special event time, e.g., being photographed for an annual school picture.
- The day a substitute teacher arrives.
- The day of report cards.
- Pre- and/or post-assembly period.

What experiences have interrupted your classroom routines? What specifically could you plan to help avert some of these potentially interrupting days? _____

_____

_____

_____

_____

_____

_____

_____

_____

After the beginning of the school day, teachers demonstrate their ability to make smooth transitions from the opening exercises into a following lesson. What transition statements have you heard during your classroom observations? Were these transitions clear and concise? Did the teacher state his/her expectations? From your point of view, which transition statements seem to be the most effective? Write your selected statements below and discuss them with your classmates.

EXERCISE 14.2: HOW CAN I MAINTAIN EFFICIENCY IN RESPONDING TO ROUTINES AND CLERICAL RESPONSIBILITIES?

Record your responses to the following statements. Use these statements as a focus for a class discussion, after you have completed the list. These suggestions may promote your efficiency and help you to use your time more productively.

	I Can Do This?	*Not Yet!*
1. I can develop a quick and accurate procedure for taking attendance, and for reporting students who are tardy.	_____	_____
2. I understand the value of beginning the academic day with a lesson—instead of requiring the students to wait quietly while I take attendance—and realize I can accomplish that task five or ten minutes later when the students are busy.	_____	_____
3. I understand the importance of *my* reading information from the school bulletin to the students.	_____	_____
4. I can organize the distribution and collection of materials and supplies quickly, with the help of a teaching aide and/or selected students.	_____	_____
5. I can keep an up-to-date account of the materials, supplies, equipment, and furniture in my classroom.	_____	_____
6. I can provide accurate information about materials that are loaned.	_____	_____
7. I can enforce school and district policies when books, equipment, or furniture are damaged.	_____	_____
8. I understand my gradebook is a legal document that should be accurate, a complete record of each student's educational progress, and should not be left open for all to read.	_____	_____
9. I can evaluate all student assignments in an efficient manner and return their evaluated work promptly.	_____	_____
10. I can maintain due dates for homework and other special assignments, remembering to acknowledge illnesses, emergencies, and other special reasons for absences.	_____	_____
11. I understand that a student's improvement may be a signal for a phone call to interested parents, just as much as a student's difficulties may be.	_____	_____
12. I understand that notes to parents can convey positive messages more often than negative ones.	_____	_____

EXERCISE 14.3: CONVEYING A POSITIVE MESSAGE TO PARENTS

Indeed, a note to the parents of one of your students can convey a positive message. Consider one example of a positive note you might write. Describe briefly the situation that could initiate a positive message from you to the parents. Practice writing one example of a positive message below. Ask another student teacher to react to your message. Does your message convey what you intended for it to say?

Situation _____

_____

Practice note to parents _____

_____

_____

_____

_____

Reaction comments _____

_____

_____

_____

_____

_____

_____

_____

Review your responses. What are the areas you want to focus on for your class discussion? Talk about them with others. Now turn your attention to the legal guidelines that support your teaching rights and the rights of students.

D. REVIEWING LEGAL GUIDELINES

You probably have a multitude of questions regarding that which you as a teacher can and cannot do, and about what you must and must not do. Without reading ahead write down here some of your questions.

_____

_____

_____

_____

_____

_____

_____

_____

_____

_____

_____

_____

_____

_____

Now, turn your attention to Exercise 14.4.

EXERCISE 14.4: WHAT LEGAL GUIDELINES ARE AVAILABLE TO ME?

Obtain copies of your state Education Code and of local district guidelines, or the faculty and student handbook of a secondary school in your area. You will find such topics as:

1. What is the legal status of the classroom teacher?
2. What is the legal status of the secondary school student?
3. What is the legal status of the teacher's contract?
4. What are your state's teacher dismissal and tenure laws?
5. What are your state's teacher retirement laws?
6. What are your state and local positions on teacher collective bargaining?
7. What is the position regarding teaching the course of study?
8. What are the legal requirements regarding punishment and discipline?
9. What are the legal requirements regarding teacher liability and negligence?
10. What is the legal status of the student teacher?

THE TEACHER AND THE LAW

While it would take another volume to treat fully the questions of Exercise 14.4, it is to the advantage of the teacher to keep the following in mind[3]:

Teachers have certain constitutional rights that cannot be disregarded, and it is the responsibility of administration to protect these rights. Specifically:

Teachers have the RIGHT to:

1. Receive support from the school administration assisting them to carry out their role as teachers.
2. Expect their classrooms will be free from disruption by students, parents, and others.
3. Use reasonable physical restraint to protect themselves, other students, or to maintain safe conditions in the performance of their duties.
4. Suspend a student within the limits of the Education Code.
5. Exclude from their extracurricular activity any student who does not meet the minimal standards established by the teacher of the activity for which the teacher is responsible, provided the rights of students are not violated.
6. Expect the student to come to class prepared and with the materials needed to carry out the activities for the day.
7. Request from appropriate authority that a student be considered for transfer, for specific reasons, out of their classroom.
8. Receive all available pertinent information regarding students placed in their classes.

Students have the RIGHT to:

1. Due process, which includes:
    a. a hearing within the school;
    b. explicit knowledge of charges brought against them;
    c. the opportunity to be heard in their own defense.
2. Know the behavior expected of them and the consequences of not obeying rules.
3. Be treated with courtesy and respect by staff and other students and have their constitutional rights protected.
4. Participate in school activities, provided they meet the qualifications of the sponsoring organizations.

Student Conduct and Behavior Standards

Disciplinary action for violation of school and state rules and regulations are based on the student and his/her deliberate defiance of the law. Some forms of action may be: calling in the parents for a conference, detention, suspension, transfer to another school, or expulsion. The school staff and administration shall at all times try to consider what forms of disciplinary action will be best for the student.

By penal code in most states, assaulting, attacking, or menacing another individual is an unlawful act. A student who either assaults, attacks, or menaces another student or school employee is guilty of violating the penal code and may be subjected to arrest as well as school disciplinary procedures.

[3] Excerpted from the *Sacramento City Unified School District Faculty, Parents and Student Handbook,* 1981, Sacramento, California.

Definitions

Assault: An open threat of bodily contact with someone, without his/her permission.

Attack: Any willful and unlawful use of force or violence upon the person of another.

Menace: A show of intent to inflict harm; a threatening gesture, statement, or act.

Extortion: It is a criminal act to ask another person for money or other valuables and at the same time threaten to harm the person or his property in any way. If a student is approached by another student or students in this manner, he/she should report it to the office immediately. Any student who takes or attempts to take money or valuables from another by force or intimidation is subject to school disciplinary penalties as well as arrest.

Removal of Students from School

Students may be removed *involuntarily* from school for these reasons:

A. *Suspension*
    1. *Definition:* Suspension is a temporary removal from school attendance and school activities for misconduct. Generally, a student may be suspended for behavior harmful to the welfare of other students or behavior that adversely affects school discipline.
    2. *Types:* There are two types of suspension:
        a. *Teacher suspension:* A teacher may suspend, for good cause, any student for the remainder of the class period the day of the suspension and the class period on the following day. Note that the student does not leave school (but only the teacher's class) under this type of suspension.
        b. *Principal suspension:* The principal, or his designee, is given the right to suspend for a period not to exceed 5 days at one given time and not to exceed more than 20 days in a school year except that the student shall first be transferred and enrolled in either one other regular school for adjustment purposes, an opportunity school, or a continuation high school.

B. *Expulsion*
    1. *Definition:* Expulsion is the most serious action that can be taken against a student. It is a disciplinary measure that removes a student from school for a specified period of time and that, after that time, allows the student to return to school only if he/she has met the conditions imposed by the Board of Education.
    2. *Reasons:* A student may be expelled for behavior that harms or threatens to harm other students or for behavior that seriously disrupts school discipline, whether such behavior takes place on or off the school grounds.
    3. *Procedure:* Because expulsion is such a serious action, the procedure is explicit and such as to give a student full protection of due process and of a fair hearing. Generally, the procedure is that the initial action is a recommendation by the principal, this being done on the Suspension Notice form, supplemented with case documentation. The next action is a hearing before an administrative panel which the student and his/her parent attend and give testimony and in which all testimony is recorded. If the panel recommends expulsion, the next step is for the superintendent to present the case to the Board of Education for approval or disapproval.

Teacher Liability

As indicated in the *Code of Ethics of the Education Profession* (in Chapter 2), the teacher must "protect the health and safety of students." With this in mind, the teacher is looked upon as *"in loco parentis"* (in the place of parents) in the classroom or as "substitute parents" at school. While the teacher can be dismissed for various reasons such as incompetence, immorality, unprofessional conduct, and/or negligence, the last category is by far the most frequent cause for legal disputes resulting in teacher dismissal. The central question here is whether or not the school and/or the teacher has exercised adequate supervision and whether there is evidence for negligence of duty on the part of the school and the teacher in the execution of their assigned duties. Some liabilities are likely to arise when the teacher is either unaware of or being imprudent in situations such as these:

1. Some states and Boards of Education allow teachers to administer corporal punishment. However, when there are some evidences that this is done in anger, unreasonably, or has caused some degree of permanent injury, the teacher is liable.
2. Teachers in special courses and activities should be especially well aware of safety precautions to prevent accidents or injuries. These would include exercising care during science demonstrations/experiments, and when handling tools and equipment in arts and crafts, home economics, or industrial arts classes. Extra care should be exercised by the physical education instructors and coaches about checking apparatus and equipment. Any teachers who take the students to field trips or who sponsor any extra-curricular activities, either on campus or outside the campus, must also be prudent in this matter.

Your Contract

What will it mean to you when you sign your first teaching contract?

1. Your contract is a legal agreement between you and the governing school board in the district.
2. Your contract guarantees you employment, a teaching assignment, a salary, and your expected length of service.
3. Your length of service is identified, i.e., service for one year, or that of continuing service to the district.
4. You are legally required to perform your assigned duties as specified in your teaching contract.
5. There is a probationary period before a tenure contract is offered to you.
6. A district's tenure laws will vary from state to state; however, the tenure law is regarded as due process for you, the teacher. This protects you against any unfair assignment change, unjust transfer, a demotion, a reduction in salary, and other changes.
7. A district's tenure law is not regarded as a safeguard against reduction in force policies, or a protection against job loss. Tenure is *not* a guarantee that your job will continue regardless of what events or financial situations arise in the district.

EXERCISE 14.5: WHAT DO I KNOW ABOUT LEGAL GUIDELINES IN MY STATE FOR THE SECONDARY SCHOOL TEACHER?

We have prepared the following 25-item true-false quiz merely as a focus for your class discussion. In no way is the quiz comprehensive, but it may serve well its purpose as stated. The items and their "answers" originate from California law and *should be compared with the legal guidelines of your own state.* We recommend that you first read and answer the statements and check your answers first against those of other members of your class, then against existing laws of your state.

True-False

_____ 1. Classroom teachers may not be assigned supervision duties outside of their classroom teaching assignments.

_____ 2. A student was struck in the eye by a student-thrown object. The incident occurred during class while the teacher was present. Because the teacher was present he/she cannot be held for negligence.

_____ 3. A teacher has the responsibility to break up even a friendly "slap fight."

_____ 4. Teachers have the responsibility to see to it that disciplinary offenses are met with disciplinary punishments.

_____ 5. If a teacher is attacked, assaulted, or menaced by a student, and the teacher's supervisor does not report the incident to law enforcement authorities, the supervisor is then guilty of a misdemeanor and is subject to a fine of up to $200.

_____ 6. If a student has assaulted your teacher colleague and you have advised your teacher friend not to report the incident, then you are guilty of a misdemeanor.

_____ 7. The Education Code forbids corporal punishment.

_____ 8. Recently (July 1984), teacher tenure was abolished.

_____ 9. If a student pulls down the pants of another student in public, then the offender is subject to a penalty of up to 6 months in jail and a fine of $50 to $500.

_____ 10. If a student taunts and challenges another to fight, this could be a disturbance of the peace and the student could be arrested by a witnessing teacher.

_____ 11. Extortion is a felony.

_____ 12. If a student is asked to stand and salute the flag and refuses, he/she may be punished for "disobedience."

_____ 13. Suspension may be imposed by a teacher, a principal, or a governing body. However, a teacher may suspend the student only from class for that day and the day following and must immediately report the suspension to the school principal.

_____ 14. A student threatens a teacher with, "I'll get you one day after school." The student could be punished with a fine up to $5,000 and sentenced to state prison for up to 5 years.

_____ 15. If a student throws a "stink bomb" into your room, he/she is guilty of a misdemeanor.

_____ 16. A teacher may arrest a student; a student may arrest another student.

_____ 17. If a student uses forces to resist an arrest, this itself is cause for a charge of assault and battery.

_____ 18. Teachers and/or administration may search students or lockers at random.

_____ 19. It is illegal to administer a test, questionnaire, or a survey, concerning a student's beliefs or practices in sex or family life unless the parent or guardian gives consent in writing.

_____ 20. It is permissible for you to request that your students purchase a weekly news supplement as long as you provide free copies to those students who cannot afford it.

_____ 21. A teacher may not receive royalties for a textbook he/she has written.

_____ 22. Teachers must maintain attendance records.

_____ 23. A teacher may be dismissed for not following the course of study.

_____ 24. Substitute teaching, summer school teaching, and adult teaching are not included in computation for permanent teaching status.

_____ 25. State law permits giving women teachers less compensation than men teachers for like services when holding the same credentials.

Answers to Quiz as related to California Education Code:

1. False	Ed. Code 13557		13. True	Ed. Code 10601
2. False	*Biggers v. Sac City USD*		14. True	Penal Code Sec. 71
	25 Cal App 3d 269		15. True	Penal Code Sec. 403
3. True	*Daily v. Los Ang USD*		16. True	Penal Code 837
	2 Cal.ed. 741, 747		17. True	
4. True	Ed. Code 13557		18. False	
5. True	Ed. Code 12916		19. True	Ed. Code 10901
6. True	Ed. Code 12912		20. False	Ed. Code 9552, 9851
7. False	Ed. Code 10853-54		21. False	Ed. Code 9256
8. False			22. True	Ed. Code 10951
9. True	Ed. Code 10852		23. True	Ed. Code 13556
10. True	Penal Code 415		24. True	Ed. Code 13332, 13333
11. True	Penal Code 520		25. False	Ed. Code 13501
12. False	*West Va. v. State Bd. of Ed.*			
	319 U.S. 624			

QUESTIONS FOR CLASS DISCUSSION

1. What are some of the tasks you will perform to maintain the physical environment of your classroom(s)?
2. What are some ways you can increase your efficiency in performing routine and clerical tasks?
3. On what grounds may a secondary student be suspended or expelled from your class? from school?
4. Which legal guidelines interest you the most? The least?
5. What changes in your state's legal guidelines do you think need to be made?
6. Is it okay for you, the teacher, to touch a student? What are the limitations?
7. What safety precautions should you make for teaching in your discipline area?
8. Would it be wise for you to take out your own teacher liability insurance policy?
9. What events have you observed that have interupted teachers during that "teachable moment?"
10. What other questions do you have regarding the content of this chapter? How might answers be found?

15

What Do Some Authorities Suggest as Approaches to Classroom Discipline?

In Chapter 14, you learned of the legal guidelines within which the classroom teacher must work, and of certain guidelines for effective classroom management. In this chapter that list will be expanded as we address the ever important topic of classroom discipline.

Classroom discipline has always been a topic of concern to teachers and for which volumes of literature are available. Let us unfold for you what the term "classroom discipline" means.

A. WHAT IS THE MEANING OF "CLASSROOM DISCIPLINE?"

In the 1800s discipline in this country meant punishment, an interpretation that was consistent with the then popular learning theory that assumed children were essentially bad and that misbehavior could be prevented by strictness, or treated with punishment.[1] Schools in the middle of that century have been described as being "wild and unruly places," and "full of idleness and disorder."[2]

By the early 1900s, educators were asking "why are the children still misbehaving?" Their answer was that the children were misbehaving *because* of the rigid, punitive system.[3] Thus entered the progressive education era, which provided the children opportunity (freedom) to decide for themselves what (if anything) they would learn. The teacher's job then became one of providing a rich classroom environment of resources and materials to stimulate the children's natural curiosity. And since the system no longer would be causing misbehavior, punishment would be unnecessary.

[1] Robert R. Reilly and Ernest L. Lewis, *Educational Psychology* (New York: Macmillan Publishing Company, 1983), p. 557.
[2] Irwin A. Hyman and John D'Alessandro, "Oversimplifying the Discipline Problem," *Education Week,* Vol. 3, No. 29 (April 11, 1984), p. 24.
[3] Reilly, op. cit., p. 558.

However, as was learned, "a completely permissive class appears to be more anxiety producing than a traditional class"[4] (traditional as in the practice of the 1800s).

Today, *discipline refers to the process of controlling student behavior in the classroom*. It involves
1. Steps in *preventing misbehavior*.
2. Ideas for *handling misbehavior*.

Discipline is an important aspect of the larger area of classroom management procedures. (Classroom management or classroom control, to us, mean the same thing although both terms are found used interchangeably in the literature.)

Today's secondary teacher is probably eclectic in his/her approach to classroom management, perhaps leaning toward the traditional. The teacher's behavior (in management) does reflect his/her philosophy about how children learn (refer to Chapter 3) and those behaviors represent that teacher's concept of effective management technique.[5] Perhaps a reflection of a school's concept of effective discipline can appear from children's responses to questions about discipline. Here are some replies we received by talking with young people.

When asked what she thought of when she heard the words class management and discipline, one junior high school student said: "If you break a rule, you get suspended or expelled. You can't goof off. You can't get into drugs like marijuana or coke. It means no fighting. You get suspended for five days. It means no cheating on tests because you get a referral to the principal. Then the principal tells you not to cheat anymore or he might give you a work-study assignment. That's when you report after school for a certain number of hours. If you are late to class three times, you could get a work-study assignment. If you are late to class more than three times, you get suspended for a couple of days. It means no food fighting. If you fight with food in the cafeteria, you can't go to any school activities for the rest of the year. It means no talking in class because your citizenship grade drops. If you swear, you get a behavioral referral (a message to the principal, who gives you a warning before calling your parents). If you steal or break into someone's locker, you get suspension for three days."

A tenth-grade student replied: "Well, first of all, I want to know what degrees of discipline you are talking about. In P.E. we are disciplined for coming in late to class. That means doing a lap around the field. We are disciplined for not dressing down. That means either running laps or picking up garbage on the field during P.E. class. In other classes, if we come in late, the teacher takes something off our citizenship grade. For cheating, fighting, and swearing, they send you down to the office. They don't waste any time with you. One class I have is a kickback class. We're not required to do all that much. All the kids are cool and the teacher is cool. We all get along with the teacher. In one class the biggest deal is you have to have a certain materials card turned in to the teacher or something comes off your citizenship grade. In another class the teacher never controls the class so there are no problems with discipline. Stuff goes on all the time but she is powerless to do anything about it. In another one, when we talk, the teacher moves you. Talking is the biggest offense in that class. Drugs will get you kicked out of the district. Stealing is usually dealt with by expelling you from school. Your parents are called and you have this 'way-hanging-big' conversation with everybody. They'll call the cops if you nabbed something from the teacher. If you steal

---

[4] Reilly, op. cit., p. 559.

[5] See C. Wolfgang and C. Glickman, *Solving Discipline Problems* (Boston, MA: Allyn, 1980).

something from another student, they'll call your parents. See, they figure that's the toughest thing they can do to you. Nine-tenths of the time they are right. Fighting? If you started it, planned it, they'd expel you out of the district. They consider who started the fight, how bad the fight was and what each fighter's intention was. It usually means five days suspension. Weapons? If you've got any sort of weapon, they'll call the police. And alcohol? If they catch you with alcohol on the school grounds or at a school function, it's an instant call to the police."

When asked to discuss "the best teacher she has met," one seventh-grade girl selects a male teacher. "He would stand outside the classroom as we came to class. When we went inside he went to his desk. He stood in the front of the room. Each day, he told us what we would learn. Then he'd help us out and explain everything. After that he'd tell us a story. He would tell jokes. Then he let us go to work. He gave us homework every night and we would correct it the next day. It took me (from) one and one-half hours to two hours every night. What I liked best about him was that he was helpful."

An eighth-grade boy mentions a particular male teacher as "best": "He was good but not too friendly. He was harsh. Had a business sense. As we came into class, he would stand at the door of the classroom. If you were late, you had to go to the office to get a tardy pass. He was always organized and had everything ready. He always laid everything out "on the line." It was all dead serious from the second you walked in the door to the second you walked out the door. He moved around the class. He explained it all first. We asked questions and then we did our work. We corrected in class that same day. We had more work (homework) every night. It would take me an hour, max. (maximum amount of time). I didn't like him but I appreciated what I learned."

A tenth-grade student rates a particular female teacher as the "best": "It's hard to pin down what she did do and what she didn't do. She would wait until we got quiet. She explained what was going to be, how far we'd get, and how short we'd fall from getting there. She handed us a slip of paper with the rules on it. Usually, she was at her desk. She always had everything ready and organized. She got upset (but in a joking way) if we weren't ready and organized. She explained things as we went along. Then she moved around the room a lot. Mostly, she moved around in front of the room because there were usually a lot of things going on in the front of the room. Once in a while she would review things, especially if we were doing something in a series, something she was quite fond of. She was interesting. Businesslike. Had humor. But she also had a theory of 'get it done.' Sometimes we had homework every day. It would take me from an hour to an hour and one-half to do. I liked her."

It seems clear that these young people's reflections demonstrate emphasis on rules, control, and punishment. More subtle perhaps, but there nevertheless, is understanding. The eclectic approach we mentioned earlier sees discipline as involving:

1. *Control* from within the child and also from outside factors.
2. *Understanding* the child and the child's perceptions of his/her behavior.
3. *Referral* to "specialists" when appropriate.
4. *Prevention* through effective teaching techniques.
5. *Individualized* instruction because of the unique needs of each individual child (see Chapters 1 and 9).[6]

Our intention in this chapter is to provide certain background information that may guide you toward the development of your own successful management system and that is consistent with your own beliefs (philosophy). Let's now look at the approaches to classroom management as suggested by some of today's leading authorities.

[6] For further description and analysis of these five elements, see: Reilly, op. cit., Chapter 16, pp. 559-566.

B. WHAT DO EXPERTS SAY?

In *Assertive Discipline: A Take-Charge Approach for Today's Educator* (Canter and Associates, 1976), Lee and Marlene Canter emphasize that: (1) you have professional rights in your classroom and should expect appropriate student behavior; (2) your students have rights to choose how to behave in your classroom, and you should plan limits for inappropriate student behavior; (3) your assertive discipline approach means you clearly state your expectations in a firm voice and explain the boundaries for behavior; and (4) you establish consequences for student misbehavior and you follow through in a consistent way.

Rudolf Dreikurs, M.D., in *Psychology in the Classroom,* 2nd ed. (Harper, 1968), *Maintaining Sanity in the Classroom* (Harper, 1971), and *Discipline Without Tears* (Harper, 1972) emphasizes that there are six points to consider in determining if you are an effective teacher. You are successful: (1) if you are a democratic teacher, fair, firm, and friendly, and involve your students in developing and implementing class rules; (2) if you arrange your classroom so that students know the rules and the consequences for misbehavior; (3) if you allow the students to be responsible not only for their own actions but for influencing others to maintain appropriate behavior in your classroom; (4) if you encourage the students to show respect for themselves and others and provide each student with a sense of belonging to the class; (5) if you recognize and encourage student goals of belonging, acquiring status, and recognition; and (6) if you recognize but do not reinforce correlated student goals of getting attention, seeking power, taking revenge, and asking to be left alone.

In his book, *Schools Without Failure* (Harper, 1969), William Glasser moves his ideas of reality therapy (i.e., the condition of the present contributes to inappropriate behavior) into the classroom. He points out that: (1) your students have a responsibility to learn at school and to maintain appropriate behavior while there; (2) with your help, the students can make better choices about their behavior in school; and (3) your classroom meetings can be devoted to establishing class rules, student behavior, matters of misbehavior, and the consequences.

In *Teacher and Child* (Macmillan, 1971), Haim G. Ginott shares his views on ways for you and a student to communicate: (1) by sending a clear message (or messages) regarding a situation instead of to the student's character; and (2) by your modeling of the behavior you expect from the students. Ginott's suggested messages are those that express feelings appropriately, acknowledge students' feelings, give appropriate direction, and invite cooperation.

Jacob Kounin, author of *Discipline and Group Management in the Classroom* (Holt, 1970), is best known for his identification of the "ripple effect" (i.e., the effect of your response to one student's misbehavior on students whose behavior was appropriate), and of "with-itness" (i.e., correcting misbehavior as soon as it has occurred, and correcting the right student). Kounin challenges you to: (1) realize the influence the ripple effect has on students; (2) exhibit "with-itness" by remaining alert to all students in your classroom at all times; (3) keep the teaching-learning momentum going during educational activities; (4) plan a smooth transition time from one activity to another; and (5) see that each student is responsible for learning the lesson's content.

In addition to the approaches to discipline presented by Dreikurs, Glasser, Ginott, Kounin, and the Canters, you are probably familiar with the term *behavior modification*—a number of popular techniques effective in changing the behavior of others in an observable and predictable way—and with B. F. Skinner's principles of behavior modification. Although it is true that Skinner did not specifically advocate a particular approach to classroom discipline or to class management, Skinner's ideas about how a student learns, how behavior can be modified by reinforcements (rewards), and his principles of behavior shaping have been extended by others. We suggest you review the following works to see how this was done: S. Axelrod, *Behavior Modification for the Classroom Teacher* (McGraw-Hill, 1977); F. Hewett, *The Emotionally Disturbed Child in the*

Classroom (Allyn, 1968); and D. Gast, *Schooling, Teaching, and Learning: American Education* (Mosby, 1978).

Behavior modification begins with four steps: (1) identifying the problem behavior that you wish to modify; (2) recording how often and under what conditions that particular behavior occurs; (3) arranging for a change to occur by reinforcing a behavior you want repeated by following the behavior with a rewarding consequence (a positive reinforcer); and (4) considering the different types of positive reinforcers to award—auditory (music), edibles (food and drink), manipulatives (toys), social reinforcers (attention, praise), tactile (clay), and visual (pictures).

As you review these classroom approaches to discipline, you read of expert opinion as well as research evidence to point out the importance of quickly attending to a student's misbehavior, being aware of what is going on in your classroom, providing smooth transitions, maintaining group alertness, and involving students by providing challenges, class meetings, ways of establishing rules and consequences, opportunities to receive and return compliments, and to build self-esteem.

The following chart illustrates the main ideas from each authority and allows you to compare the recommended approaches.

COMPARING DISCIPLINE APPROACHES

Authority	To Know What Is Going On	To Provide Smooth Transitions	To Maintain Group Alertness	To Involve Students	To Attend To Misbehavior
Canter	Realize that the student has the right to choose how to behave in your class with the understanding of the consequences that will follow his or her choice.	Insist on decent, responsible behavior.	Set clear limits and consequences; follow through consistently; state what you expect; state the consequences, and why the limits are needed.	Use firm tone of voice; keep eye contact; use non-verbal gestures as well as verbal statements; use hints, questions, and direct messages about requesting student behavior; give and receive compliments.	Follow through with your promises and the reasonable, previously stated consequences that have been established in your class.
Dreikurs	Realize that the student wants status, recognition, and a feeling of belonging. Misbehavior is associated with mistaken goals of getting attention, seeking power, getting revenge, and wanting to be left alone.	Identify a mistaken student goal; act in ways that do not reinforce these goals.	Provide firm guidance and leadership.	Allow students to have a say in establishing rules and consequences in your class.	Make it clear that unpleasant consequences will follow inappropriate behavior.
Ginott	Communicate with the student's feelings about a situation and about his/ herself.	Invite student cooperation.	Model the behavior you expect to see in your students.	Build student's self-esteem.	Give a message that addresses the situation and does not attack the student's character.

COMPARING DISCIPLINE APPROACHES *(continued)*

Authority	To Know What Is Going On	To Provide Smooth Transitions	To Maintain Group Alertness	To Involve Students	To Attend To Misbehavior
Glasser	Realize that the student is a rational being; he/she can control their behavior.	Help the student make good choices; good choices produce good behavior and bad choices produce bad behavior.	Understand class rules are essential.	Realize that class-room meetings are effective means for attending to rules, behavior, and discipline.	Accept no excuses for inappropriate behavior; see that reasonable conse-quences always follow.
Kounin	Develop "with-itness," a skill enabling you to see what is happening in all parts of the class-room at all times.	Avoid jerkiness which consists of thrusts (giving directions before your group is ready); of dangles (leaving one activity dangling in the verbal air and starting another one and then returning to the first activity); of flip-flops (termin-ating one activity, beginning another one, and then return-ing to the first activity you terminated).	Avoid slowdowns (delays and time wasting) that can be caused by over-dwelling (too much time spent on explanations) and by fragmentation (breaking down an activity into several unnecessary steps); develop a group focus through format (active participation by all students in the group); through accountability (holding all students accountable for the concept of the lesson) and by attention (seeing all the students and using unison responses as well as individual responses).	Avoid boredom by providing a feeling of progress for the students, by offering challenges, by vary-ing class activities, by changing the level of intellectual chal-lenge, by varying lesson presentations, and by using many different learning materials and aids.	Understand teacher correction influences behavior of other nearby students (the ripple-effect).

COMPARING DISCIPLINE APPROACHES *(continued)*

Authority	To Know What Is Going On	To Provide Smooth Transitions	To Maintain Group Alertness	To Involve Students	To Attend To Misbehavior
Skinner	Realize value of nonverbal interaction (i.e., smiles, pats, and handshakes to communicate to students that you know what is going on).	Realize that smooth transitions may be part of your procedures for awarding reinforcers (i.e., points and tokens), to reward appropriate behavior.	Set rules, rewards, and consequences; emphasize that responsibility for good behavior rests with each student.	Involve students in "token economies," in contracts, and in graphing own behavior performance.	Provide tangibles to students who follow the class rules; represent tangibles as "points" for the whole class to use to "purchase" a special activity.

Using the criteria of your own philosophy, your feelings, your values, and your perceptions, we encourage you to devise a classroom management system that is effective for you. (Remember: you must have the attention of the children before you can teach them.) Here are twenty general guidelines for your consideration in the development of your management system.

GENERAL GUIDELINES FOR ESTABLISHING AND MAINTAINING CLASS CONTROL[7]

1. Establish control early, in the best way available.
2. Have as few rules and regulations as possible.
3. Enforce whatever rules and regulations you make.
4. Involve students in making and enforcing rules and regulations.
5. Learn the students' names early and use them.
6. Make all threats clear and understandable (see Deutch, 1973).
7. Do not make threats that you cannot carry out.
8. Maintain a sense of humor about misbehaviors.
9. Find out about policies, attitudes, and practices of fellow teachers and administrators (see Curwin and Mendler, 1980).
10. Use your eyes, voice, feet, and posture to communicate nonverbal cues (see Fast, 1970; also, Howell and Howell, 1979).
11. Discuss misbehavior in private with the student whenever feasible.
12. Be yourself—only the real you can succeed in the classroom.
13. Use reason and logic in your behavior requests and punishment.
14. Vary classroom activities, with occasional breaks and change of pace (see Kounin, 1970).
15. When you use punishment, make it as immediate as possible (see Tanner, 1978).
16. Don't punish the entire class for the misbehavior of a few.
17. Be careful with the use of sarcasm in the classroom.
18. Do not misbehave personally. You are a model.
19. Be aware of personality conflicts and don't feel guilty about them.
20. Spend time outside of class diagnosing problems and planning strategies.

These guidelines to classroom management can help you build a strong foundation for your own classroom discipline techniques. Now, on the basis of what you have learned in this chapter, try the exercises that follow.

[7] Reilly, op. cit., pp. 579-593. Used by permission.

EXERCISE 15.1: CASE STUDIES FOR CLASS DISCUSSION

The cases that follow have been provided for analysis and discussion in your class. Study the cases and decide what you would do in similar situations. For your convenience, here is a brief statement of what each case is about:

1. A slow learner in junior high school, a boy who hangs around the teacher.
2. A bully in the tenth grade, an active-destructive type.
3. A lonely, unhappy, disinterested girl in Grade 10, a potentially passive-destructive type.
4,5. Accidents at school.
6. "Please stop baiting and harrying me."
7. "Five points deducted for your name!"
8. Write your own case for class discussion.

We hope that use of these case studies will add depth to your perceptions and insight about the day-by-day events that occur in teaching.

CASE 1: THE BOY WHO HANGS AROUND

Background

Bill is male, age 13, in general science. He is tall and awkward. He has a poor skin condition. He is considered "crazy" by his classmates. He has minor police offenses and is in apparent conflict with his father. He has taken an apparent liking to the general science teacher and spends many extra hours in the classroom. He is energetic and displays an inquisitive nature. He is quick to get interested in projects but almost as quick to lose interest. He likes to run the film projector for the teacher, but he does not like to participate in discussions with the rest of the class. He likes personal chats with the teacher but feels that the other students laugh at him.

The Situation

Bill's IQ is 95. The teacher attempted to work with Bill in improving his apparent feelings of inadequacy. The teacher had frank talks with Bill about his gangliness and his acne. What follows is actual material as written by Bill during the course of the first semester of school.

September: "I want to make the best out of the time I am on earth. I want to be somebody, not just exist either. . . . The members of this class influence me and what I think of doing. . . . They also make me feel real low. Their teasing me has changed me. . . . The teacher of my science class has helped me very much. . . . My greatest problem is in holding my head up and fighting for myself. . . .

October: "I have made a lot of headway in the past weeks. . . . I think I have done a good choice in the subject I am studying. . . . I also thank my teacher's actions toward me, that we may get to be very good friends, and learn a lot to know that teachers are human too, that they also have problems to solve and goals to head for.

November: "I don't have to fear anybody or anything on the idea of getting up and saying what I feel I have accomplished in this class and I have learned to make my own dissisions on what I will study or maybe do when I get out of school.

December: "I have learned that I have confidence in others only when I have confidence in myself.

January: "I have my report on the afect of geabriilic acid on plants. . . . I told (the class) about all my failures and they were quite interested. I told them that I had failed four times . . . that my science teacher told me I should not give up at this point and that a seintice (scientist) does not give up. I had no longer stated that fact and they all seemed like they could help in some way. I think the report went over well."

So the student developed courage to stand in front of his peers, holding his head high, and confidently reporting to the class how he kept at his plant experiment, even after four failures. He was proud of what he had learned about the work of the scientist. And he was even more proud that the students no longer teased and laughed at him.

QUESTIONS FOR CLASS DISCUSSION

1. How did you feel after reading this case?
2. Did Bill learn anything that semester? What?
3. Did he learn science?
4. What did the teacher do to facilitate Bill's learning?
5. What is ahead for Bill in school?

CASE 2: THE CASE OF THE BULLY

Background

Tony is considered by his peers as one of the "tough guys." He is 15 and in the tenth grade at Green High. Tony is prone to bullying, frequently quarreling with his fellow students and teachers; is considered by his parents to be disobedient. He has a record of minor offenses that range from truancy to destructiveness of property to drunkenness and offensive behavior. In general, Tony gets his satisfactions in ways that are damaging and unfair to others.

It is obvious to school officials that Tony is beyond parental control. He is frequently beaten by his father. Tony's mother has no apparent ability to control Tony's behavior.

Tony is not a member of any school organization of an extracurricular nature. His midquarter progress shows that he is failing in three subjects.

The Situation

One of the subjects Tony is failing is tenth-grade English. Tony is a discipline problem in your class and although it makes you feel guilty, you cannot help but be pleased when Tony is absent from class.

QUESTIONS FOR CLASS DISCUSSION

1. Where is the problem?
2. Where is Tony heading?
3. What can and should be done, if anything? By whom?
4. What is the role for Tony? His teachers? His peers? The school administration? His parents? Society in general?
5. Is it too late for Tony?

CASE 3: THE CASE OF MARY

Background

Mary has been characterized by her peers and by her teachers as being lonely, indifferent, and generally unhappy. She avoids both students and teachers. She will lie and cheat to avoid attention. Her "close" friends describe her as thoughtless and unkind. She often uses damaging remarks about members of her class, calling them conceited, teacher's pets, and so on. She considers members of her class as thoughtless, unkind, and uninterested in her.

Mary will do what she has to do in order to achieve average success in her studies. Her association with adults, her parents, and her teachers would be described as one of "merely getting along," doing what "I have to do in order not to get too much attention."

The Situation

One of Mary's friends is another 15-year-old girl, Jane. Jane is an above-average student in school, seemingly well adjusted, interested in people, and has gotten to know Mary because they are neighbors and walk together to school. Because of Jane's interest in other people and her closeness to Mary, she has become interested in "trying to bring Mary out of her shell."

Mary has told Jane that she feels her teachers are unreasonably severe. Mary said, "The teachers are only interested in the popular kids." Jane disagreed. Mary said, "You only disagree because you are pretty and popular." At this point, the conversation was broken by a boy running up and saying, "Hey, Jane, you're late for the council meeting."

QUESTIONS FOR CLASS DISCUSSION

1. Where is the problem?
2. What if you were Mary's teacher?
3. How did you feel after reading this case?

CASE 4: THE CASE OF THE STABBING VICTIM

Ron King, 16, who claims he was stabbed in the back during an English class, wants $100,000 in damages from North High School, Central Union High School District, and student Richard Decarlo.

According to the action, filed by King's mother, Lee, of 460 Bowman Avenue, the incident occurred last February. King says he was stabbed by Decarlo and lost his spleen as a result.

The suit says there was no teacher in the classroom when the stabbing took place and that the school was negligent in not providing supervision.

The action also contends that school officials knew that Decarlo secretly carried deadly weapons with him on the school grounds.

CASE 5: "MY STUDENTS ARE NICE YOUNGSTERS, BUT . . . ."

I have a feeling that my tenth-grade class sees through my youth and inexperience to my hidden fears and insecurity. I often feel that they are giggling while my back is turned. I catch glimpses of quickly hidden notes. Little things go on that I sense but do not see. My students are nice youngsters, really, but these minor annoyances are making me a nervous wreck. How can I stop these actions without alienating the children?

CASE 6: "PLEASE STOP BAITING AND HARRYING ME!"

I was fortunate enough to get an appealing and able seventh-grade class as my first teaching assignment. However, one boy is ruining my progress with them and my happiness in my work. He is a constant noise maker and trouble instigator. No special incident or difficulty precipitated his attitude, but he seems to take an actual delight in baiting and harrying me. I don't know how to change his attitude. What would you do?

CASE 7: "FIVE POINTS DEDUCTED FOR YOUR NAME!"

I was having difficulty explaining the solution of a problem because of continual talking among the students. I announced to the class, "I have reminded you students several times about our earlier discussion on courtesy in the classroom. Apparently it hasn't meant much to you, so from now on I shall write on the board the names of anyone talking out of place, and those individuals will have five points subtracted from their next examination grade—yes, five points for each time their names appear on the board."

CASE 8: WRITE YOUR OWN CASE FOR CLASS DISCUSSION

Perhaps you have a case in mind that you would like to bring up for class discussion and analysis, perhaps a particular incident that has happened recently in the school where you are observing, student teaching, or teaching.

_____

_____

_____

_____

_____

_____

_____

_____

_____

_____

_____

_____

_____

_____

_____

_____

_____

_____

_____

_____

_____

_____

_____

_____

_____

_____

_____

EXERCISE 15.2: ROLE-PLAYING MANAGEMENT PROBLEMS

Teams of approximately five each will develop and present role-playing skits. A skit will be performed and followed by time given for team formation and implementation. Teams will present skits and each skit will last approximately 10 minutes.

Skits should illustrate that the team has researched the topic. Topics should include such things as: a classroom incident, a private student-teacher confrontation, a campus incident, a faculty room incident, an incident during planning an extracurricular function, teacher-departmental chairman incident, student-teacher-administrator confrontation, student-teacher incident, faculty meeting incident, faculty member-parent confrontation, PTA meeting incident, an incident in which the student makes his first mistake.

Here are some sample skits:

1. Group is half-asleep, dreaming, looking out of window, slumped in seats. Some put their heads down on desks.
2. Group is moderately attentive but one boy gradually slumps, finally falls asleep, snoring peacefully. He persists and group is amused.
3. Teacher is talking to a J.H.S. group. Two girls farthest from teacher continually whisper and giggle and others are distracted, turn around, and get the giggles too.
4. Tardy bell has rung but no one is seated and no one is even thinking about sitting down. Look out window, draw on board, talk, etc.
5. Students are reading quietly. Two boys exchange notes, one says loudly "Oh yeah?" and hits other on upper arm with fist.

C. THE QUESTION OF ADOLESCENT SMOKING, ALCOHOL, AND DRUG USE (S-A-D)

Ever since the "social revolution" of the college students in the 1960s, the influence of smoking, alcohol, and drugs among secondary-school students has been of serious concern to parents, to teachers, and to law enforcement agencies. There is no question that drug use can and does affect the attitudes and behaviors of students in the classroom. Recalling your own experiences as a secondary-school student, ask yourself the following questions:

1. Were cigarettes, alcohol, or drugs used by me when attending secondary schools?
2. If yes, when did I start it? And, why?
3. And, what effect did it have on my own learning and behavior?
4. How do my own answers to these previous three questions compare with the following?

AGE OF FIRST DRUG USE REPORTED BY HIGH SCHOOL SENIORS

Substance	Jr. High or Earlier	10th Grade	11th Grade	12th Grade
Marijuana	26%	12%	11%	6%
Alcohol	53	18	14	7
Barbiturates	8	7	6	3
Amphetamines	5	5	4	2

Source: H. J. Parry, "Sample Surveys on Drug Abuse," in R. L. Dupont, A. Goldstein, and J. O'Donnel (Eds.), *Handbook on Drug Abuse* (Washington, DC: U.S. Government Printing Office, 1979).

How do these statistics of 1979 compare with most recent statistics that you can find? How do you think they compare to those, if available, from the school where you are currently observing, student teaching, or teaching? Why do young people use smoking, alcohol, or illegal drugs? Here are possible reasons:

1. Miniature/instant adulthood. "I am a grown-up; I feel more like an adult when I do it."
2. Experiment/curiosity. "I just want to try and see what it is like."
3. Peer conformity and pressure. "My friends do it, and I want to be accepted by them, so I join in."
4. Rebellion/depression. "Nothing works for me, nobody cares about me, so this is the way I get some pressure off."

What Can the Classroom Teacher Do?

First of all, you should be a model to your students, as we have said over and over again in this resource guide. Next, you should observe your students—watch for the odor of alcohol, the dilation of pupils, students acting "high," and for sudden changes in behavior, such as grades dropping, assignments suddenly not being done, a student suddenly withdrawing from his/her friends. If and when you observe any of these possible signs, then you should do any or all of the following:

1. Talk with your colleagues who have the same student and compare their observations.
2. Talk with the school counselor for his/her advice.
3. Report your observations to the school principal.

What Can the School Do?

Classroom teachers can be encouraged to talk about alcohol and drug abuse, to build lessons around the topics of smoking, alcohol, and drugs. This is particularly relevant for social studies teachers, who can develop lessons around the socio-psychological and/or legal frameworks, and for physical education and science teachers, who can develop lessons about the physiological and health standpoints.

Many secondary schools regularly invite law enforcement officials as guest speakers. Their presentations are realistic and the legal ramifications educational for students. Effective drug education is never too late, but should most likely begin before junior high school age.

Related to the issue of smoking, alcohol, and drug usage is the issue of "searches" by school officials. Consider the following news item:

Schools Get More Power for Searches[8]

WASHINGTON—The Supreme Court, calling drug use and violent crime in public schools "major social problems," Tuesday gave school officials more legal power to search students.

By a 6-3 vote, the court said public school teachers and administrators do not need court warrants nor the same justifications police officers need before searching a student.

Searches of students are justified "when there are reasonable grounds for suspecting that the search will turn up evidence that the student has violated or is violating either the law or the rules of the school," Justice Byron R. White wrote for the court.

One of the dissenters, Justice John Paul Stevens, said the decision allows searches for "even the most trivial school regulation."

"For the court," Stevens said, "a search for curlers and sunglasses in order to enforce the school dress code is apparently just as important as a search for evidence of heroin addiction or violent gang activity."

The court unanimously ruled that school officials, like police officers, must adhere to the Constitution's ban on unreasonable searches and seizures. School authorities act as "representatives of the state," not merely as surrogates for parents, and cannot claim the same kind of immunity from the Constitution as parents, it said.

But the court then divided on the question of how much protection to grant students, with the majority choosing to limit such protection in order to ensure discipline.

The court said it would permit searches based on the simpler but lesser standard of "reasonable suspicion," rather than the higher but more complex standard of "probable cause," to believe a crime has been committed. The simpler standard, White wrote, would spare teachers and administrators from mastering the "niceties" of the law and permit them to act on "reason and common sense."

The court cautioned school officials against "excessively intrusive" searches.

White noted that "maintaining order in the classroom has never been easy." He added that in recent years, "school disorder has often taken particularly ugly forms . . . ."

[8] *Source: Sacramento Bee,* Sacramento, CA, January 13, 1985. Reprinted by permission.

Some Relief on S-A-D

Parents and teachers these days hear so much about the S-A-D behavior of youth, and they feel that there isn't much that can be done for improvement. The following article, however, provides a different account:

High School Seniors Turn Away from Drugs, but Not to Alcohol[9]

ANN ARBOR, Mich. (AP) — High school students are turning away from drug use, and they do not seem to be exchanging narcotics for alcohol as some people feared, according to a government-sponsored survey released Monday.

Although the percentage of seniors who have tried an illegal drug has fallen only slightly — from 1982's 65 percent to 62 percent last year — there have been substantial declines in active or current use, according to the University of Michigan study.

Lloyd Johnston, one of three social psychologists who conducted the nationwide study of high school seniors for the National Institute on Drug Abuse, said there also has been a gradual decline in alcohol use since 1979.

"There was a concern in some circles that alcohol use would rise as illicit drug use declines," Johnston said. "But they both have been dropping, though alcohol use has been dropping much more slowly."

The percentage of seniors who said they used any illegal drug in the month before the survey declined from 38 percent in 1979 to 29 percent last year, Johnston said. The percentage reporting use of an illegal drug other than marijuana in the month before the survey fell from a peak of about 20 percent in 1981 to 14 percent last year, he said.

According to the study, the percentage of high school seniors using cocaine has not changed since 1979, despite a growing aversion to marijuana, alcohol and cigarettes, Johnston said.

"We observed a sharp increase in cocaine use between 1976 and 1979, but since 1979, the rates of use in this age group have been relatively stable," Johnston said. "Still, usage levels are troublesomely high."

Sixteen percent of the seniors surveyed last spring had used cocaine at least once, 12 percent had used it some time in the previous year and 6 percent were monthly users, he said.

Johnston, of the university's Institute of Social Research, said more seniors view cocaine as dangerous and disapprove of its use, but there is an indication of increasing use, especially in the Northeast.

Meanwhile, 85 percent of the seniors disapproved of regular marijuana use in 1984, compared with 65 percent in 1977, the study said.

"Concern about both the psychological and physical effects of regular marijuana use has shifted dramatically over the last seven years," resulting in "an increasing number of young people terminating or reducing their use after some initial period of involvement," Johnston said.

"This substantial downturn in use of marijuana in the face of continuing widespread availability illustrates the critically important fact that drug abuse can be dealt with effectively through reducing the demand for drugs, not just the supply," Johnston said.

The National Institute on Drug Abuse, part of the Department of Health and Human Resources, annually surveys 17,000 seniors in about 140 public and private high schools nationwide.

[9] *Source: Los Angeles Times*, January 13, 1985. Reprinted by permission.

QUESTIONS FOR CLASS DISCUSSION

1. It has been said the teacher should practice the "three Fs": be firm, be fair, be friendly. Do you think this is sound advice?
2. It has been said that "hostility begets hostility." How do you feel about that? Does it have meaning for the classroom teacher and his/her behaviors?
3. What are the sources for extrinsic motivation? For intrinsic motivation? What are the values of each?
4. It has been said that the professional responsibility of the teacher is to diagnose and prescribe, not to label. What meaning does this have for the classroom teacher?
5. One of the twenty guidelines for classroom control, as presented in this chapter, is to establish classroom control early in the school year. Specifically how will you do this?
6. Identify your own subject field, select a level (junior high or high school), and list the specific classroom rules you would establish. How would you communicate those rules to your students?
7. How can students help enforce the rules? Give some specific ways.
8. What "threats" are permissible (or inevitable) for the teacher to make? Is announcing a test a threat?
9. Can nonverbal cues ever miscommunicate? Give an example.
10. Is there ever a time when punishment can or should be delayed?
11. Do you need to "like" all the students? How can a teacher effectively teach a student he/she does not like?
12. Have any of the schools you have visited used the concept of a "holding area"? (See Carducci, 1984.)
13. When is it appropriate for a teacher to temporarily remove a student from the classroom?
14. What other questions do you have regarding the content of this chapter? How might answers be found?

SELECTED READINGS AND REFERENCES FOR CHAPTERS 14 and 15

Baker, Keith. "Research Evidence of a School Discipline Problem." *Phi Delta Kappan,* Vol. 66, No. 7 (March 1985), pp. 482-488.

Brooks, Douglas M. "The Teacher's Communicative Competence: The First Day of School." *Theory Into Practice,* Vol. 24, No. 1 (Winter 1985), pp. 63-70.

Carducci, Kewey J., and Judith B. Carducci. *The Caring Classroom.* Palo Alto, CA: Bull Publishing Company, 1984.

Curwin, R. L., and A. N. Mendler. *The Discipline Book: A Complete Guide to School and Classroom Management.* Reston, VA: Reston, 1980.

Doyle, W. *Classroom Management.* West Lafayette, IN: Kappa Delta Pi, 1980.

Dreikurs, Rudolf, B. B. Gruenwald, and F. C. Pepper. *Maintaining Sanity in the Classroom: Classroom Management Techniques.* New York: Harper & Row, Publishers, Inc., 1981.

Emmers, Edmund T., and Carolyn M. Evertson. "Synthesis of Research on Classroom Management." *Educational Leadership,* Vol. 38, No. 4 (January 1981), pp. 342-347.

Evertson, Carolyn M., and Edmund T. Emmer. "Effective Management at the Beginning of the School Year in Junior High Classes." *Journal of Educational Research,* Vol. 74, No. 4 (August 1982), pp. 485-498.

Fast, J. *Body Language.* New York: M. Evans, 1970.

Gnagey, William J. *Motivating Classroom Discipline.* New York: Macmillan Publishing Company, 1981.

Medland, Michael, and Michael Vitale. *Management of Classrooms.* New York: Holt, Rinehart and Winston, 1984.

Reilly, Robert R., and Ernest L. Lewis. *Educational Psychology: Applications for Classroom Learning and Instruction.* New York: Macmillan Publishing Company, 1983.

Rinne, Carl H. *Attention: The Fundamentals of Classroom Control.* Columbus, OH: Charles E. Merrill, 1984.

Strain, Phillip S., ed. *The Utilization of Classroom Peers as Behavior Change Agents.* New York: Plenum Press, 1981.

Wolfgang, C., and C. Glickman. *Solving Discipline Problems.* Boston, MA: Allyn & Bacon, 1980.

Part V

Evaluation of Teacher Performance and Student Achievement

You, therefore, who teach another, do you not teach yourself?
—Romans 2:21

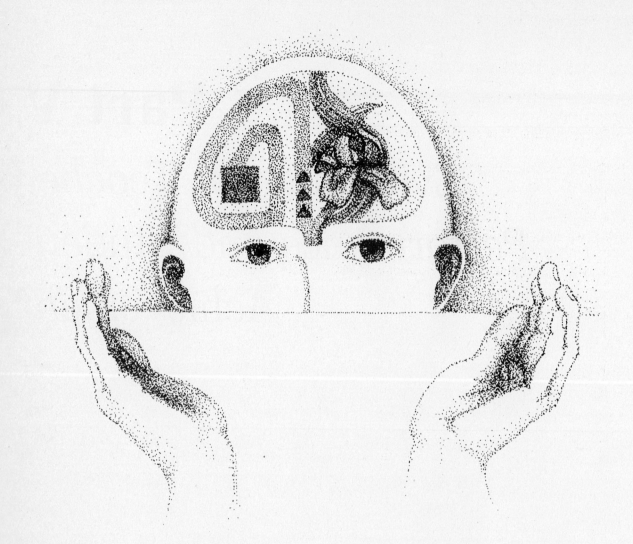

Drawing by Carol Wilson, unpublished material. Reprinted by permission.

Part V assists you with

- Tools of evaluation.

- Grading and its alternatives.

- Self-evaluation through micro-teaching.

- Self-evaluation through verbal interaction analysis.

- Knowledge of your growth in competency development.

- Knowledge of evaluation forms used by educators.

- Guidelines for meeting and conferencing with parents.

How Do I Evaluate and Report Student Achievement?

Earlier sections of this text addressed the *why, what,* and *how* of secondary school teaching. We now focus on the fourth and final component of the teaching/learning reciprocal process—the *how well* component. The four components are the essentials of competent teaching. The *how well* comprises the assessment component, and should accomplish all of the following:

1. To evaluate how well the students are learning.
2. To identify their strengths and weaknesses in order to restructure the learning activities.
3. To assess the effectiveness of a particular teaching strategy.
4. To evaluate the effectiveness of the curriculum.
5. To evaluate the effectiveness of the teacher.
6. To be able to communicate to parents the student's progress.

This chapter is concerned with techniques for evaluating and reporting student achievement. Techniques for evaluating are wide and varied, as are those for recording and reporting. Evaluation is as critical a component of your planning as any of the others. When used inappropriately it can have a terribly damaging consequence. Teaching/learning is a complex human activity, and when evaluating that activity we can never be absolutely sure of the *validity* and *reliability* of our techniques. *Validity is the degree to which the chosen technique measures that which is intended. Reliability is the accuracy with which a technique measures.* A technique must have reliability before it can have validity. Consequently, although a technique may have reliability (it is on target), it may not be very valid (it is poorly designed). Entire texts are devoted to the topics of measurement and evaluation.

The next chapter addresses the strategies of teacher-centered evaluation, that is, those designed for the evaluation and improvement of teaching. Included are samples of instruments used by supervisory personnel for evaluation of practice teaching, and those of school districts for their evaluation of teachers: instruments that illustrate the criteria by which the beginning teacher is likely to be evaluated.

Evaluating and reporting student achievement may consume a large portion of your time. This involves selecting and designing evaluative instruments, implementing the evaluation, checking and analyzing results, recording, reporting, arranging and conducting conferences with students and parents.

A. EVALUATING STUDENT ACHIEVEMENT: SOME AVENUES

There are three types of student behavior that provide means by which the teacher may evaluate a student's learning: (1) what the learner *says,* (2) what the learner *does,* and (3) what the learner *writes.*

No matter which avenue you might be using, *you must evaluate against the instructional objectives.* Any given objective may be checked by using more than one avenue, and by using more than one instrument. Subjectivity, inherent in the evaluation process, may be reduced as you check validity, comparing the results of one technique against those of another.

B. EVALUATING A STUDENT'S VERBAL AND NONVERBAL BEHAVIORS

When evaluating what the learner says, you should:

1. Listen to the student's questions.
2. Listen to the student's responses.
3. Listen to the student's interactions with other students.
4. Observe the student's attentiveness.
5. Observe the student's involvement in class.
6. Observe the student's responses to challenges.

Notice that the teacher should listen and observe. While listening to what the student is saying, you should, simultaneously, be observing the student's nonverbal behaviors. For this avenue you may use:

1. Checklists and rating scales.
2. Behavioral-growth record forms.
3. Observations of the student's performance of classroom activities.
4. Periodic conferences with the student.

We remind you that, with each technique used, you will operate from an awareness of anticipated learning outcomes, and will evaluate the learner's progress toward meeting these objectives. Here are guidelines to follow when evaluating the student's verbal and nonverbal behaviors in the classroom.

Guidelines for Evaluating What the Learner Does and Says

1. *Make a list* of desirable behaviors.
2. *Check the list* against the specific instructional objectives.

3. *Record your observations* of the student as quickly as possible following your observation. Tape or video recordings can assist you in checking your memory accuracy, but if this is inconvenient, we recommend that you spend some time during school, immediately after, or later that evening, recording your observations, while they are still fresh in your mind.
4. *Record your professional judgment* regarding the learner's progress toward the desired behavior (see form that follows), but think it through before writing it down (see Section D of this chapter).
5. *Write comments* that are reminders to yourself, such as:
    "Check validity by further testing."
    "Discuss my observations with student's parents."
    "Discuss my observations with the student's counselor."

EVALUATING AND RECORDING STUDENT VERBAL AND NONVERBAL BEHAVIORS: SAMPLE FORM

Verbal and Nonverbal Behaviors
Observation Form

_____   _____   _____
          Student   *Grade*   *School*

_____   _____
          Observer   *Period or Subject Observed*

_____
          Date

Objective for Time Period or Subject:	*Desired Behavior*	*What Student Did, Said, or Wrote*

Your professional comments: _____

_____

_____

_____

_____

_____

_____

_____

_____

_____

_____

_____

_____

_____

_____

_____

_____

_____

_____

_____

_____

_____

_____

_____

_____

C. EVALUATING A STUDENT'S WRITTEN BEHAVIORS (ANECDOTAL RECORD)

To follow the anecdotal avenue of evaluation you will use worksheets, written homework, and tests. Worksheets and homework assignments are most often used for the ongoing evaluation of a learner's progress. Tests, too, should be a part of this ongoing evaluation, but are also used for "terminal" evaluation at the end of a unit or period of learning. Review Chapter 11, Section G, for the guidelines for using assignments.

What a teacher writes about a student can have an enormous impact upon the development of that student; we give special attention to that topic in the following section.

D. RECORDING MY OBSERVATIONS AND JUDGMENTS: A WORD OF CAUTION ABOUT THE ANECDOTES I WRITE

It is important that you consider carefully the written comments you make regarding a student. We have seen anecdotal comments in a pupil's permanent school record that said more about the teacher who made the comment than we learned about the pupil. Sometimes comments that go into a student's permanent record can be quite detrimental to the student's welfare and progress, in school and beyond. Teacher comments must be professional, that is, *diagnostically useful to the further development of the student*. This is true for any comment you write, whether on a student paper, a note to the student's parents, or one that becomes a permanent comment on the student's school record.

Here is an example of an *unprofessional comment* observed in one student's school record: "John is lazy." Describing a student as "lazy" could be done by anyone! It is nonproductive, and is certainly not a professional diagnosis. Moreover, it could be detrimental to the future of the student by causing prejudicial behaviors from the student's future teachers and/or employers. Saying that a student is lazy merely *describes* behavior as observed by the teacher who wrote the comment. More important, and productive, would have been an attempt by the teacher to analyze *why* the student was behaving that way, then *prescribing* activities that would have been more likely to activate the student to behave in a more acceptable way.

Teachers' comments should be useful, productive, analytical, diagnostic, and prescriptive, for the continued development of the learner. The professional teacher performs diagnoses and prepares prescriptions; the teacher does *not* label students as "lazy," "vulgar," "slow," "dumb," or "unmotivated"—no matter how great the temptation to do so. The competent teacher sees the behavior of students as being goal-directed; perhaps the "lazy" student has developed that behavioral pattern in order to gain attention. That student's goal, then, is attention (we all like and need attention), and that student has assumed negative, perhaps even destructive, behavioral patterns to accomplish that goal. The task of the professional teacher is to facilitate the student's understanding (perception) of his/her goal, and then identify acceptable behaviors positively designed to reach it.

That which separates the professional teacher from "anyone off the street" is the teacher's skill in going beyond the mere description of student behavior. Always keep this fact in mind as you write comments that will be read by the student, the student's parents or guardians, other teachers, and by future employers of the student. Let us now reinforce this concept with Exercise 16.1.

EXERCISE 16.1: AN EVALUATION OF WRITTEN TEACHER COMMENTS

Instructions: Here are some written teacher comments as drawn from student records. Check those you consider to be professionally useful, then compare your responses against the key. Discuss your results with your classmates.

		Professionally Useful	
		Yes	No
1.	This year, I have observed that Patty performs her math assignments much better when done in class than when they are given as homework.	( )	( )
2.	Anthony has been consistently disruptive this year in my class.	( )	( )
3.	Dick has a lot of difficulty staying in his seat.	( )	( )
4.	Sue seems most responsive in "hands-on" learning activities.	( )	( )
5.	Stanley seems to have an excess of nervous energy and I have developed a concern about his eating habits.	( )	( )
6.	Emily did very well this year in science laboratory activities but seems to have reading difficulties.	( )	( )
7.	Mark does not get along well with the other students.	( )	( )
8.	Gretchen seems unable to understand my verbal directions.	( )	( )
9.	I am recommending special remediation in mathematics for Noreen, perhaps through private tutoring, before she is promoted.	( )	( )
10.	I do not appreciate Eugene's use of slang expressions in the classroom.	( )	( )

Key to Exercise 16.1

1. This is useful information.
2. Not useful, as there are no helpful specifics. It could provide a bias to the student's next teacher. "Disruptive" is merely descriptive, not prescriptive.
3. Could be useful to the next teacher.
4. Useful.
5. Useful.
6. Useful, although more specifics would help.
7. Not useful; could bias the next teacher.
8. Not useful. Tells more about the teacher than about Gretchen.
9. Useful.
10. Not useful.

E. CONSTRUCTING TESTS

Construction of a good test is a critically important professional responsibility. Tests can be designed for several purposes, and a variety of kinds of tests can keep your testing program interesting and reliable. Purposes for which tests are used include:

1. To provide review and drill to enhance teaching and learning.
2. To serve as motivational devices.
3. To assist in decision-making regarding promotion and classification.
4. To provide information for planning for individualization.
5. To help determine teaching effectiveness.
6. To serve as a source of information for student counseling and guidance.
7. To assess and aid in curriculum planning.
8. To measure student achievement.

As a college student, perhaps you are most experienced with testing for the purpose of measuring achievement (Purpose No. 8), but as a secondary-school teacher you will use testing in a number of different ways.

After determining the purpose for which you are designing a test, you should identify the specific instructional objectives the test is being designed to measure. *This is criterion-referenced testing.* Your written instructional objectives are specific so that you can write test items to measure against those objectives. So, the first step in test construction is identification of the test purpose. The second step is to identify the objectives to be measured, and the third step is to prepare the test items.

General Guidelines for Test-Item Preparation

1. *Use a variety* of kinds of test items.
2. Be sure that *content coverage is complete,* that all relevant objectives are being measured.
3. Each item of the test should be *reliable,* that is, measures the intended objective.
4. Each test item is *clear and unambiguous.*
5. The test is *difficult enough* for the poorly prepared student, but easy enough for the student who has learned.
6. Prepare your test, put it aside, and think about it, then work it over again. The test should represent your very best professional efforts. A quickly and poorly prepared test is likely to be more damaging than beneficial to student learning.

Test items are categorized as to *verbal* (written words), *visual* (pictures and diagrams), and *manipulative* (requiring the learner's manipulation of materials). Manipulative tests are important when measuring for psychomotor skill development. Visual tests are useful when working with students who lack fluency with the written word. The category of test you use depends upon your purpose and objectives. Carefully consider the alternatives within that framework. A good testing program will likely include items from all three categories, in order to provide validity checks and to account for the individual differences among your students.

What follows is a review of 14 types of tests[1] defined by the nature of the test items. (We encourage you to practice writing these different kinds of test items when appropriate for your own subject field.) Within our discussion of each item type we will attempt to provide a sample item, designed each time to measure the same desired learning outcome. The objective we have frequently selected is one regarding your understanding of the importance of set induction body, and closure to a good lesson plan. This objective may not fit so well with certain item types, but its use is meant to give you a basis for comparison.

F. ANALYZING ITEMS FOR PREPARING WRITTEN TESTS IN SECONDARY SCHOOL TEACHING

I. PERFORMANCE ITEMS

Performance tests measure a pupil's ability to carry out certain operations. The needed materials are placed before the student together with a statement of the problem to be solved. The student is expected to solve the problem and demonstrate the end result. He/She may or may not be expected to explain the reasons for his/her operations. He/She may be scored on the end product only, or on each step, or on his/her explanations, or on all three. Performance tests come closer to measuring certain desirable outcomes of the program than do most other tests. Unfortunately, not much experimentation with this type of test has been carried out.

Objective:

The student is to show understanding of set induction, lesson body, and closure.

Sample Item

Performance Test

Student is given a class of ten students and asked to prepare and implement an effective lesson with the three required components.

Advantages:

Little or no verbalization is required. Manipulative ability is tested. Understandings that are difficult to verbalize are tested. Students who do poorly on verbal tests may receive recognition for their achievements.

---

[1] Our appreciation to Professor Alfred T. Collette who granted permission to use in this chapter some material originally printed in his out-of-print textbook, *Science Teaching in the Secondary School*, Allyn & Bacon, 1973, pp. 598-610.

Disadvantages:

This type of test is difficult to administer to large groups. If duplicate sets of equipment are used, a large amount of materials is needed. Otherwise, cumbersome rotation systems must be used so that each student gets a turn.

Common in the arts and physical education.

II. IDENTIFICATION ITEMS

This type of test measures a student's ability to carry out identification procedures. He/She is given one or more unknown specimens and the materials he/she will need to test their properties. He/She is scored on the accuracy of his/her identification.

Sample Item

Identification Test

When viewing a teaching demonstration, the student is to correctly identify the beginning and end of each component.

Advantages:

As with performance tests, students are working with actual materials. The test measures their true understandings of procedures. Verbalization has little place in the test.

Disadvantages:

As with performance tests, adequate materials must be provided. To be fair, the specimens must be unfamiliar to all students; this may be difficult to arrange.

Common in biology.

III. COMPLETION DRAWING ITEMS

Students are given a drawing that is incomplete and are asked to add the proper lines to complete the drawing.

Sample Item

An electric bell, a push button, and a dry cell are pictured on the question sheet. Accompanying directions read, "Draw lines to represent the wires needed for making the bell ring when the button is pushed."

Advantages:

This type of test requires less skill than a standard drawing test. Time needed for completion is short. The answers are usually simple to correct.

Disadvantages:

Students may misinterpret the diagrams provided for them. Students need prior practice in completing the same types of drawings.

IV. ESSAY ITEMS

In constructing the essay item, the teacher asks a question or presents the student with some type of *problem;* the student composes the response in the form of some kind of sustained prose. The student is free to choose his/her own words and to organize his/her ideas in his/her own phraseology *within the limits of the question posed.*

The essay item is still widely used by high school teachers although it has been the object of much criticism, especially by experts in the field of testing.

Advantages:

1. It measures the higher mental processes, such as ability to think, to understand large concepts, to organize information, and to express ideas clearly and concisely in good English.
2. It requires a useful and rewarding kind of study on the part of the pupil and stimulates creativity and freedom of expression.

Disadvantages:

1. It requires a great deal of time to read and score, if the teacher is conscientious and the results are to have any significance.
2. It tends to provide an unreliable sampling of student achievement. Because the number of essay test items must be small owing to the time factor, the teacher must draw inferences as to student achievement from a limited sample.
3. It tends to be vulnerable to unreliable scoring, in that:
   a. Different teachers tend to assess the same response differently.
   b. The same teacher tends to assess the same response differently at different times.
   c. The essay item is especially vulnerable to the "Halo Effect."
   d. The scorer may be unduly influenced by legibility, beauty of handwriting, quality of grammar, punctuation, diction, spelling, general neatness, and verbose answers.
   e. Teachers are prone to write essay items hurriedly, without careful thought.
4. The student who writes slowly and laboriously may not be able to complete the test although his/her achievement is high and his/her learning profound.

Suggestions for the Construction and Scoring of the Essay Item

1. The teacher must devote a good deal of time and thought to the construction of an essay test item. Unfortunately, too many teachers strongly favor the essay test over the objective test simply on the grounds that it is "easier" to construct.
2. The question should *precisely define* the *direction* and *scope* of the response desired. It should include instructions on how much coverage the student should give the item and how much detail is desired. If the question is not clearly defined, the students "are not running the same race." Please refer to *Suggestions for the Use of Key Words in Essay Items*, later in this section.

Sample Items

Faulty:

Discuss standardized and teacher-made tests.

(The student very likely will write in an aimless fashion, not knowing how the item will be evaluated, until he/she feels that he/she has used up enough space or has consumed his/her time allotment. What does "Discuss" mean? "Explain"? "Evaluate"? "Define"? "Compare"? "Contrast"? "Describe"?)

Improved:

Explain two (three, four) essential similarities and two (three, four) essential differences between standardized tests and teacher-made tests.

Faulty:

Discuss the steps in processing milk.

Improved:

What are the important steps in processing milk from dairy farm to consumer? Describe each step and explain its function.

3. A large number of questions, each of which requires a reasonably short prose response, is generally preferable to a small number of questions requiring long prose answers. (The large number of items provides more adequate sampling of the content, and briefer answers tend to be more precise.)
4. The teacher should very carefully take into consideration the time required for adequate response to the item in relation to the amount of time available in the testing period.
5. In a normal class, the practice of providing optional items is generally indefensible. Different qualities of performance are more likely to be comparable if all students face the same set of test situations.

6. When the test item is constructed, the teacher should make a tentative scoring key. The teacher should decide how many points at most will be allotted to each item. This number of points should appear to the left of the number of the item on the test so that the student will also be informed of the item's value.

   The teacher should also inform his/her students in advance whether he/she is going to include in the score an evaluation of errors in grammar and spelling, punctuation, organization, etc.

7. In order to reduce the "Halo Effect" one question should be graded seriatim for all students rather than all questions for one student. In other words, grade all Question 1's, then all Question 2's, etc.

8. The level of the following student performances is commonly measured by means of the essay item:

   a. Comparison of two (or more) things on a given basis.
   b. Comparison of two (or more) things in general.
   c. Decision for or against.
   d. Statement of causes or effects.
   e. Explanation of meanings, use of words, phrases, or longer portions of given passages.
   f. Summary.
   g. Analysis.
   h. Statement of relationships.
   i. Original illustration or exemplification of rules, principles, procedures, usages, etc.
   j. Classification.
   k. Applications of rules, laws, and principles to new situation.
   l. Statement of aims of author in selection or organization of material.
   m. Criticism as to adequacy, correctness, or relevance of words, phrases, or statements.
   n. Outlining.
   o. Reorganization of facts previously encountered in different arrangements.
   p. Formulation of new questions and problems.
   q. Suggestion of new methods of procedure.

SUGGESTIONS FOR THE USE OF KEY WORDS IN ESSAY ITEMS

In our observations secondary-school teachers are inclined to use subjective tests (essay tests) more frequently than objective tests for various reasons. It must be noted here that there are a number of key words for essay questions that the tester could use; however, the connotation and/or the meaning of each key word may be different. Please note the following:

"Compare"—asks for analysis of similarity and difference, with greater emphasis on *similarities* or *likenesses*.

"Contrast"—asks more for *differences* than for *similarities*.

"Criticize"—asks for the "goods" and "bads" of an idea or a situation.

"Define"—asks student to express clearly and concisely the meaning of a term (as in the dictionary, or in the writer's own words).

"Describe"—asks student, writing sequentially, to give an account of or to sketch a specified topic.

"Diagram"—asks student to put quantities or numerical values into the form of a chart, a graph, or drawings.

"Discuss"—asks student to explain or argue, presenting various sides of events, ideas, or situations.

"Enumerate"—asks student to count over or list one after another; different from "Explain briefly" or "Tell in 2-3 words."

"Evaluate"—asks student to express worth, value, judgment.

"Explain"—asks student to describe with emphasis on cause and effect, in an open manner.

"Illustrate"—asks student to describe by means of examples, figures, pictures, and/or diagrams.

"Interpret"—asks student to describe or explain a given fact, theory, principle, or doctrine in a specific context.

"Justify"—asks student to show reasons, with emphasis on "right," "positive," and "advantageous."

"List"—asks student to simply name items in a category or to include them in a list, without much description.

"Outline"—asks student to give a short summary with headings and subheadings.

"Relate"—asks student to tell how specified things are connected or brought into some kind of relationships.

"Summarize"—asks student to recapitulate the main points without examples or illustrations.

"Trace"—asks student to follow a history or series of events step by step by going backward over the evidence.

"Prove"—asks student to present materials as witnesses, proof, and evidence.

V. SHORT EXPLANATION ITEMS

This type of question is but a shortened version of a standard essay question, the subject being limited so that the answer may be given in a single sentence.

Sample Item

Explain with one sentence the following statements: (1) The lowest string of a violin has a larger diameter than the highest string. (2) A trombone player lengthens his horn to play a low note.

Advantages:

This type of question tests a student's understandings in the same fashion as an essay question but is more economical of time for both the student and the teacher. By using several of these instead of a single essay question, a greater coverage of material is possible.

Disadvantages:

Some students cannot express themselves well enough with single sentences; many have difficulty in writing concisely enough to give an answer in such a limited fashion.

VI. COMPLETION STATEMENT ITEMS

Students are given a set of statements that lack a word or phrase for meaning. The student is supposed to add a word or phrase in the blanks provided, either within the sentence or at the side.

Sample Items

1. Fill in the blank in each of the following with the proper word:
    a. An explosive gas that is lighter than air is _____ .
    b. The product resulting from the combustion of sulfur and oxygen is _____ .
2. Write in the space in the left-hand margin the word that best completes the following sentence.

    (1.) _____ The part of the automobile engine where air and gasoline are mixed is the __(1)__ .

Advantages:

These tests measure how well students can recall words or phrases, and when recall is important they make an excellent testing device, easy to take, and relatively easy to score. Wider coverage is possible in a short time.

Disadvantages:

The test does not measure understandings, only recall of words. It cannot be scored mechanically; the teacher must be alert for the possible significance of each separate answer.

VII. MULTIPLE-CHOICE ITEMS

A multiple-choice test is somewhat like a completion test in that statements are presented in incomplete form. Several possible choices are given and the student is to choose one or more from them. This format stresses recognition rather than recall.

Sample Items

1. Underline the word that best completes the following statement.
    The alloy of copper and tin is called (solder, zinc, bronze, brass).

2. Write in the space at the left the letter of the word that best completes the following:
    _____ (1.) The portion of the sun's spectrum that causes sunburn is:
            a. infrared
            b. yellow
            c. ultraviolet
            d. Hertzian
            e. orange.

Advantages:

Multiple-choice items can be answered and scored rapidly. A wide range of subject matter can be tested in a short time. The questions are fairly easy to write. By using four or five alternates in each question, the effect of guessing is rendered relatively unimportant. These tests are excellent for all purposes—motivation, review, and evaluation.

Disadvantages:

These questions tend to measure only on the recognition level. Because the scoring is mechanical, there is danger that the problems of the students will be overlooked.

Suggestions for Constructing the Multiple-Choice Item

1. If the item is in the form of an incomplete statement, it should be meaningful in itself and imply a direct question rather than merely lead into a collection of unrelated true/false statements. For example:
   Faulty: The United States of America
   a. has more than 200,000 people.
   b. grows large amounts of rubber.
   c. has few good harbors.
   d. produces most of the world's automobiles.
   Improved: The population of the United States is characterized by
   a. an increasing birth rate.
   b. varied nationality backgrounds.
   c. its even distribution over the area of the United States.
   d. an increasing proportion of young people.

2. Use a level of English that is simple and clear, easy enough for even the poorest readers to understand. Avoid unnecessary wordiness. For example:
   Too Wordy: Which of the following metals is characterized by extensive utilization in the aircraft industry?
   a. Chromium.
   b. Uranium.
   c. Aluminum.
   d. Beryllium.
   Improved: Which of the following is most often used in making airplanes?
   a. Chromium.
   b. Uranium.
   c. Aluminum.
   d. Beryllium.

3. The length of the alternatives—that is, the number of words each contains—should not vary significantly. Otherwise students may note that long alternatives tend to be correct, or vice versa.

4. The distractors should be plausible. They should be closely related to the same concept as the correct alternative and should be as reasonable and natural as the correct response. Humorous and absurd distractors have no measuring value.

5. The arrangement of the alternatives should be uniform throughout the test. If the incomplete-statement form of stem is used, the alternatives should come at the end of the statement. All alternatives should be listed in column form rather than in paragraph form. For example:
   Faulty: The cheapness of land and scarcity of labor in the West created a. an aristocratic class of landowners, b. a large class of wage-earning men, c. a system of servitude, d. a large class of small freeholders.
   Improved: The cheapness of land and scarcity of labor in the West created
   a. an aristocratic class of landowners.
   b. a large class of small freeholders.
   c. a system of servitude.
   d. a large class of wage-earning men.

6. Every item should be grammatically consistent. If the stem is in the form of an incomplete sentence, it should be possible to form a complete sentence by attaching any of the alternatives to the stem. For example:
   Faulty: One of the basic essentials in experimental research is
   a. the researcher should have a science background.
   b. the identification and statement of the problem.
   c. animals must be available for experimentation.
   d. variables that need to be clarified.
   Improved: One of the basic essentials in experimental research is
   a. the researcher's background in science.
   b. the identification and statement of the problem.
   c. the availability of animals for experimentation.
   d. the need to clarify variables.

7. Generally, there should be four to five alternatives to reduce chance responses and guessing. However, occasionally the number of alternatives might be reduced to three if it is impossible to construct more without including absurdities or obviously false distractors. It is not necessary to maintain a fixed number of alternatives for every item. But the use of fewer than three alternatives is definitely not recommended.

8. As a general principle, the stem should be expressed in *positive* form. The negative stem presents a psychological disadvantage to the student, often confusing and irritating him/her at a time when he/she is already under great stress. Negative items are those which ask what is *not* characteristic of something, what is the *least* defensible reason for something, what is the *least* frequent occurrence, etc. It is good practice to discard the item if it cannot be expressed in positive terms.

9. Responses such as "all of these" or "none of these" should be used *only* when they will contribute more than another plausible distractor. Care should be taken that such responses answer or complete the stem. "All of the above" is a poorer response than "none of the above" because items that use it have four or five correct answers; also, if it is the right answer, knowledge of any two of the distractors will cue it.

10.   There must be only one correct or best response.

11.   The stem must mean the *same thing* to everyone who reads its. For example:
       Ambiguous: Which of the following household appliances would use the most electrical power?
         a.   the vacuum cleaner.
         b.   the electric fan.
         c.   the electric iron.
         d.   a fluorescent tube.
       (Does the test-maker refer to frequency of use, duration of use, or power used by each appliance over the same period of time?)
       Improved: In one hour of operation, which one of the following household appliances would use the most electric power?
         a.   a vacuum cleaner.
         b.   an electric fan.
         c.   an electric iron.
         d.   a fluorescent tube.

12.   Understanding of definitions is better tested by furnishing the name or word and requiring choice between alternative definitions than by presenting the definition and requiring choice between alternative names or words. For example:
       Faulty: Water enters the air by a process called
         a.   osmosis.
         b.   filtration.
         c.   condensation.
         d.   evaporation.
       Improved: Evaporation is a process in which
         a.   vapors turn into liquids.
         b.   liquids pass between the porous surfaces.
         c.   solids dissolve in liquid.
         d.   liquids turn into vapors.

13.   The stem should state a single, specific problem.

14.   The stem must not *include any clues* which will indicate the correct alternative.
       Faulty: A four-sided figure whose opposite sides are parallel is called
         a.   a trapezoid.
         b.   a parallelogram.
         c.   an octagon.
         d.   a triangle.

VIII. MATCHING ITEMS

The matching item consists of three parts:

1.   The directions.
2.   A list of stems or numbered items (statements, incomplete sentences, phrases, or words).
3.   A list of lettered choices or items (words, phrases, or numbers).

Sample Item

Directions: Identify by using the associated letter the name of the man who accomplished each of the following:

_____ 1. organized the Standard Oil Trust.

_____ 2. became a millionaire steel industrialist.

_____ 3. contributed to consolidation and efficiency in railroading.

_____ 4. invented the light bulb and phonograph.

_____ 5. laid the first transatlantic cable.

_____ 6. discovered a process to make steel cheaply.

A. Edwin L. Drake

B. Cornelius Vanderbilt

C. Cyrus W. Field

D. Alexander Graham Bell

E. John D. Rockefeller

F. F. W. Woolworth

G. Henry Bessemer

H. Thomas Edison

I. Andrew Carnegie

Advantages:

1. When properly constructed, the matching item can effectively measure the ability to judge simple relationships between somewhat similar ideas, facts, definitions, and principles.
2. It is relatively easy to score because students do not construct their own responses.
3. The range of material tested can be broad.
4. Guessing is reduced, especially if one column contains more items than the other.

Disadvantages:

1. The matching item is not well adapted to the measurement of the understanding of concepts and conceptual schemes, the ability to organize and apply knowledge and other elements of higher learnings.
2. It emphasizes the identification of relationships between or among memorized content.
3. Because all parts of a matching item must be homogeneous it is difficult for the test maker to avoid giving clues which tend to reduce validity.
4. Too many items become confusing.

Suggestions for Constructing Matching Items

1. The number of items in the column from which matching items are to be selected should always exceed the number of items in the stem column. (See the example.)
2. The number of items to be identified or matched should not exceed ten or twelve.
3. There should be a high degree of homogeneity in every set of matching items. All items in both columns should be in the same general category. For example, events and their dates should never be mixed with events and the names of famous persons.
4. If choices may be used more than once, the directions should so state.

IX. CORRECTION ITEMS

Students are given sentences or paragraphs with a number of italicized words that reduce the meaning of the statements to absurdity. Students are to replace the italicized words with others that make sense of the statements.

Sample Item

Change the italicized words in the following paragraph so that the paragraph has meaning:

Tom went down to the *garden* to go fishing. The fish were swimming about with their *hands* and *feet* looking for *chickadees* and other insects. Tom baited his hook with a *carrot* and tried to catch one of the trout.

Advantages:

This type of test is a welcome variant to standard tests and students like its absurdities. It measures recall in the fashion of completion tests.

Disadvantages:

This type of exercise has the same disadvantages as completion tests, with the added problem that the wrong words may distract the thinking of the students. Perhaps it should not be used for determining grades.

X. GROUPING ITEMS

This type of test requires students to recognize several terms that are associated with each other. In a list of several items the students are to select those that are related in some way and to discard those that are not.

Sample Item

Below are sets of four terms, only three of which are alike in some way. Cross out the word that does not seem to belong with the others.
   set induction
   closure
   insight
   introduction

Advantages:

This is an interesting type of test and it stimulates discussion. It tests knowledge of groupings.

Disadvantages:

Alternative groupings may suggest themselves to students unless suggestions are given.

XI. ARRANGEMENT ITEMS

The students are given a list of terms that are to be arranged in some specified order.

Sample Item

The names of the planets are given below.
List these in order of their distance from the sun, beginning with the closest:

Mars	Earth	Uranus
Pluto	Saturn	Jupiter
Mercury	Neptune	Venus

Advantages:

This type tests knowledge of sequence and order. It is good for review and for starting discussions.

Disadvantages:

It is difficult to give partial credit in scoring this test. Probably it should not be used in determining grades.

XII. TRUE-FALSE ITEMS

In this familiar type of test, students are given a number of statements that they are to judge for accuracy. They may accept a statement or refuse to accept it, signifying their decisions with *true* or *false, yes* or *no,* or a plus or minus sign. Sometimes a student is permitted to qualify his/her answer with a sentence telling why he/she cannot answer either way.

Sample Items

1. Write the word *true* or *false* in the blank at the left side of each statement:

    _____ (1) White pines have five needles in each cluster.

2. Read the following statement. Circle the letter T at the left if you believe it to be true. Circle the letter F if you believe it to be false.

     T   F   (1) A ship will sink deeper as it passes from the Hudson River into the Atlantic Ocean.

Advantages

A great number of items can be answered in a short time, making broad coverage possible. The answers can also be checked rapidly, particularly with the use of a key. This type of test is good for initiating discussions and makes a good pretest.

Disadvantages:

It is very difficult to write items that are strictly true or false without qualifying them in such a way that students can guess what is expected of them. Much of the material that lends itself to this type of testing is relatively unimportant. If students guess the answers, they have a one-in-two chance of selecting the right answer. Mechanical grading makes it impossible to know why a student made his/her choice. True-false items are not well suited for determining grades.

Suggestions for the Construction of True-False Items

1. Write the item out first as a true statement; you can then make the statement false by changing a word or phrase.
2. Avoid negative statements. If they must be used, the word or phrase that makes the statement negative should be underlined.
3. Do not include more than a single idea in one true-false item.
4. Use approximately an equal number of true and false items.
5. Avoid specific determiners, that is, strongly worded statements containing words such as "always," "all," or "none," which may indicate that the statement is likely false.
6. Avoid words that may have different meanings for different students.
7. Avoid using the exact language of the text. The use of exact words would indicate your preference for rote learning.
8. Avoid trick items that appear to be true but are false because of some inconspicuous word or phrase.
9. You can move the true-false type question beyond the guessing realm to higher-level thinking by requiring the student to either correct the false statements so they are true or to explain why the statement is false.

XIII. MODIFIED TRUE-FALSE ITEMS

True-false tests may be modified to reduce the guessing prevalent in standard true-false tests and to encourage students to think more. The statements made are the same but students are to rewrite false statements so that they are true. Usually some clue as to the desired change must be given.

Sample Items

If you judge the statement below to be true, write "True" in the space at the left. If you judge it to be false, rewrite it so that it is true.

_____ 1. Chlorine added to drinking water removes dissolved minerals.

_____

_____

Below are some statements, some of which are true and some of which are false. If you believe a statement is false, change the underlined word to make the statement true, by writing the correct word in the space at the left.

_____ (1) Butterflies have *four* wings.

_____ (2) Houseflies have *four* wings.

Advantages:

This modification of a true-false test is useful in stimulating discussion.

Disadvantages:

The time needed for checking the answers is increased. It is also difficult to assign credits for giving grades.

XIV. SOMETIMES-ALWAYS-NEVER ITEMS

This type of test is much like the true-false test but with a third alternative offered.

Sample Item

For the statements below, if you believe it to be *always true,* circle the letter A at its left. If you believe it is *never true,* circle the letter N. If you believe that it may *sometimes* be true, circle the letter S.

A S N   1. A magnet has two poles.

A S N   2. An electric current sets up a magnetic field.

A S N   3. Like magnetic poles attract each other.

Advantages:

The addition of the third alternative reduces the chances for guessing to one in three. The test is speedily answered and scored. The questions may stimulate a good deal of discussion while being scored.

Disadvantages:

When writing the items it is difficult to avoid giving clues to the answers expected. The fairly high chances for guessing correctly reduce the value of these items for giving grades.

FINAL GUIDELINES ON TESTING

1. Just as the objectives and test items must correlate, so must the activity and evaluation. For example, if you use an inquiry approach to teach the interrelationship of land, climate, and products, you should probably ask an essay type question rather than a matching which calls for memorization.
2. For major tests, use a variety of types of test items.
3. Tested areas should be represented on the test in proportions similar to time spent on each area in class.
4. Improve your tests each year.
5. Give clear directions as to what students are to do if they finish the test while others are still working on it.
6. Checking and grading of tests should be done by you.
7. Prepare the test/quiz as much in advance as you can; review and try it yourself first. Avoid last-minute preparation, and prepare model answers or the keys for the test.
8. Provide enough time for the students to complete the test and review their answers rather than relying on your own time judgment.

You are now ready for the next exercise, where you will practice writing your own test questions.

EXERCISE 16.2: PREPARING MY OWN TEST ITEMS

For your subject field:

1. State the purpose(s) for which your test is intended. (Refer to the beginning of this chapter).

    _____

    _____

2. List one specific objective the test is designed to measure. _____

    _____

    _____

3. Write test items designed to measure this objective—one item for each of the types listed below and discussed in the preceding section.

    Performance item: _____

    _____

    _____

    _____

    Identification item: _____

    _____

    _____

    _____

    Completion-of-Drawing item: _____

    _____

    _____

    _____

    Essay item: _____

    _____

    _____

    _____

    Short explanation item: _____

    _____

    _____

Completion statement item: _____

_____

_____

_____

Multiple-choice item: _____

_____

_____

_____

Matching item: _____

_____

_____

_____

Correction item: _____

_____

_____

_____

Grouping item: _____

_____

_____

_____

Arrangement item: _____

_____

_____

_____

True-false item: _____

_____

_____

_____

4. Share and discuss your test with your classmates and/or instructor.

G. GRADING STUDENT ACHIEVEMENT

If conditions were ideal, and if we teachers were doing our jobs perfectly well, all of our students would receive top marks (mastery learning), and there would be no need to further address this topic of grading. However, as conditions are not perfect, let us proceed with guidelines on this topic, one that is of considerable interest to you and to your students.

As mentioned earlier, the teacher must first ask, What is this thing we call *achievement*? Is it achievement of the objectives against some preset standard, or is it simply achievement itself? Most likely it is the former, in which case it is possible for the teacher to arrive at appropriate symbols (letters, numbers, grades) that serve to report to students and their parents the progress being made by the student. The grade symbol, then, may be said to be the teacher's subjective estimate of the percentage of the objectives the student has reached thus far, or by the end of the semester or school year. Regardless of the objectivity of your grading system, it is ultimately based upon your personal subjective judgment. Your task is to make it as objective as possible so that students and parents will understand how grades are determined by you. Grades are extremely important to the lives of many high school students; you need to carefully plan your procedures for determining those symbols, which will be used by many different people in a variety of ways that have a long-term impact on the lives of students. The following general guidelines are provided to help you in this important endeavor.

GUIDELINES TO PREPARE YOU FOR GRADING

1. Each student is an individual and should not be converted to a statistic on a frequency-distribution curve. You can periodically do frequency-distribution studies of your grades for your own information, but *do not grade your secondary-school students on a curve.*

2. At the beginning of the school year, *explain your grading policies to yourself,* then to your students and their parents.

3. The achievement grade *should be tied to a performance level* (see Chapter 7).

4. Build your grading system around the *concept of success* rather than failure, as students proceed from one success to another.

5. *Use the point system for determination of grades,* where students receive points for everything they do, say, and write. If you use the standard breakdown of a certain percentage of points necessary for an A (90 percent), B (80 percent), C (70 percent), and so on, then you and your students can, at any time during the grading period, determine exactly and quickly what a student's grade is. As the individual student can keep a running total of his/her own point count, and knows what the possible total is, then that student is always aware of how he/she is doing. We favor this system over one where the teacher records checks and/or letter grades for everything and then, later in the semester, such as at the end of the grading period, tries to average those symbols. With that system, it is difficult or impossible for the student to maintain a steady and accurate awareness of how he/she is doing with respect to an exact grade.

6. A first- and third-quarter grade is in fact a *progress report! It is the final semester grade that counts the most*—the one that ends up on the student's transcript and may eventually be used to determine success or failure for the course, to determine college entrance, and in the awarding of scholarships. Keep that important fact in mind as you work with the students through each grading period.

7. The items used in determining the students' final quarter and semester grades should be a *good balance of homework, classwork, quizzes, major tests, and exams*. In many classes, the number of major tests (including exams) should be a minimum of six for an entire semester. The number of quizzes would be much greater. The total grade should be determined by approximately 50 percent test (including quiz) scores, and 50 percent classwork and homework. This is a general guideline only; just be cautious if you develop a system that counts too heavily on students' scores on major tests.

8. To minimize your own headache resulting from having to deal with *makeup exams* (and quizzes) we suggest you consider this: if you give many quizzes and several tests during the semester, then you might simply allow the absent student the choice of taking a makeup test *or* allowing the next test to count double for that student.

9. Especially when you grade using a point system, you will encounter students who will ask for *extra-credit* assignments, and this will occur with increased frequency as the grading period draws to a close. Our recommendation: *do not burden yourself with having to devise extra assignments for students who did not do the regular assignments.* Extra assignments may have a reasonable place for students who *need* extra work because of legitimate absences or who are above and beyond where the rest of the class is, or who have special needs (see Chapter 1), but in most cases those will be discerned much earlier during the grading period.

10. A special hint that will perhaps make your job a bit easier is to *consider giving your quarter exams* (first and third) *a week before the end of the grading period*. This is not the norm for secondary-school teachers, but if it is possible, it will give you an extra week to read the exams, score them, make final grade determinations, and mark the computer printout grade report forms. Doing so might help preserve your home life!

11. *Grading procedures in performance classes,* such as art and music, will vary from many of the previous guidelines, particularly those dealing with the administration of tests that can be measured objectively. In these courses the teacher will perhaps rely more heavily on subjective items, such as classroom participation. Is the student demonstrating a positive attitude toward trying? Does the student respect other students and the correct use of materials, instruments, and supplies? Are assignments neat and turned in on time? Does the student's performance (see acceptable verbs in Section D of Chapter 7) satisfy the concept of the task? A point scoring system can still be utilized for the final determination of student grades.

12. A final guideline concerns the fact that you will also be arriving at a mark that represents the student's social behavior in your class—commonly referred to as the "citizenship grade." Although the student's social behavior will likely affect his/her academic achievement, the two marks are separated on reporting forms (see next section). Our advice to you: *Do not deduct academic accomplishment points from the student's total points just because his/her citizenship is less than satisfactory to you!* Unless you are teaching in a particular area of social studies where you can safely combine the grades, they should be kept separate, and reported separately. You might have a student in your class who is a real "smart alec" and whose behavior you abhor but who still achieves well academically. The academic grade reflects his/her academic achievement, not necessarily his/her immature behavior in your classroom.

H. REPORTING A STUDENT'S ACHIEVEMENT

One of the teacher's responsibilities is to report the student's achievement. In most secondary-school districts this is done in either of two ways: some junior high schools and even some senior high schools continue to use the traditional "report card," which is marked and sent home either with the student or by mail; but many high schools today use the more modern method of reporting by computer printouts, which are often sent by mail directly to the student's home address. Such printouts might include all of the courses taken by the student while enrolled in that high school, as well as the student's current accumulation of units and grade point average to date.

Whichever reporting form is used, it will separate the social from the academic behaviors of the student. In high schools, the academic achievement is usually indicated by a letter grade (A through F) and the social behavior (citizenship) simply by a "satisfactory" or an "unsatisfactory." Junior high school reporting forms may be more specific regarding the social behavior items.

In either case, please note the following.

SUGGESTIONS FOR MAKING OUT REPORT CARDS

1. Study Report Card/Progress Report/Quarterly Report used in your school. Be familiar with the policies/regulations governing the report card.
2. If you have to grade "Citizenship," be extra careful to guard against the "Teacher Subjectivity" (biases and prejudices).
3. You should always make separate assessments of Achievement and Citizenship.
4. If you are not satisfied with the report card established by the school, create your own for your students or a more detailed one for the parents. Let your administrators know you are doing this.
5. Invite your students and parents to talk about the report card with you.
6. Keep in mind and be clear about the "gradable categories" (quizzes, tests, assignments, project(s), etc.).

I. CONFERENCING WITH A PARENT

As a secondary-school teacher you are likely to be meeting many of the parents early in the school year during "Back to School Night" and throughout the year in individual parent conferences. Frequently these are anxious times for the beginning teacher. Here are some guidelines to help you with those experiences.

Guidelines for the Teacher Meeting Parents

1. When discussing your method of operation during "Back to School Night," remember the parents are anxious to learn about their child's new teacher. Tell them a little about yourself and then make some straightforward remarks about your expectations of the students in your class. The parents will be glad to learn that you (1) have your program well planned, (2) are a "task master," (3) will communicate with them frequently. The parents will be delighted to find that you are from the school of the three F's—firm, friendly, and fair.

Parents will expect to learn about your curriculum, about any long-term projects, and about your grading procedures. They will need to know what you expect of them: will there be homework, and if so, should they help their children? Try to anticipate questions there are likely to be—such as how they can contact you. Your principal may be of assistance in helping you anticipate and prepare for these questions. But of course you can never prepare for the question that comes from left field. Just stay calm and don't get flustered. Parents will be reassured to know you are an in-control person.

2. Later in the year, when meeting parents in individual conferences, our advice is for you to be as specific as possible when explaining to the parent the progress of his/her child. Be helpful to their understanding, and don't bombard the parent with more information than he/she needs. As a group, teachers tend to talk too much. Resist that tendency and allow time for the parent to ask questions. Keep your answers succinct. Never compare one child with another, or even with the entire class. If the parent asks a question for which you do not have an answer, tell the parent you will try to find the answer and phone him/her as quickly as you can. And do it! Have the child's work with you during parent conferences so you can *show* the parent examples of what is being discussed.

3. When a parent asks how he/she may help at home, here are some suggestions for *consideration:*
   a. Limit television viewing.
   b. Save all of the student's papers, digging them out once in a while to review progress with the student.
   c. Establish a regular time each evening for a family discussion about school.
   d. Ask your child to share with you each evening one specific thing learned that day in school.
   e. As needed, plan short family meetings *after* dinner, but while you are still seated at the table. Ask for a "tableside" report of "What's happening in your school life?" Ask, "How can I help?" When your child expresses a concern, emphasize ways to solve problems that occur, e.g., problems with classes, teacher, peers, homework, and social interaction.

4. When a parent is angry and hostile toward you and/or the school, here are a few general guidelines:
   a. Remain calm in your discussion with the parent, allowing the parent to talk out his/her hostility while you say little. The parent may just need to vent frustrations that might have very little to do with you.
   b. Do not allow yourself to be backed into a corner. If the parent tries to do so by attacking you personally, do not press your defense at this point. Perhaps the parent has made a point that you would like some time to consider and now is a good time to arrange for another conference with this parent in about a week.
   c. Generally, the less you say the better off you probably will be, and what you do say must be objective and to the point of the student's work in the classroom.
   d. It is important that you not talk about other students in the class; keep the conversation about this parent's child's progress. Have objective data at hand that you can refer to during the conversation.
   e. The parent does not really need to hear about how busy you are and about how many other students you are dealing with simultaneously, unless he/she asks.
   f. This parent is not your rival, or should not be. You both are interested in the education of the child. Try and establish an adult conversation with the parent with a focus on a mutual diagnosis of the problem, with mutually agreed upon steps you both will undertake to resolve the problem. To this end you may need to solicit help from the principal or another third party. Do not hesitate to take that step when it appears necessary.

QUESTIONS FOR CLASS DISCUSSION

1. Can a teacher be too objective in evaluating a student's achievement? Explain.
2. The best evidence for student achievement is a variety of evidence. Explain the importance of this statement to you as related to your own subject field.
3. Why do you suppose so much is written about the "slow learner" and about the "gifted learner," but so little about the "average learner?" In school, which were you?
4. Do you believe in the use of "therapeutic" grading? Why or why not?
5. Pretend you are a secondary-school teacher and are getting ready to meet the parents of your students for the first time (perhaps at a "Back to School Night"). What will you say to them? Try it out on your classmates.
6. What standardized tests are administered to the secondary-school students at the schools you have visited? What are their purposes? How are they used?
7. Do you believe students should be failed or held back in grades? When, if ever, should parents be involved in the decision?
8. Outline and defend the grading procedure you will use in subjects you plan to teach. Share your plan with your classmates.
9. What question would you like to raise for class discussion? How might answers be found?

17

How Can I Continue to Evaluate My Developing Competency?

The evaluation of your own teaching proficiency is an ongoing process that we trust will continue throughout your teaching career. Whether you are a teacher candidate or an experienced teacher, the material in this chapter should help you to improve your competency level.

We begin this chapter with a skill-development strategy especially useful in teacher education.

A. A LOOK AT MY PRESERVICE SKILL DEVELOPMENT: MICRO-PEER TEACHING

Micro-peer teaching (MPT) is a useful skill-development strategy. In this technique, the "teacher" prepares and teaches a brief lesson to a small number of peers. The teaching demonstration is followed by immediate feedback and diagnosis. It is a scaled-down teaching experience involving:

1. A limited objective.
2. A brief period of time for teaching the lesson.
3. A lesson taught to a limited number of students (8-10).

Research indicates that this training can be an excellent predictor of subsequent teacher behavior in a regular classroom. But more important, MPT can provide the opportunity to develop and improve specific teaching behaviors. The teaching demonstration is videotaped, allowing the "teacher" to observe him/herself in action and also viewing an immediate replay for self-evaluation and diagnosis.

Evaluation of the MPT is related to the following criteria:

1. What was the quality of "teacher" preparation and presentation? For example, did the lesson appear well-prepared and creative? What were the quality of the teacher's voice and mannerisms?

2. What was the quality of the planned and implemented "student" involvement?
3. Were the teacher's objectives reached?
4. Was the cognitive level appropriate? The secondary teacher candidate prepares and teaches to his/her peers a lesson that might be a lesson he/she would use for an actual secondary-school class, but he/she prepares the lesson as a presentation to peers. That is, as opposed to teaching the lesson to peers as though they are secondary-school children.

Guidelines for the Use of the MPT

We emphasize the following important elements in the use of this strategy.

1. The MPT exercise provides the preservice teacher an opportunity to prepare and implement a mini-lesson.
2. The exercise calls for constructive feedback in the form of (a) peer evaluation, (b) self-evaluation, and (c) instructor evaluation, *in that order.*
3. If there is time in your course for each student to do several MPT demonstrations, then each MPT might focus on specific strategies, such as questioning, discussion, and inquiry.
4. There are *three ingredients for the completed MPT.* They are:
   a. The preparation and implementation.
   b. The packet turned in by each "teacher" upon completion, which is in effect a summative peer and self-evaluation, including statements of what the "teacher" would change were he/she to repeat the presentation.
   c. The instructor's evaluation of the "teacher's" participation in the total class exercise, i.e., *teaching, playback, student, evaluator.* We emphasize the scope of learning encompassed as you perform each of these four roles, as indicated in Exercise 17.1: Micro-Peer Teaching: My Final Evaluation Form.

Instructions for the MPT Exercise (Exercise 17.1)

In this exercise, you are to prepare and implement a teaching lesson to a group of your peers. Some members of your class will be your students, others will be evaluating your teaching demonstration. The lesson duration should be 20 minutes, at most. Your instructor will specify the exact length. You will be videotaped, for your later self-evaluation. Try to ignore the camera while teaching. (Warning: if you have never seen yourself on television, you will observe that black and white makes you look ten pounds heavier, color even more).

Forms that follow may be used for preparation and evaluation of the MPT.

NOTE TO THE INSTRUCTOR

With the aid of a split-screen generator and two or more cameras, you can record, simultaneously on one screen, both "students" and "teachers." During playback, this affords an opportunity for the "teacher" to view student reactions during the teaching, without losing the picture of himself/herself.

EXERCISE 17.1: MICRO-PEER TEACHING: MY PREPARATION

Instructions: Use this form for initial preparation of your lesson. After completing this form, and after receiving the approval of your instructor, you should then prepare a lesson plan using one of the forms from Chapter 8 (or another approved by your instructor).

MPT PREPARATION FORM

1. Lesson I will teach: _____

_____

_____

_____

2. Specific instructional objectives: _____

_____

_____

_____

3. Strategies I will use: _____

_____

_____

_____

4. Student experiences I will provide: _____

_____

_____

_____

5. Materials and equipment I will need: _____

_____

_____

_____

EXERCISE 17.1: MICRO-PEER TEACHING: MY PEER EVALUATION

Peer evaluators may use either of the following forms. Peer evaluators should not be students during the teaching demonstration; eight to ten evaluators should be off to the side of the classroom. The evaluations are collected by the "teacher" upon completion of her/his teaching demonstration, and taken to another room for her/his own tape viewing and self-evaluation.

MPT EVALUATION: FORM I

Teacher: _____ Topic: _____

Rate the following by circling the appropriate number; 1 is very poor, 7 is excellent.

Content: (Was this of help to you? Did it extend your knowledge of the area?)

   1   2   3   4   5   6   7

Comment: _____

_____

_____

Presentation: (Did the presentation hold your interest? Was it clear and logical?)

   1   2   3   4   5   6   7

Comment: _____

_____

_____

Improvement: (How could the presentation have been improved?)

   1   2   3   4   5   6   7

Comment: _____

_____

_____

MPT EVALUATION: FORM II

Teacher: _____ Subject: _____ Date: _____

I. Organization of Lesson:	5	4	3	2	1
A. Lesson Preparation	Very evident		Somewhat evident		Not evident
B. Lesson beginning	Effective start		Effectiveness somewhat lacking		Poor start
C. Subject-matter knowledge	Well informed and much to offer		Some knowledge evident; valuable		Needs to be more informed
D. Closure	Effective ending		Effectiveness somewhat lacking		Poor finish

Comments: _____

_____

II. Lesson Presentation:

	5	4	3	2	1
A. Audience contact	Excellent eye contact		Needs to look at audience more		Relies heavily on notes; does not maintain eye contact
B. Enthusiasm	Intense		Somewhat evident		Lacking (another job to be done)
C. Speech quality and delivery	Very articulate and natural		Clear and appropriate but with minor problems		Monotone; boring
D. Use of language (vocabularies)	Well chosen		Appropriate		Inappropriate
E. Use of aids and materials	Well chosen and effective		Effectiveness doubtful		None evident; could use some
F. Examples and analogies	Excellent and logical		Needs better selection		None evident; could use some
G. Involvement of audience	Excellent and tactful		Somewhat passive		No involvement
H. Responses to audience	Very personal and accepting		Somewhat passive or indifferent		Impersonal; no response
I. Directions and refocusing	Extremely clear and to the point		Somewhat vague or not too evident		Confusing or vague
J. Transitions	Very smooth and clear		Somewhat disjointed and unclear		Abrupt or unclear
K. Closing	Excellent		Rough		Too abrupt

Comments: _____

_____

What to Look for in Video Playback Session for Your Self-Evaluation

Upon collection of your peer evaluations, you will move to another room where you will view the playback of your teaching demonstration. During the playback, there are specifics you should look for. These are:

1. Effective use of verbal responses.
2. Effective use of nonverbal responses (gestures).
3. Fluency in use of questioning.
4. Use of voice inflection and nonverbal cueing.
5. Use of set induction.
6. Stimulus variation (variety of materials and experiences).
7. Use of time and closure.
8. Examples and analogies.
9. Eye contact.
10. Peripheral awareness (overlapping).
11. Acceptance.
12. Listening.
13. Use of names.
14. Sense of humor.
15. Pertinence of MPT (nonfrivolous).
16. Keeps you relaxed but interested.
17. Overall creativity.
18. Effective use of body, hands.
19. Mobility.
20. Listen to your questions—clear and understood?

During the playback, you may stop the tape at various times, and backwind to see certain things a second time. Also, you should be reviewing the peer evaluations for any characteristics frequently mentioned and which you can see during the playback. Later you may wish to do a frequency-distribution analysis on the peer evaluations. A single comment from one evaluator may not be as informative as one mentioned by many of the evaluators.

Preparing the MPT Packet

Upon completion of your viewing of the playback, you should then prepare the MPT Packet to give to your instructor (perhaps a week after viewing playback). The packet should include:

1. Your lesson plan.
2. The peer evaluations.
3. Your self-evaluation.
4. Your summary analysis, which will include your selection and description of items that were strengths and weaknesses, and what areas you would improve if you were to repeat the presentation.

Upon receipt of your packet, your instructor will then provide a final evaluation of your MPT, perhaps using the form that follows.

EXERCISE 17.1: MICRO-PEER TEACHING: MY FINAL EVALUATION

_____

Student

Packet Due _____ Rec'd. _____

Criterion I: The Presentation

Lesson Objective:

1. Preassessment   10 9 8 7 6 5 4 3 2 1 N.A.
2. Materials   10 9 8 7 6 5 4 3 2 1 N.A.
3. Application   10 9 8 7 6 5 4 3 2 1 N.A.
4. Student Involvement   10 9 8 7 6 5 4 3 2 1 N.A.
5. Post Assessment   10 9 8 7 6 5 4 3 2 1 N.A.
6. Cognitive Level   10 9 8 7 6 5 4 3 2 1 N.A.
7. Poise, Voice, etc.   10 9 8 7 6 5 4 3 2 1 N.A.

Subtotal Criterion I _____

Criterion II: The Packet

8. Summary Analysis   10 9 8 7 6 5 4 3 2 1 N.A.
9. Selection and Description 10 9 8 7 6 5 4 3 2 1 N.A.

Subtotal Criterion II _____

Criterion III: Participation in MPT

10. In Playback Session   10 9 8 7 6 5 4 3 2 1 N.A.
11. As Student   10 9 8 7 6 5 4 3 2 1 N.A.
12. As Evaluator   10 9 8 7 6 5 4 3 2 1 N.A.

Subtotal Criterion III _____

Final MPT Grade _____ _____ Reteach: YES   NO

EXERCISE 17.2: HOW CAN I FURTHER ANALYZE MY VERBAL INTERACTIONS WITH STUDENTS?

Instructions: Analyze your verbal interactions. There are two ways that observations may be made—by you as you listen to a recording (audio or audio-video) made during your teaching, or by another observer who sits in your room during class. While observing, tallies are made of those behaviors observed. Observations and their corresponding tallies could be made at regular intervals of 15 seconds, or each time there is a new teacher or pupil behavior.

An analysis of tallies can provide a picture of the percentages of class time spent in:

Teacher-initiated talk
Pupil-initiated talk
Teacher-response talk
Pupil-response talk
Silence
Confusion

and of the cognitive levels of those activities.

An analysis of tallies of praises or compliments you express to your students can also provide a picture as to what kind of and how frequently you use the said expressions in the classroom. From recording and analyzing your teacher talk and your interaction with the secondary students, you will be able to determine:

- If you are accepting and clarifying the positive or negative feelings and attitudes of students.
- If you are praising and encouraging students, and using humor.
- If you are criticizing, directing, commanding, ordering, and lecturing.
- If students have the freedom to express their ideas, and to share their opinions and thoughts.
- If there are periods of confusion, of planned or unplanned silence, and of pausing.

Knowledge gained from an interaction analysis of your classroom gives you teaching power, power that will help you examine the effects of your verbal teaching behavior on the student's verbal behavior.

B. ANOTHER LOOK: MY SECONDARY TEACHALOGUE, WITH 20 TEACHING SUGGESTIONS

What additional advice can we give you as a beginning teacher? Can this advice be compacted into some special hints, ideas, or secrets? We have summarized them in this "teachalogue," containing 20 teaching suggestions for secondary teachers to help you further evaluate yourself.

SECONDARY TEACHALOGUE CHECKLIST

Before the Lesson

1. Did you write specific, concrete goals, aims, and objectives, and will you share them with your students?
2. Did you refer to the established course of study for your subject and grade level, and review state framework documents, teacher's manuals, and scope and sequence charts?
3. Is your motivation relevant to your lesson? Do you know the difference between a topic that is interesting to students and a topic that needs additional motivation?
4. Are you taking secondary students' interest in a topic for granted, or does your motivational component of the lesson meet the needs and interests of your students?
5. Did you order audiovisual materials pertinent to your lesson, and did you preview the material?
6. Did you prepare demonstration materials and display them so that all students can see?
7. Have you planned very carefully your lesson transitions from one topic/activity to another, and from one lesson to the next, and do you have the required supplies and materials ready and available for each lesson?
8. Have you established efficient, orderly routines and procedures for your class management tasks, such as collecting homework, taking roll, sharpening pencils, distributing and collecting books and materials, using the wastebasket, and dismissal at the end of the period?

During the Lesson

9. Are you beginning each period with a clean chalkboard?
10. Are you remembering that sometimes the material is clearer to students when they can see it than when they hear it?
11. Are you remembering to write legibly and boldly, and orderly, so all can read your writing on the chalkboard?
12. Are you being empathic to your students, indicating that you know that they *can* learn?
13. Are you allowing your students to participate in discussions (to talk), and be heard, and are you giving each one the quiet praise that he or she deserves?
14. Are you setting the mental stage, varying your class activities, and, when possible, building upon each student's contributions during the lesson?
15. Are you making clear all relationships between main ideas and details for your students, and presenting examples of abstract concepts in a simple, concrete way?
16. Are you explaining, discussing, and commenting on audiovisual materials you use in your lesson?

17. When asking questions of students, are you giving students time to review the topic; to hear your frame of reference for your questions; to recognize that your question is on their level of understanding; and to participate in "think-time" or "brainstorming time" before they respond to your questions? Are you remembering never to answer your own questions?

18. Are you introducing materials to the students *before* they are needed in the lesson?

19. Are you evincing enthusiasm in your speech, keeping a moderate pace in your delivery, and insisting that all students give you their attention when you begin the lesson?

20. Are you properly attending to the needs of special students in your class, attempting to individualize their learning according to their individual needs, interests, and abilities?

C. STILL ANOTHER LOOK: SECONDARY PRACTICE-TEACHING EVALUATION FORM AND COMPETENCY DESCRIPTIONS

EVALUATION FOR MID-TERM _____ FINAL _____

_____ _____ _____
Student Teacher   Grade   School

_____
Cooperating Teacher

_____
Date

_____
College or University Supervisor

Place a check ✓ in one of the categories for each evaluative competency.*

1. The teacher candidate will exhibit professional traits such as showing enthusiasm for learning and teaching, for self-evaluation, and for correcting behaviors that affect teaching.

   Needs Improvement _____ Progressing Satisfactorily _____ Toward Competency _____

2. The teacher candidate plans lessons ahead, identifies objectives, and selects a variety of appropriate activities to develop objectives.

   Needs Improvement _____ Progressing Satisfactorily _____ Toward Competency _____

3. The teacher candidate demonstrates a knowledge of the subject matter that is taught in the secondary school.

   Needs Improvement _____ Progressing Satisfactorily _____ Toward Competency _____

4. The teacher candidate successfully carries out a variety of instructional techniques.

   Needs Improvement _____ Progressing Satisfactorily _____ Toward Competency _____

5. The teacher candidate has an effective classroom management style that is consistent with his/her behavioral requirements of students.

   Needs Improvement _____ Progressing Satisfactorily _____ Toward Competency _____

6. The teacher candidate constructs a variety of teacher-made instructional materials that are clear and appropriate and function as good models.

   Needs Improvement _____ Progressing Satisfactorily _____ Toward Competency _____

* At the end of the semester, a teacher candidate whose teaching competency receives an "inadequate" rating in one or more of the competency areas is not ready to be recommended for a teaching credential.

Competency Descriptions for Each Evaluative Criterion

1. **The teacher-candidate will exhibit professional traits, such as showing enthusiasm for learning and teaching, for self-evaluation, and for correcting behaviors that affect teaching negatively.**

____ *Needs Improvement:* Has a poor attendance record; gives excuses when evaluated; does not attempt to correct behaviors that affect teaching-learning environment; does not seek help and suggestions; has ineffective voice control; is dependent upon others to plan and prescribe lessons.

____ *Progressing Satisfactorily:* Has an average attendance record; responds to constructive evaluation; attempts to correct behaviors that affect teaching negatively; often seeks help and suggestions; has effective voice control; plans independently.

____ *Toward Competency:* Is responsive to evaluations of the candidate's work; self evaluates; has a good attendance record; is a good model for students; seeks suggestions and help; plans independently; shows enthusiasm for teaching and learning; always corrects any habits or manners that may negatively affect teaching.

2. **The teacher candidate plans lessons ahead, identifies objectives, and selects a variety of appropriate activities to achieve objectives.**

____ *Needs Improvement:* Uses only one instructional activity; is reluctant to plan; has difficulty in identifying objective; is not interested in varying activities.

____ *Progressing Satisfactorily:* Is aware of the value of varying the learning activities; maintains lesson plans ahead; knows objectives.

____ *Toward Competency:* Always plans lessons ahead; identifies objectives for students' as well as teacher's goal; stimulates learning environment by offering a variety of activities; can change instruction, using different approaches and procedures.

3. **The teacher candidate demonstrates a knowledge of the content that is taught in the subject discipline.**

____ *Needs Improvement:* Knowledge is somewhat superficial; sometimes makes errors or gives misinformation in statements; relies on the school textbook, teacher's guides, or courses of study alone for information and ideas.

____ *Progressing Satisfactorily:* Has reliable information; shows an awareness of recent developments or materials in subject area; has broad knowledge.

____ *Toward Competency:* Introduces reliable, pertinent information; has a wide background of experience; is accurate; resourceful; has a command of content taught at the secondary-school level.

4. **The teacher candidate successfully carries out a variety of instructional techniques.**

____ *Needs Improvement:* Seems to follow the same teaching technique regardless of topic, students, or classroom conditions.

____ *Progressing Satisfactorily:* Usually selects an instructional technique that is appropriate for a lesson; recognizes that different instructional techniques help or hinder a teacher's effectiveness under differing classroom conditions.

____ *Toward Competency:* Consistently selects an instructional technique that is effective for the topic, the students, and the classroom condition; is ready to change the technique quickly if necessary; can successfully implement directed reading lessons, lectures and demonstrations, guided discovery, experiments, and informal group discussions; is able to give individual help.

5. **The teacher candidate has an effective classroom management style that is consistent with behavioral requirements of students.**

____ *Needs Improvement:* Often lacks group control; allows disruptive noise and other conditions to interfere with learning; seems unaware of school and district policies and procedures about student conduct; teacher behavior often results in student hostility, resentment, or lack of respect.

____ *Progressing Satisfactorily:* Manages group so that learning continues; understands and accepts district and school policies and procedures about student conduct; shows an improvement in teacher-student relationships during the practice teaching assignment.

____ *Toward Competency:* Strong group management is evident with friendly and cooperative teacher-student relationships; students work toward educational goals; teacher accepts students' individual differences and needs; group and individual respect is evident; is comfortable with this age group; gives precise directions, does not over-react, uses eye contact, gestures, uses appropriate pacing, always has activities for emergency situations; can teach a small group while being aware of the rest of the class; is fair.

6. **The teacher candidate will construct a variety of teacher-made instructional materials that are clear, appropriate, and function as good models.**

____ *Needs Improvement:* Is unconcerned about preparing instructional aids (or is unaware of the need to prepare them).

____ *Progressing Satisfactorily:* Occasionally prepares an instructional aid with urging from the cooperating teacher and/or supervisor; appears hesitant to prepare any materials independently.

____ *Toward Competency:* Identifies lessons where instructional aids are appropriate; consistently selects and prepares a matching aid that will provide an effective learning experience; relates difficulty level of the material to the level of the students.

EXERCISE 17.3: SECONDARY PRACTICE TEACHING: WHAT DOES MY SECOND SELF-EVALUATION TELL ME?

Turn back to the "Secondary Practice-Teaching Evaluation Form" immediately preceding. Read the descriptions of the competencies that follow it, then complete your own competency self-evaluation check. What does this second self-evaluation tell you?

Now compare your evaluation with the earlier evaluation done in Exercise 4.1. Can you identify progress that has been made in your own competencies development? Discuss your comparisons with your classmates.

D. LOOKING AHEAD: SAMPLE FORMS USED BY SCHOOL PERSONNEL TO EVALUATE TEACHERS

From district to district, the teacher-evaluation forms vary. We consider the forms that follow to be representative enough to give you a good idea of their form and content.

TEACHER BEHAVIOR CHECKLIST

Teacher _____ Grade _____ Students _____ Minutes _____

Observer _____ Date _____

Unit or Lesson

A. LEARNING ENVIRONMENT	COMMENTS

1. Presence
   a. The teacher displays a sense of self-confidence in the classroom.
   b. The teacher is business-like and authoritative in the conduct of the class.
   c. The teacher consistently monitors the progress of the students.	

2. Organization
   a. The teacher presents a lesson that has a clear, logical structure.
   b. The teacher is well-organized throughout the lesson.
   c. The teacher has available well-prepared or well-chosen materials for students.	

3. Clarity
   a. The teacher speaks in a clear, easily understood voice.
   b. The teacher tells the students what is expected of them.
   c. The teacher gives clear, easily understood feedback to students.
   d. The teacher's directions to students are clear and easily understood.	

4. Enthusiasm
   a. The teacher makes the lesson interesting.
   b. The teacher seems to enjoy the lesson.
   c. The teacher displays a personal interest in the lesson.
   d. The teacher displays a sense of humor in a positive manner.	

(continued)

A. LEARNING ENVIRONMENT	COMMENTS
5. Student Dignity a. The teacher provides good support of student dignity.	
6. Academic Learning Time a. The majority of the students are actively engaged in learning tasks which are related to goals and objectives from the curriculum.	

7. Discipline
   a. The majority of the students are responsible for their behavior.
   b. The teacher's management of the students is clearly established.
   c. The teacher consistently monitors the behavior of the students.	

8. Other	

TEACHER OBSERVATION FORM

Teacher _____ Grade _____ Students _____ Minutes _____

Observer _____ Date _____

Unit or Lesson

B. INSTRUCTION	COMMENTS

1. Interaction
    a. The teacher displays an awareness of each student.
    b. The teacher is actively engaged with the students.
    c. The teacher actively seeks student participation.	

2. Optimism
    a. The teacher expresses faith in the student's ability to perform well.
    b. The teacher helps students form a good self-concept.
    c. The teacher shows respect for student ideas.
    d. The teacher praises the class for good performance.	

3. Knowledge of Students
    a. The instruction is differentiated for each student's level of achievement.
    b. The teacher demonstrates a knowledge of each student's level of achievement.
    c. The teacher demonstrates good rapport with the students in the class.	

4. Intellectual Stimulation
    a. The teacher's questions require student responses at various cognitive levels.
    b. The teacher's responses to students' answers are accepting and encouraging.	

5. Evaluation
    a. The teacher has a systematic way to evaluate the progress of students.
    b. The teacher uses the results of formal testing to evaluate student progress.
    c. The teacher gives students ways in which they can improve their achievement.
    d. The teacher has a systematic way to evaluate his/her performance.	

6. Consistency a. The teacher is consistent.	
7. Other	

CLASSROOM OBSERVATION

Name _____ Date _____

Class(es) _____

Critical Teacher Behaviors

	Observed	Not Observed	Comments
A. Clarity			
1. The teacher speaks clearly.			
2. The teacher's instructions are given clearly.			
3. The teacher's objectives are clearly stated to students.			
B. Organization			
1. The teacher presents materials in an orderly manner.			
2. The teacher integrates, relates, and categorizes to aid in student comprehension.			
C. Enthusiasm			
1. The teacher is energetic, stimulating, and involved.			
2. The teacher appears to enjoy both content and process of the lesson.			
D. Support of Student Dignity			
1. The teacher establishes a classroom climate where the basic dignity of students is supported.			
2. The teacher avoids embarrassing or criticizing students.			
E. Personalization			
1. The teacher uses personal examples in dialogue.			
2. The teacher refers to each student by name.			
3. The teacher has contacts with students outside of the instructional program.			

(continued)

	Observed	Not Observed	Comments

F. *Knowledge of Subject Matter*
   1. The teacher projects command of material.
   2. The teacher answers the student questions and concerns, or redirects them to appropriate resources.
G. *On Task Time—Teaching Inventory*
   1. The teacher actively engages in the teaching/learning act.
   2. The teacher actively supervises seat work and makes himself/ herself easily available to students.
   3. The teacher keeps the majority of the students involved in the lesson, most of the time.
H. *Articulation Expectations for Students*
   1. The teacher spells out his/her expectations for student achievement.
   2. The teacher expresses faith in the students and their ability to achieve.
I. *Interaction*
   1. The teacher provides opportunity for expression of opinion, assenting and dissenting.
   2. The teacher uses student ideas and comments.

STATEMENT OF GOALS, OBJECTIVES, AND ASSESSMENT TECHNIQUES

Evaluatee: _____ Date Submitted: _____

Goal Classification No.: _____ Goal No.: _____

Note: The statement of Goals, Objectives, and Assessment Techniques is to be submitted by the evaluatee, reviewed by the evaluator, if necessary revised by the evaluatee, agreed upon and signed by both. Due date October 15. With the concurrence of the evaluator, objectives or assessment techniques may be changed during the year.

Goal Classifications: A.   Student Progress
                        B.   Control of Educational Environment
                        C.   Adjunct Duties
                        D.   Self-improvement

Statement of the Goal: _____

_____

_____

_____

Why the Goal Has Been Selected: _____

_____

_____

_____

Objective(s) (Includes Assessment Techniques and Timeline)	*Instructional Strategies (How I Will Go About It)*	*Resources Required*	*Progress to Date*

E. LOOKING WITHIN: A SUMMARY OF GUIDELINES THAT PERMEATE THE ASSESSMENT COMPONENT

Here is a list of ten guidelines that should permeate the total evaluation program.

1. The teacher needs to know how he/she is doing.
2. The learner needs to know how he/she is doing.
3. Evidence, feedback, and input for Items 1 and 2 should come from a variety of sources.
4. Evaluation of a learner's progress should be ongoing.
5. If grades are given, the student should at all times know where he/she stands.
6. Self-evaluation is an important aspect of the total process.
7. Much of the evaluation process should be systematized.
8. The evaluation process should contribute to the improvement of the teacher and to the growth of the learner.
9. Evaluation is a reciprocal process; that is, it includes evaluation of teacher performance as well as evaluation of student progress.
10. The teacher's professional responsibility is to teach and to assess the progress, and he/she will be held accountable for this responsibility.

QUESTION FOR CLASS DISCUSSION

1. What do *you* want to talk about? Write your question below, tear off, drop in a box or other container provided by your instructor. Your question: _____

_____

_____

_____

_____

_____

Then mix forms around, select a class representative to reach into the box, select one question, and begin the discussion.

SELECTED READINGS AND REFERENCES FOR CHAPTERS 16 AND 17

Alper, Michael. "All Our Children Can Learn." *University of Chicago Magazine,* Vol. 74, No. 4 (Summer 1982).

American Association of School Administrators. *Time on Task: Using Instructional Time More Effectively* (1983). 1801 North Moore St., Arlington, CA 22209.

Bloom, Benjamin S. *All Our Children Learning, A Primer for Parents, Teachers, and Other Educators.* New York: McGraw-Hill Book Co., 1981.

Comer, James P. "Parent Participation in the Schools." *Phi Delta Kappan,* Vol. 67, No. 6 (February 1986), pp. 442-446.

Gronlund, N. F. *Constructing Achievement Tests,* 3rd ed. Englewood Cliffs, NJ: Prentice-Hall, Inc., 1982.

Hills, J. R. *Measurement and Evaluation in the Classroom.* Columbus, OH: Charles E. Merrill, 1981.

Hopkins, K. D., and J. C. Stanley. *Educational and Psychological Measurement and Evaluation.* Englewood Cliffs, NJ: Prentice-Hall, Inc., 1981.

Newton, R. R. "Teacher Evaluation: Focus on Outcomes." *Peabody Journal of Education,* Vol. 58, No. 1 (October 1980), pp. 45-54.

Paschal, Rosanne A., Thomas Weinstein, and Herbert J. Walberg. "The Effects of Homework on Learning: A Quantitative Synthesis." *Journal of Educational Research,* Vol. 78, No. 2 (November-December 1984), pp. 97-104.

Patton, M. Q. "Truth or Consequences in Evaluation." *Education and Urban Society,* Vol. 13, No. 1 (November 1980), pp. 59-74.

Reilly, Robert R., and Ernest L. Lewis. *Educational Psychology.* New York: Macmillan Publishing Company, 1983.

Part VI

What Should I Know About the Secondary Practice-Teaching Experience and Beyond?

Too many people quit looking for work when they find a job.
—Hillsborough *(Illinois)* Rotarian

Part VI provides information about

- The paraprofessional experience.

- The practice teaching experience.

- Getting your first teaching job.

- Writing a résumé.

- Interviewing for a job.

- Credential requirement information sources.

- Educational associations related to secondary-school teaching.

18

What Should I Know About the Secondary Practice-Teaching Experience?

You're excited about the prospect of being assigned to your first classroom as a teacher candidate (a student teacher), but you are also very concerned. Will your host teacher like you? Will the two of you get along? Will the students like you? Will you be assigned to a subject and grade level you want? What will the students be like? Will there be many behavioral problems? What about mainstreamed youngsters? Will your responsibilities be different from those you had as a paraprofessional?

Indeed, you should be excited and concerned, for this experience, the experience of practice teaching, is one of the most significant and important facets of your teacher education program. In some programs, the practical teaching experience is planned as a coexperience with your college or university theory classes. In other programs, your practical teaching is a culminating experience. Different sequences are represented in different programs. For instance, at one college or university you may have a practice-teaching experience that extends over a two-semester or a three-semester time period. In other colleges or universities, you may take part in a theory-class-first arrangement, followed by a full semester of practice teaching. Regardless of when and how your practice teaching occurs, the experience is a bright and shining opportunity to improve your teaching skills in a real classroom environment. You will be supported by an experienced college or university supervisor and by carefully selected cooperating teachers, who will share their years of classroom experience with you. Teacher education programs refer to these fine cooperating teachers in various ways—host teachers, master teachers, or mentors.

Everyone concerned in the teacher education program—your cooperating teacher, your course instructors, and your supervisor—realize that for you, this is practice in learning how to teach. During practice teaching, you will, no doubt, create some teaching errors, and you will benefit and learn from those errors. Sometimes, your fresh approach to motivation, your ideas for learning activities that support the concept being learned, and your energy and enthusiasm make it possible for the cooperating teacher to learn from you! What is of value to both of you on this educational team is that students who are involved with you in the teaching-learning process will benefit from your role as the teacher candidate in their classroom.

We offer the following guidelines to you, to your cooperating teacher, and to the school principal, to help make these classroom experiences beneficial to everyone involved.

A. THE PARAPROFESSIONAL EXPERIENCE

Prior to practice teaching we believe the preservice teacher should have had classroom experience as a paraprofessional. The following list provides information as to the kinds of experiences a preservice teacher might have while serving in this capacity as a paraprofessional. These help to familiarize the trainee with the many wide-ranging facets of a teacher's real life, before the trainee actually begins the phase we call "practice teaching."

Clerical Experience

1. Sending for free and inexpensive classroom materials.
2. Keeping attendance records.
3. Entering evaluative marks in the teacher's marking book.
4. Averaging academic marks and preparing report cards.
5. Keeping records of class schedules.
6. Keeping inventory of classroom stock-equipment, books, instructional supplies.
7. Managing classroom libraries.
8. Setting up and maintaining seating charts.
9. Typing, duplicating, and collating instructional materials.
10. Typing and duplicating the class newspaper.
11. Duplicating students' writings and other work.
12. Typing and duplicating scripts for plays and skits.
13. Finding resource materials for various teaching units.
14. Compiling information for teacher reports.
15. Preparing bulletins for parents to explain school programs, events, and rules.
16. Managing instructional materials for accessibility.
17. Keeping bulletin boards current and neat.

Noninstructional Experience

18. Gathering supplementary books and materials for instruction.
19. Distributing books and supplies.
20. Collecting homework and test papers.
21. Checking out library books in central library for students and teacher.
22. Assisting committees engaged in special projects—constructing, researching, or experimenting.
23. Helping settle student disputes and quarrels.
24. Setting up special classroom exhibits.
25. Accompanying a student to the office, nurse's room, etc.
26. Monitoring study hall.
27. Helping teacher supervise students on field trips.

28. Running errands relevant to classroom work.
29. Reading student bulletin to class.

Audiovisual Assistance

30. Ordering and returning films, filmstrips, and other AV materials.
31. Procuring and returning AV equipment.
32. Setting up and operating overhead projectors, slide viewers, and other instructional equipment.
33. Previewing films and other AV materials.
34. Preparing introductions to give students background for viewing AV materials.
35. Correcting standardized and informal tests and preparing student profiles.
36. Correcting homework and workbooks, noting and reporting weak areas to teacher.
37. Interviewing students with specific learning problems.
38. Observing student behavior and writing reports.
39. Preparing informal tests and other evaluative instruments.
40. Preparing instructional materials—cutouts, flash cards, charts, transparencies, etc.
41. Collecting and arranging displays for teaching purposes.
42. Preparing special learning materials to meet individual differences—developing study guides, taping reading assignments for less able readers, etc.
43. Teaching a small class group about a simple understanding, skill, or appreciation.
44. Tutoring individual students—the faster as well as the slower learners.
45. Supervising and assisting students with library assignments.
46. Teaching students who miss instruction because they were out of the room for special work—remedial reading, speech therapy, etc.
47. Preparing and teaching a short lesson to the class.
48. Repeating lessons for slower learners.
49. Helping students who were absent to get caught up with others in their group.
50. Listening to the student's oral reading.
51. Assisting students with written compositions—especially with spelling, punctuation, and grammar.
52. Instructing in the safe and proper use of tools.
53. Teaching etiquette and good manners.
54. Assisting the teacher in special demonstrations.
55. Providing accompaniment in music classes.
56. Reading and storytelling.
57. Helping students find reference materials.
58. Preparation of reading, spelling, or vocabulary lists.
59. Supervising laboratory work.
60. Putting written work on the blackboard.
61. Assisting in drill work with word and phrase flash cards (e.g., remedial reading).
62. Assisting and checking students in seat work.

Some of the Paraprofessional's Duties

63. Supervising the halls between classes.
64. Supervising recess.

65. Supervising extracurricular activities.
66. Visiting the teachers' lounge.
67. Visiting the principal's office.
68. Visiting the attendance office.
69. Visiting the counselor's office.
70. Observing in nonstandard classes (e.g., shop classes, special education, student government, agriculture).
71. Observing assemblies, student government.
72. Observing teacher meetings, department meetings, etc.

Paraprofessionals should *not* be expected to:

1. take work home, i.e., to grade papers at home.
2. do work for cooperating teachers of a personal nature unrelated to classroom responsibilities.
3. bring coffee to the teacher.
4. be left alone with the class.
5. do the entire routine for regular teachers, i.e., filing, typing dittos, duplicating, etc.

B. THE PRACTICE-TEACHING EXPERIENCE

1. *Is practice teaching like "real" teaching?*
   The answer to this is both yes and no. *Yes*, because you will have real live students and the opportunity to try your skills at teaching. *No*, because your cooperating teacher still has the ultimate responsibility for the class.
2. *How do I prepare for it?*
   By preparing well! Learn all you can about the school, the community, the students, the nature of the course(s) you will be teaching, what is expected of you, how you will be supervised. And plan your lessons well.
3. *What kind of experiences can I anticipate?*
   Rewarding, frustrating, and neutral. You will perhaps have fewest neutral days. Most will be good, bad, or a combination of both. You will become emotionally spent, elated, and tired. Students will give you a "honeymoon period," then test you, try you, go along with you, and like you. You will be scared, anxious, insecure, but will overcome. Confidence will develop. You might be mistaken for just another senior in high school. You will earn your "status." Parents will ask questions. You will be expected to attend games, dances, and faculty meetings. You will spend hours preparing lessons that might flop or go untaught. Textbooks will be outdated. Films will be late in arriving. Guest speakers may not show. You will laugh and cry and find out what makes teaching exciting, frustrating, enriching, and dull—simultaneously. There are no two days alike.
4. *What kind of support can I expect?*
   Perhaps little; one hopes, a great deal. But be prepared to stand alone. Be thankful when it is there, perhaps from the master teacher, or the librarian, the custodian, the student who smiles with you.
5. *What kind of supervision can I expect?* (See also Chapter 4, Section B.)
   Your students are there every day. You will know from their responses how you are doing. Your cooperating teacher will offer critiques, and occasionally or perhaps often your college or university supervisor will observe and offer critiques. Except for, perhaps, a drop-in by another

teacher or administrator, you are alone with your class. If you don't believe you are getting proper help then seek it out. There are many people around who will be most happy to offer suggestions if asked.

6. *What kind of criticisms can I expect?*
   The more the better. Some will be helpful, others not so. Listen to all! Try new ideas and suggestions. Practice teaching is the time to try new skills and to get feedback. It is important for you to take the initiative in soliciting feedback. Don't wait until someone comes and offers you criticism.

7. *What dangers should I be on the watch for?*
   Student restlessness, inattentiveness, poor attendance. These symptoms might be a reflection on you or they might not. Investigate and find out. Be cautious of starting out trying to be too "buddy-buddy" with students. Respect and friendship are earned and occur gradually and slowly. Your students may tell you that they like you better than some other teacher. That sounds good for your poor ego but it may also mean little. If you must decide between being on the "tough" side or the "easy" side, then choose the tough.

C. THE PRACTICE-TEACHING EXPERIENCE FROM THE COOPERATING TEACHER'S POINT OF VIEW: HOW CAN I HELP MY STUDENT TEACHER?

1. *What is my role?*
   Your role is to assist when necessary. To provide guidance. To look at lesson plans before presented. To facilitate the learning of the student teacher. To help the student teacher become and feel like a member of the profession.

2. *How can I prepare for it?*
   Get to know your student teacher ahead of time. Develop a collegial rapport with the student teacher.

3. *Who is my student teacher?*
   One who is making the transition from a college student to a professional teacher. He or she is perhaps in his or her mid-twenties, and scared to death, anxious, knowledgeable, and somewhere between being a romantic idealist and a pragmatic realist. Don't destroy the idealism—help the student teacher with understanding and dealing with the realism.

4. *What kind of support, criticism, and supervision should I give?*
   You will have to decide this yourself. Generally speaking, lots of support, helpful criticisms, and supervision are wanted by the student teacher. But by all means, try not to put the student teacher into a total sink-or-swim situation. Your students deserve more.

5. *What dangers should I look for?*
   Your student teacher may be very different from you in both appearance and style, but may be potentially just as effective. Judge his/her effectiveness slowly and cautiously. Offer suggestions, but do not make demands. A student teacher who is not preparing well is likely heading for trouble, as also is one who seems to show no interest in the school outside of the class. The student teacher should be prompt, anxious to spend out-of-class time with you, and be aware of the necessity of school clerical tasks. If you feel there is a lurking problem, then let the student teacher know your feelings. Poor communication between cooperating teacher and student teacher is a common danger signal.

6. *What else should I know?*
    Your student teacher is likely to be partially employed elsewhere and to have other demands on his or her time. Become aware of the situation. Be sure that the student teacher becomes a member of the total faculty, is invited to faculty functions, has his/her own mailbox, and has total awareness of school policies, procedures, curriculum guides, and so forth. Once your student teacher is well grounded, then he/she should be left alone with the class most of the time. This time can afford you the opportunity to work on papers and curriculum matters.

D. THE PRACTICE-TEACHING EXPERIENCE FROM THE PRINCIPAL'S POINT OF VIEW: HOW CAN I HELP?

1. *What is my role?*
    It is your obligation to meet the teacher candidate when the candidate arrives at school on the first day; to give a brief verbal orientation about the school and important policies; and to arrange a short introductory tour of the building. Introduce your cooperating teacher to the candidate. Invite the candidate to participate in various school meetings, activities, and events.
2. *How can I prepare for it?*
    Schedule the needed time for the day that the teacher candidate or candidates arrive on the campus.
3. *Who are the teacher candidates?*
    The teacher candidates are college or university students who are preparing a role change from that of student to one of professional teacher. Most of them are in their twenties, somewhat nervous, but knowledgeable. Some of the candidates are idealistic about helping students to learn. Their experiences with your credentialed staff, along with the active responses of the students, will lead each candidate toward ways of understanding and coping with the reality they find in a practice-teaching experience.
4. *Should I give constructive evaluation?*
    Because you are responsible for everything that goes on at your campus, we suggest that you make every effort to visit the teacher candidate and observe the candidate's teaching during the practice teaching. This gives you first-hand information about the competency of the beginning candidate and gives the candidate some insight about the beginning years when evaluation is made by the school administrator. If your busy schedule permits a follow-up conference with the candidate, then it is of value to arrange a short discussion time with the candidate after the classroom observation. Some principals share their district's credentialed-employees evaluation form with the candidate. Others mention the strengths they observed and indicate, gently, any area of teaching that seems to need additional attention. Remember, the teacher candidate may be terrified about all this because it represents a "first" for him or her. It is each teacher candidate's *first* real classroom, a *first* challenge about teaching and class management, a *first* experience in being observed and evaluated by a cooperating teacher, college or university supervisor, and school administrator. All of these "first" experiences create a great deal of stress for the beginning teacher.
5. *What cautions should I look for?*
    Keep in close contact with your cooperating teachers. Listen to what they are saying. Are they discussing a teacher candidate's looks? style of dress? teaching effectiveness? Is the student preparing adequately? Does the candidate show an interest in your school, outside of the classroom instruction time? Is the student arriving on time each morning? If you read the

verbal and nonverbal communications of your cooperating teacher in such a way that you believe there is a problem looming, then let the teacher candidate know your feelings. Keep the channels open between your cooperating teacher, the teacher candidate, and the college or university supervisor.

6. *What else should I know?*

Does the teacher candidate commute from a great distance? Does the candidate have heavy family responsibilities? Is there a financial problem? Is the candidate working part-time in another job? What is the additional college or university workload? Has there been a severe illness or recent death in the family? A divorce? Or an engagement called off? Is the candidate riding a bike to your school because of lack of transportation? Any and all of these situations may affect a candidate's competency in the classroom. Know what is going on. When the cooperating teacher in your building indicates to you that the teacher candidate is ready because the candidate appears competent in planning and implementing lessons and in maintaining class management, then the candidate may begin to be left alone for ever-increasing periods of time, with your approval. For a specified amount of time, a teacher candidate's goal is to work toward a competency that enables the candidate to begin the school day, teach all morning or all day, and close the school day—with an increasing responsibility for everything! This means the cooperating teacher is nearby and on call in case of an emergency but out of sight of the students. Sometimes the cooperating teacher is near your office, working on files, papers, and curriculum responsibilities.

**EXERCISE 18.1: THE PRACTICE-TEACHING EXPERIENCE FROM THE STUDENT
TEACHER'S POINT OF VIEW: HOW CAN I CONTINUE MY SELF-
EVALUATION AS A SECONDARY-SCHOOL TEACHER?**

1. Repeat Exercise 17.3.
2. Repeat Exercise 4.1.
3. Share and discuss the results of the above with your cooperating teacher and with your university supervisor.
4. Record your thoughts about your discussion.

_____

_____

_____

_____

_____

_____

_____

_____

_____

_____

_____

_____

_____

_____

_____

_____

_____

_____

_____

_____

_____

_____

QUESTIONS FOR CLASS DISCUSSION

1. You must have a lot of questions related to the content of this chapter. Identify them, pool yours with those of other members of the class, and arrange to have them all answered reasonably well before completion of this course on your practice-teaching experience.

19

What Do I Need to Know That May Help Me in Getting My First Teaching Job?

You have spent four or five years in a college or university preparing yourself for a teaching credential. Now that you have that credential, or are about to receive the credential, you are ready to embark upon finding your first paid teaching job. The prospects look good for you, because predictions are that our nation's teacher-education programs are only producing about three fourths of the 12.6 million new teachers expected to be needed between the years 1988 and 1992.

We hope the following guidelines will be helpful to you as you pursue the first job of your exciting new career.

A. GENERAL GUIDELINES TO HELP ME IN GETTING MY FIRST TEACHING JOB

1. The *personal interview* is perhaps the most important factor once you are a candidate for a teaching position. During the interview you are going to be observed carefully in (a) motivation for teaching, and (b) your ability to communicate. Be prepared in both areas; among other things "ability to communicate" probably includes your initial physical appearance.
2. Your *area of preparation* and the extent of preparation is important. You are most likely to be hired if you are a "total English teacher" rather than a specialist in Elizabethan literature. As an example: the prospective science teacher should be prepared to teach at least three of the five common science courses taught in secondary schools. In other words, the principal of a school with an opening is more likely to want a teacher with academic mobility. If you can teach history, that is fine, but if you can also coach swimming, that may be even better.
3. A third area of major importance has to do with *student-teaching recommendations*. The potential employer wants to know that: (a) you are an effective teacher, (b) you have good rapport with students, (c) you can manage a classroom.

In summary, you can help yourself in getting a teaching job by (1) preparing yourself to teach in several areas, (2) doing a good job in your practice teaching, and (3) preparing and showing well in the personal interview.

MY CHECKLIST: HOW TO LOOK FOR A JOB

Resources for Locating a Position

1. College placement.
2. Local school and district.
3. County agency.
4. State department of education.
5. Private schools.
6. Commercial placement agencies.
7. Out of state and overseas.

The Interview

1. Phone.
2. Write letter of application.
3. I may be asked questions about
    a. experience with children.
    b. hobbies.
    c. extracurricular activities.
    d. attitudes toward discipline.
    e. subject matter.
    f. the purpose of education.

Administration Will Be Looking for My Answers to:

1. Will I be able to maintain classroom control?
2. Will I maintain good human relations with the staff and parents?
3. Will I efficiently and punctually carry out tasks assigned?
4. Will I be able to teach with competence?

Decision Factors

1. My transcript.
2. Letters of recommendation.
3. College extracurricular activities.
4. Attitudes.
5. Character traits.
6. Nature of my personality.
7. My accent on the positive.
8. What questions I ask.

The Followup

1. What could I do?

The Contract

1. Legal document.
2. When I commit myself, I must inform any district which may be awaiting my decision that I am no longer available for consideration.

B. SPECIFIC GUIDELINES TO HELP ME IN GETTING A TEACHING JOB

1. *What types of placement services does my college or university offer?*
   Locate the Job Placement Center or Career Counseling Service on your campus. Arrange a meeting with a career counselor. Ask about the procedure for opening a job-placement file. Obtain copies of required forms, if needed. Review the regulations governing your job-placement file.
2. *Where can I obtain information about new positions and teaching vacancies?*
   Visit your Job Placement Center regularly. Often there are printed lists identifying available teaching positions. Sometimes correspondence from districts is kept in a binder that is available to you. Ask about a teaching "hot line" service—a number that you are given at the placement office to call every two weeks or so, to hear a recorded message indicating the available positions. Visit the local district office to see if job announcements are posted regularly on en entry bulletin board. You state department of education may be able to provide you with a list of school districts in your state.
3. *Is more information available?*
   Yes, consider reading the newspapers and newsletters from teacher organizations, and journals in your special interest area. Some associations offer a placement service during their annual conventions. (See listing of educational associations in the U. S. related to secondary-school teaching.) Consider subscribing to an annual summer employment guide, the *Journal of Overseas Teaching Opportunities,* or the annual *educators placement directory,* all available from The Advancement and Placement Institute, 167 N. 9th St., Dept. NEM, Brooklyn, N.Y. 11211.

4. *Are there teacher employment agencies?*

   Yes, but the service will require a fee. Consider Global Teacher Placement Services, 2100 Culver Blvd., Baltimore, MD 10021. For help in placement in the Southeast, write Haworth Teachers Agency, Box 1808, High Point, NC 27261.

5. *Are teaching contacts valuable?*

   Yes, and if you are acquainted with a teacher or principal in a district where you would be interested in teaching, then contact them and keep in touch by phone or letter to find out information about job possibilities.

6. *Can I apply by letter?*

   Yes, write to the districts where you want to teach; send a short cover letter and a copy of your résumé.

7. *What if there are no available teaching jobs?*

   Apply for substitute teaching, long-term or short-term; indicate your interest in the district's Home Tutoring Program or in summer school teaching. Would you consider a position as an aide or as a teaching assistant?

8. *Should I apply outside a school district?*

   If this interests you, apply for a position in the Job Corps, in Peace Corps, in Teacher Corps, or in the Volunteers In Service Through America (VISTA). Are there hospitals that are interested in a teaching service for children who are ill? Does your state's Youth Authority Agency indicate a need for teaching service? Is there a private learning clinic nearby? Are there drug or alcohol rehabilitation programs that require a teaching service? Does any local business (phone company, computer service) have a training program that would require the services of a credentialed teacher?

9. *Is the competition great?*

   The competition for teaching jobs is great in only certain disciplines and in certain school districts. Nationwide there is a critical shortage of teachers. If your teaching field is one in which there is still a surplus of teachers, then you may wish to enhance your job prospects by developing a second teaching field, or applying for a position in an area that may not be as popular. Would you be willing to teach in an urban school system, to move to a desert area, to a mountain zone, or out of state? Consider the reciprocity of credentials that your state has with other states. Consider reviewing your state's Public School Directory and Private School Directory. A directory gives you a name, an address, the principal's name, a telephone number, grade-level range, and enrollment figures for each school in the state. Sometimes the schools are listed by school districts for each county. Additional information is often included: names, addresses, and telephone numbers of county and district administrators, state board of education members, advisory committees, and/or commissions to the state board of education, major state school officers for each state in the United States. For California, both the *Public School Directory* and the *Private School Directory* may be ordered from: California State Department of Education, P.O. Box 271, Sacramento, CA 95802.

MY CHECKLIST: HOW TO WRITE AN EYE-CATCHING RÉSUMÉ

1. Plan an outstanding appearance for your résumé. Consider asking your career counselor's opinion about your decisions, or perhaps discuss choices with a local printing shop. Do you want 8½″ x 11″ pages, or a 7″ x 10″ size? Be professional in your choice of stationery color. Consider pages of off-white, cream, light gray, or beige. One personnel officer indicates that he automatically discards résumés printed on bright colors such as passionate pink, brilliant blue, sunshine yellow, lime green, or fascinating fuschia.
2. Prepare sentences in your résumé that are concise. Avoid educational jargon, awkward phrases, and unfamiliar words.
3. Plan a forceful appearance for your résumé. Begin with a short statement about your educational objectives.
4. Identify your experiences; list from the present and move back in chronological order through the years. Avoid abbreviations.
5. Write a cover letter to accompany your résumé. Do you want your letter to be typed on the same stationery as your résumé? Do you want matching envelopes? Your cover letter should:
   a. be well-written. (Ask a friend to proofread it for you.)
   b. be prepared individually. Avoid photocopies or form letters.
   c. be addressed to the personnel officer *by name*.
   d. be no more than one or two pages of single-spaced sentences.
   e. be a letter that emphasizes *you*, and your educational interests.
6. Practice writing your résumé on the blank form that follows.
7. Have someone else look at your résumé and get feedback.

RÉSUMÉ FORMAT

(for you to practice on)

_____
(name)
_____
(address)

_____
_____
(phone)

EDUCATIONAL POSITION OBJECTIVE
(What Kind of Teaching Position Are You Seeking?):

EDUCATIONAL POSITION HISTORY
(What Kind of Teaching Job Have You Had Previously?):

OTHER EMPLOYMENT HISTORY
(What Kinds of Jobs Have You Had Other Than Teaching?):

EDUCATION:

PERSONAL (optional):

    age: height: weight: married:

    children:

    professional affiliations:

    military service:

    hobbies:

    civic interests:

MY CHECKLIST: HOW TO DEVELOP INSIGHTS ABOUT AN INTERVIEW

1. Whenever possible, telephone the day before to confirm your arrival for the interview.
2. Be on time for the interview.
3. Dress with good taste.
4. Be friendly and enthusiastic; shake hands firmly; start the conversation with a friendly comment (perhaps about school construction work you noticed, road work you encountered during the drive to the interview, or something that impressed you as you entered the building, met the receptionist, briefly chatted with someone in the waiting room, or discussed with a colleague recently).
5. Be professional at all times; show you interest, your enthusiasm, your confidence, and your professional goals.
6. In advance, plan one, two, or three professional questions you would like responses about, and plan to ask these questions when the opportunity arises.
7. When possible, share a comment about the official's achievements, the district's achievements, or a particular school's achievements, to show your interest in the district, or to express your admiration for some of the district's educational plans to meet certain local needs.
8. If possible, follow up your interview with a thank-you letter. Mention a comment stated by the interviewer to indicate how observant and attentive you are, or refer to some interests discussed during the interview. Remember that very few personnel officials will make a judgment about hiring immediately, and your follow-up letter may be an influential factor in his or her final decision.
9. Prepare ahead for your interview. One teacher candidate conducts a mirror interview (practices in front of a mirror). Another asks a friend to play the role of a personnel officer. Still another audio-tapes selected questions and the responses, replays, restates, and reviews what has been said. What are some questions that might be asked in an interview situation?
    a. Tell me a little about yourself.
       (Will you tell me about yourself?)
    b. What is your basic philosophy about education?
    c. What is your strong area? Your weak area?
    d. What are your plans for classroom management?
    e. What grades do you prefer to teach? Subjects within your field?
    f. What do you want to be doing five years from now?
    g. Do you feel comfortable writing behavioral or performance objectives?
    h. What interests you most about working in the _____ school district?
    i. What was the last book you read? Educational journal?
    j. To what professional organizations do you belong?
    k. Why are you interested in this teaching position?

EXERCISE 19.1: MAKING TOUGH DECISIONS ABOUT "WHOM TO HIRE"

Here is an exercise that might take courage for you and the other members of the class to participate in. If you have been working well together during the course, you might like to try it. Read the exercise, then decide as a group whether it might be beneficial to all. Change the rules in any way that seems appropriate.

Introduction By this time you all undoubtedly know one another fairly well, have worked together in groups, and most likely have observed each other teach in micro-sessions, at least. In other words, you have as much data about one another as anyone would have who was responsible for interviewing you for a teaching position.

Procedure Seat yourselves in a circle so each person can see everyone else's face. Put your name on a card and place it in front of you, just in case others in the class might not remember your name. (We hope your instructor will join you in this activity.) Now, all ready? Pretend that you are a principal of a school and have three openings for teachers for next year. Every member of this class is an applicant for one of those three positions. List on a sheet of paper the three applicants you wish to hire. Now, as a class, decide what you will do from here. Here are some choices made by other classes:

1. Pass the papers around for all to read.
2. Pass them to one person to tally, then distribute the results in rank order.
3. Have one person tally and identify the three persons whose names appeared most often, then, as a class, discuss what qualities these people have.
4. Do not share your lists, but think about why you chose the persons you did.
5. Pass them, folded, to one person to tally, and have the complete rank-ordered list posted in the instructor's office for those who want to see it.
6. Discuss candidly your reactions to this exercise.

Peer evaluation and selection are difficult. As a teacher, in the future you might from time to time expect your students to do something similar to this. It is important that you remember how difficult this experience was for you. As a teacher, you may eventually find yourself in a position where you will be asked to make judgments about your colleagues—who gets hired, promoted, and so on. So you see, this exercise will have given you some insight about the kinds of qualities an interviewer might look for and be attracted to. It would be interesting and worthwhile to follow up this exercise with research to find out which of your classmates do in fact get hired first.

C. INFORMATION SOURCES ABOUT CREDENTIAL REQUIREMENTS STATE BY STATE

Alabama
 State Department of Education
 Montgomery, AL 36104

Alaska
 State Department of Education
 Juneau, AK 99801

Arizona
 State Department of Public
  Instruction
 Phoenix, AZ 85007

Arkansas
 State Department of Education
 Little Rock, AR 72201

California
 State Department of Education
 Sacramento, CA 95814

Colorado
 State Department of Education
 State Office Building
 Denver, CO 80203

Connecticut
 State Department of Education
 P.O. Box 2219
 Hartford, CT 06115

Delaware
 State Department of Public
  Instruction
 Dover, DE 19901

Florida
 State Department of Education
 Tallahassee, FL 32304

Georgia
 State Department of Education
 Atlanta, GA 30334

Hawaii
 State Department of Education
 Honolulu, HI 96804

Idaho
 State Department of Education
 Boise, ID 83702

Illinois
 Office of the Superintendent of
  Public Instruction
 302 State Office Building
 Springfield, IL 62706

Indiana
 State Department of Public
  Instruction
 Indianapolis, IN 46204

Iowa
 State Department of Public
  Instruction
 Des Moines, Iowa 50319

Kansas
 State Department of Public
  Instruction
 Topeka, KS 66612

Kentucky
 State Department of Education
 Frankfurt, KY 40601

Louisiana
 State Department of Education
 Baton Rouge, LA 70804

Maine
 State Department of Education
 Augusta, ME 04330

Maryland
 State Department of Education
 Baltimore, MD 21201

Massachusetts
 State Department of Education
 Boston, MA 02111

Michigan
 State Department of Education
 Lansing, MI 48902

Minnesota
 State Department of Education
 St. Paul, MN 55101

Mississippi
 State Department of Education
 Jackson, MS 39205

Missouri
 State Department of Education
 Jefferson City, MO 65101

Montana
 State Department of Public
  Instruction
 Helena, MT 59601

Nebraska
 State Department of Education
 Lincoln, NE 68509

Nevada
 State Department of Education
 Carson City, NV 89701

New Hampshire
 State Department of Education
 Concord, NH 03301

New Jersey
 State Department of Education
 Trenton, NJ 08625

New Mexico
 State Department of Education
 Santa Fe, NM 87501

New York
 State Education Department
 Albany, NY 12224

North Carolina
 State Department of Education
 Raleigh, NC 27602

North Dakota
 State Department of Public
  Instruction
 Bismarck, ND 58501

Ohio
State Department of Education
Ohio Departments Building
Columbus, OH 43215

Oklahoma
State Department of Education
Oklahoma City, OK 73105

Oregon
State Department of Education
Salem, OR 97310

Pennsylvania
State Department of Public
Instruction
Harrisburg, PA 17126

Rhode Island
State Department of Education
Providence, RI 02908

South Carolina
State Department of Education
Columbia, SC 29201

South Dakota
State Department of Public
Instruction
Pierre, SD 57501

Tennessee
State Department of Education
Nashville, TN 37219

Texas
Texas Education Agency
Austin, TX 78711

Utah
Office of the Superintendent
of Public Instruction
Salt Lake City, UT 84111

Vermont
State Department of Education
Montpelier, VT 05602

Virginia
State Board of Education
Richmond, VA 23216

Washington
Office of the State Superin-
tendent of Public Instruction
and the State Board of
Education
Olympia, WA 98501

West Virginia
State Department of Education
Charleston, WV 25305

Wisconsin
State Department of Public
Instruction
126 Langdon Street
Madison, WI 53702

Wyoming
State Department of Education
Cheyenne, WY 82001

D. EDUCATIONAL ASSOCIATIONS IN THE UNITED STATES RELATED TO SECONDARY-SCHOOL TEACHING

AAHPER	American Alliance for Health, Physical Education and Recreation, 1201 Sixteenth Street, N.W., Washington, DC 20036.
AACJC	American Association of Community and Junior Colleges, One Dupont Circle, Washington, DC 20036.
AAPT	American Association of Physics Teachers, 335 E. 45th Street, New York, NY 10017.
AASA	American Association of School Administrators, 1801 North Moore Street, Arlington, VA 22209.
AASL	American Association of School Librarians, 50 E. Huron Street, Chicago, IL 60611.
ACE	American Council on Education, One Dupont Circle, Washington, DC 20036.
AHEA	American Home Economics Association, 2010 Massachusetts Avenue, N.W., Washington, DC 20036.
AIAA	American Industrial Arts Association, 1201 Sixteenth Street, N.W., Washington, DC 20036.
AVA	American Vocational Association, 1510 H Street, N.W., Washington, DC 20005.
AECT	Association for Educational Communications Technology, 1201 Sixteenth Street, N.W., Washington, DC 20036.
AFSTE	Association for Field Services in Teacher Education, c/o Dr. John J. Diabal, Jr., Division of Extension, Northern Illinois University, DeKalb, IL 60115.
ASCD	Association for Supervision and Curriculum Development, 225 W. Washington Street, Alexandria, VA 22314.
ATE	Association of Teacher Educators, 1701 K Street, N.W., Suite 1201, Washington, DC 20006.
CEC	Council for Exceptional Children, 1720 Association Drive, Reston, VA 22091.
CLR	Council on Library Resources, Inc., One Dupont Circle, Washington, DC 20036.
Home Ec.	Department of Home Economics, 1201 Sixteenth Street, N.W., Washington, DC 20036.
EMC	Educational Media Council, 1346 Connecticut Avenue, N.W., Washington, DC 20036.
ERIC	Educational Resources Information Center, One Dupont Circle, Washington, DC 20036.
IRA	International Reading Association, 800 Barksdale Road, Newark, DE 19711.
JCEE	Joint Council on Economic Education, 1212 Avenue of the Americas, New York, NY 10036.
MENC	Music Educators National Conference, 1902 Association Drive, Reston, VA 22091.
NAEA	National Arts Education Association, 1916 Association Drive, Reston, VA 22091.
NASM	National Association of Schools of Music, 11230 Roger Bacon Drive, Reston, VA 22090.
NASSP	National Association of Secondary-School Principals, 1904 Association Drive, Reston, VA 22091.
NBEA	National Business Education Association, 1906 Association Drive, Reston, VA 22091.
NCEA	National Catholic Educational Association, One Dupont Circle, Suite 350, Washington, DC 20036.
NABT	National Association of Biology Teachers, 1515 Wilson Blvd., Suite 101, Arlington, VA 22209.
NCSS	National Council for the Social Studies, 1515 Wilson Blvd., Suite 101, Arlington, VA 22209.

NCTE   National Council of Teachers of English, 1111 Kenyon Road, Urbana, IL 61801.

NCTM   National Council of Teachers of Mathematics, 1906 Association Drive, Reston, VA 22091.

NSTA   National Science Teachers Association, 1742 Connecticut Avenue, N.W., Washington, DC 20009.

Secondary Teaching Positions Overseas

For dependents schools: Department of Defense
Office of Dependents Schools
2461 Eisenhower Avenue
Alexandria, VA 22331

For developing countries: Committee on International Relations
National Education Association
1201 Sixteenth Street, N.W.
Washington, DC 20036

For independent schools: International Schools Services
126 Alexander Street, Box 5910
Princeton, NJ 08540

EXERCISE 19.2: COMPLETING MY CHECKLIST OF COMPETENCIES AS REVIEWED THROUGH *A RESOURCE GUIDE FOR SECONDARY-SCHOOL TEACHING: PLANNING FOR COMPETENCE*

Now that you have completed this course and have thoroughly read this resource guide, check yourself on the competency list below.

	Very Aware	Somewhat Aware	What? Not Aware!
I am aware of some information about today's secondary schools, can recall some informational sources about students, can share my thoughts about my own secondary-school experiences, and recently visited a nearby secondary classroom.	_____	_____	_____
I am aware of the Professional Code of Ethics.	_____	_____	_____
I am aware of the instructional and the noninstructional responsibilities facing me as a beginning teacher.	_____	_____	_____
I have identified the kind of first-year teacher I might be.	_____	_____	_____
I am aware of different teaching styles.	_____	_____	_____
I recognize some important teaching behaviors that have a positive relationship with student achievement.	_____	_____	_____
I have identified my teaching skills on a self-evaluation form.	_____	_____	_____
I have identified the characteristics of a competent secondary teacher that I display.	_____	_____	_____
I am aware of ways to make a supervisor's evaluation of my teaching a professionally rewarding one for me.	_____	_____	_____
I am aware of the importance of planning.	_____	_____	_____
I have examined state curriculum frameworks, teachers' manuals, and students' texts.	_____	_____	_____
I can write behavioral or performance objectives.	_____	_____	_____
I am aware of models to guide me when I plan units of study or daily lesson plans.	_____	_____	_____

(continued)

	Very Aware	Somewhat Aware	What? Not Aware!
I can individualize a learning experience for my students.			
I am knowledgeable about preparing self-instructional packages for the students.			
I can choose and implement several instructional strategies.			
I have developed my knowledge about where to find help and resources that will enable me to teach everything expected of me.			
I am knowledgeable about commercial and teacher-made games that might be useful to me in my teaching.			
I am knowledgeable about commercial aids and published resources that are available to me.			
I am aware of teaching behaviors that facilitate student learning.			
I can maintain the physical environment of my classroom in a satisfactory manner.			
I am efficient in my clerical routines.			
I am knowledgeable about the legal guidelines for the classroom teacher.			
I am familiar with various approaches to classroom management.			
I can cope with the classroom management responsibility.			
I am familiar with some of the experiences I will have as a teacher candidate in a secondary classroom.			
I can evaluate and report student achievement.			
I can prepare and teach a lesson for micro-teaching.			
I can analyze my micro-teaching lesson using verbal interaction analysis.			
I have evaluated my practice teaching more than once.			
I can discuss the growth I've made in my teaching skills.			

(continued)

	Very Aware	Somewhat Aware	What? Not Aware!
I'm aware of selected evaluation forms that may be used by school administrators.	_____	_____	_____
I am familiar with some of the experiences a paraprofessional will have.	_____	_____	_____
I understand the basic role of the cooperating teacher and the school administrator.	_____	_____	_____
I am familiar with some of the guidelines to help me in locating a job.	_____	_____	_____
I am familiar with some of the essentials in a résumé.	_____	_____	_____
I can locate information about credential requirements, state by state.	_____	_____	_____
I know where I can contact educational associations in the United States that support secondary-school teaching.	_____	_____	_____

QUESTIONS FOR CLASS DISCUSSION

1. Share with the class the information you can obtain regarding the retirement plans, sick-leave benefits, insurance program, and related fringe benefits now available in your state for public-school teachers. Do any of these apply to teachers in private or parochial schools?
2. What merit or incentive plans for classroom teachers can you find in existence, or in a planning stage, for your state or local districts?
3. What experiences have you had that might prepare you as a new teacher for meeting parents at an Open House, Back-to-School Night, or other school functions?
4. Congratulations! You have come to the end of this resource guide, but there are probably many questions remaining in your mind. Identify them, with ways you might still find answers.

SELECTED READINGS AND REFERENCES FOR CHAPTERS 18 AND 19

Austin-Martin, G. G. "Effects of Student Teaching and Pretesting on Student Teachers' Attitudes." *Journal of Experimental Education,* Vol. 49, No. 1 (Fall 1979), pp. 36-38.

Costa, Arthur L., and Robert Garmston. "Supervision for Intelligent Teaching." *Education Leadership,* Vol. 42 (February 1985), pp. 70-80.

Ellenburg, F. C. "You Can Pay Me Now or You Can Pay Me Later." *Clearing House,* Vol. 54, No. 5 (January 1981), pp. 200-205.

Litt, Mark D., and Dennis C. Turk. "Sources of Stress and Dissatisfaction in Experienced High School Teachers." *Journal of Educational Research,* Vol. 78, No. 3 (January-February 1985), pp. 178-185.

Reilly, Robert R., and Ernest L. Lewis. *Educational Psychology.* New York: Macmillan Publishing Company, 1983. See especially Phyllis Johnson, "Surviving in Today's Classroom," ibid., pp. 599-614.

Scherer, C. "Effects of Early Experience on Student Teachers, Self-Concepts and Performance." *Journal of Experimental Education,* Vol. 47, No. 3 (Spring 1979), pp. 208-214.

Epilogue

THE CLASSROOM TEACHER IS LIKE A SYMPHONY CONDUCTOR. You are the person ultimately accountable for the quality of the performance. You must understand the potential of the contribution of each section of the orchestra, of each individual member. You must work at getting each member to perform to full potential. You must comprehend the origin of the score, its history, the mood of the composer, and you must be able to "hear" the finished piece before it is played.

During performances you must not only be in control of the orchestra every moment, but simultaneously be several bars ahead in your thinking. There is no time to belabor the sour notes, nor fret over an occasional missed beat. You have planned and rehearsed the orchestra so well that you have confidence in its overall ability and in the quality of the anticipated performance.

You are aware of the limitations and constraints placed on you by equipment or surrounding resources and outside influences. You perceive these as providing challenges, and as evidence of a need for improved community understanding of the value of the orchestra. You respect the community support, but know of the need for improved instruments, more rehearsal time, new scores, better pay, and incentives for good performance.

Concomitant with these responsibilities is the potential for stress and professional "burn-out." Aware of this you have developed a plan for coping with stress and that plan includes:

1. taking good care of yourself physically by eating well and exercising regularly.
2. taking good care of yourself mentally by planning days of relaxation away from the orchestra and from thinking about its performances, by being aware of when you need some time off, and rewarding yourself accordingly.
3. by developing support groups that will include colleagues and other peer relationships where you can vent your feelings, discuss your work, and develop your own skills; by developing a supportive relationship with your staff and administrators.

Have a good career, the best of performances!

E. C. K.

R. D. K.

421

Index

Acceptance, 12, 179
Access mode, 202
Accountability, 178
Achievement, reporting, 353
Achievement, student, 15, 52, 323-326, 351
Adler, Mortimer J., 15
Administrators, 12, 73
Advance organizer, 51, 55
Affective domain, 96, 99, 100
Aids and resources, 233
Algebra, *see* Mathematics
Allard, Harry, 273
Alley, G. R., 156n
Anecdotal records, 327
Application questions, 180, 181
Art, 117, 252, 262
Articulated curriculum, 74
Assertive discipline, 298
Assessment component, 323, 381
Assignments, controversial, 214
Assignments, use of, 214, 352
Associations, professional, 413
Attendance taking, 281
Attitude, student, 52
Attitudinal objectives, 99, 100
Audiovisual, *see* Aids and resources
Auditory modality, 52
Average daily attendance (ADA), 25
Axelrod, S., 298

Back to basics, 206
Back-to-School Night, 25, 353
Barbe, Walter B., 52n
Beginning teacher, 5-6, 38-40, 112
Beginning the day, 274, 279, 281
Beginning the year, 10-11
Behavioral objectives, 95
Behaviorism, 44-45
Behavior, modeling, 10, 59, 298
Behavior modification, 298-299
Behavior, student, 10, 287
Behavior, teacher, 11, 140, 177, 197, 296, 298
Berquist, William H., 47n
Bigge, Morris L., 46n
Bilingual education, 262
Biology, 119, 137
Blackboard, *see* Chalkboard
Bloom, Benjamin, 155, 155n
Boyer, Ernest L., 15, 238n
Business education, 124, 252, 262

Canter, Lee, 298, 300
Canter, Marlene, 298, 300
Carroll, John, 155, 155n
Case studies, 305-309
Cavanaugh, David P., 52n
Chalkboard, 65, 239, 275

Citizenship grading, 352, 353
Clarifying, 180
Classroom behavior rules, 10, 274, 298
Classroom control, 303
Classroom environment, 51, 61, 206, 276
Classroom management, 273, 295, 303, 311, 372
Classroom meetings, 298
Classroom observations, 23, 53, 55
Claus, Calvin K., 96, 103n
Clerical responsibilities, 39, 281
Clinical supervision, 60
Closure, 140, 147
Code of Ethics of the Education Profession, 34, 289
Cognitive-experimentalism, 44, 45
Cognitive domain, 99
Collette, Alfred T., 333n
Comments, teacher, 214, 327-329
Communication, classroom, 10
Community resources, 246
Comparative organizer, 55
Competencies, teacher, 59, 370-372, 415-417
Computer assisted instruction (CAI), 235
Computer assisted learning (CAL), 235
Computer assisted management (CAM), 235
Computer experiences, 235
Computer periodicals, 237
Computer software, 236
Concept, 111n
Conferencing with parents, 353
Conferencing with supervisor, 66
Content, deciding, 81
Contract, teacher's, 289
Contract, unit plan, 137
Controversial assignments, 214
Controversial issues, teaching, 91
Cooperating teacher, 6, 391, 395
Cooperation Square Game, 219
Corporal punishment, 289
Costa, Arthur L., viii, 180n, 181n, 185n, 189n, 193n, 197n
Course of study, 85
Credential information, sources of, 411
Curriculum, 74, 83, 85, 87, 89
Curriculum documents, 81
Curriculum guides, 85

D'Alessandro, John, 295n
Delivery mode, 202
Delivery, teacher, 51, 61
Demonstration, use of, 211
Didactic teaching, 202, 204
Disciplinary action, 288
Discipline, 295
Discrepant event, 205, 206
Discussion, use of, 207
Ditto *see* Duplicator, spirit
Donlan, D., 212n
Dreikurs, Rudolf, 298, 300

Drop-out students, 17
Drug use, 313-315
Duck, Lloyd, 45n, 46n
Dunn, Rita, 52n
Duplicator, spirit, 246
Dupont, R. L., 313

Ear problems, middle, 157
Eberle, Betty M., 52n
Eclectic approach to discipline, 297
Eclectic teaching style, 44, 51, 57, 66, 177
Educational games, 217
Educational Policies Commission, 79
Educational reform movement, 16
Employment, teacher, 403, 406
Encouragement, use of, 251
English, 127, 253, 262
Environment, classroom, 51, 61, 206
Essay test items, 334-337
Evaluation, self, 60, 61, 63
Eye contact, 10
Exceptional child, 8, 9, 156 *see also* Special needs students
Exceptionality, areas of, 9
Experiences, learning, 234
Expository organizer, 55
Expulsion, 288
Extra credit assignment, 352

Facilitating behaviors, 177, 179
Feeney, Therese A., 133n
Feistritzer, Emily, 15
Field trip, 234, 246
First day, the, 10-11
Focusing, 140
Foreign language, 135, 255, 262
Framework, curriculum, 83
Free period, 7
Futrell, Mary Hatwood, 8n

Gage, N. L., 12n
Gallagher, J. J., 9n
Gallup Poll, 1983, 16
Game, cooperation square, 219
Games, use of, 217
Games, publishers of, 223-226
Gast, D., 299
Geometry, model lesson plan, 139-146
Get-acquainted activities, 11, 13
Gifted students, 158
Ginott, Haim G., 298, 300
Glasser, William, 298, 300
Glickman, C., 296n
Goals and objectives, 95
Goldstein, A., 313
Goodlad, John I., 16
Graubard, Steven R., 16
Grobman, Deborah, 119n

Grouping for instruction, 156
Guided inquiry, 204
Gustafson, Thomas, 236

Haglund, Elaine, 173
Hearing impaired, 9
Hemisphere research, 51
Hewett, F., 298
Hirschman, Penny, 12, 12n
Holding area, 316
Home economics, 255, 262
Homework, 214 *see also* Assignments
Houchins, R. R., 157n
Housekeeping functions, teacher, 37
Humor, use of, 273
Hunt, James B., Jr., 15
Hyman, Irwin A., 295n

Individualized educational plan (IEP), 156
Individualizing for instruction, 155, 159
Industrial arts, 262
In loco parentis, 289
Inquiry teaching, 204-207
Inservice teacher, 92
Instructional objectives, 95
Instructional planning, 111
Instructional responsibilities, 35, 38
Instructional strategies, 201
Interaction, classroom, 53, 187, 367
Issues, controversial, 91, 214

Job getting, 404-406
Job interview, 49, 60, 409
Johnson, Rita, 159, 159n
Johnson, Stuart, 159, 159n

Kinesthetic modality, 52
Kirk, S. A., 9n
Kounin, Jacob, 298, 301

Learning by doing, 233
Learning, definition of, 95
Learning experiences ladder, 233
Learning, philosophies of, 44-46
Learning, recall, 99
Lecture, use of, 177, 203
Lee, Helen C., 66n
Legal guidelines, 285-292
Lesson plan, evaluation of, 152
Lesson plan, model, 139-146
Lesson planning variables, 51, 61
Lesson plan, preparation of, 147
Lesson plans, sample, 117-146
Lewis, Ernest L., 295n
Library skills, 162-171
Library, use of, 245
Lindsay, Targe, Jr., 137n
Lunar survival game, 220-221

Makeup exam, 352
Mainstreaming, 9, 156
Management, classroom, 273, 295, 303, 311, 372
Mastery learning, 155
Mathematics, 139-146, 256, 262
Meeks, John, 117n
Merit pay, 16
Microcomputer *see* Computer
Micro-peer teaching, 357-365
Middle ear problems, 157
Milone, Michael N., Jr., 52n
Mitchell, J. R., 219
Modality preference, 51-52
Modeling, teacher, 10, 11, 179, 298, 313 *see also* Behavior, modeling
Morgan, Sue, 127n
Motivation, 109, 202, 249
Multilevel teaching, 157
Multiple-choice test item, 338-341
Music, 129-130, 257, 262
Mystery island lesson, 206-208

Names, learning student, 10
National Education Association, 33, 79
Nylen, D., 219n

Objects, *see* Realia
Objectives, instructional, 95
Objectives, sources of, 103
Observations, classroom, 23, 53, 55
O'Donnel, J., 313
Opaque projector, 241, 245
Open classroom, 206
Open house, 25
Openness, 206
Organizers, advance, 55
Orientation meeting, 6
Overhead calculator, 241
Overhead projector, 65, 240
Overlapping, 178
Overobjectivity, 109

Pacing, lesson, 273
Paraprofessional, 392
Parent, communication with, 281, 283, 353
Parent, hostile, 354
Parent-teacher organization, 27
Parry, H. J., 313
Pause, teacher use of, 180
Pearson, M. J., viii, 157n
Performance objectives, 95
Periodicals, professional, 262
Personalize learning, 204
Peterson, N., 157n
Phillips, Steven R., 47n
Physical education, 131-132, 258, 262
Planning, instructional, 73, 74, 111, 371
Plans, evaluation of, 115, 152

Plans, sample unit and lesson, 117-146
Plans, writing daily, 147-151
Plans, writing unit, 112-114
Plecas, Suzie, 162n
Policies, school, 15
Praise, use of, 41, 179, 196
Practice-teaching, 391, 394-399
Preparation period, 7
Principal, 12, 396
Problem solving, 204-206
Processes, inquiry, 205
Processing of data, 180-181
Professional growth, 15
Professional organizations, 413
Professional periodicals, 262, 266
Professionalism, 33, 371
Progressive education era, 295
Projector, opaque, 245
Projector, overhead, 65, 240
Props, visual, 247
Psychomotor domain, 99
Public Law 94-142, 8

Questioning, use of, 61, 180-196

Reading range, 212
Realia, 247
Reavis, George H., 71n
Records, 15
Reilly, Robert R., 295n, 297n, 303n
Reliability in testing, 323, 331
Responsibilities, teacher, 35-37
Resource file, 267
Resource unit, 91
Resume, preparing a, 407-408
Rinne, Carl H., 155n
Ripple effect, 298
Rodriguez, Gloria, 135n
Romanticism-maturationism, 44-45
Rules, classroom, 10, 274, 298
Ryans, David G., 11n, 12n

Safety, school, 289
Salary, teacher, 31
Samples, Robert E., 52n
Schedule, modular, 7
Schedule, school, 7-8
School-community activities, 37
School day, 7
School year, 7
Science, 119-123, 137-138, 259, 262
Scofield, Cristy, 124n
Self-instructional package, 155, 159-171
Set induction, 147
Shipp, David, 131n
Silence, use of, 180
Simulated experiences, 234-235
Simulations, 217

Singer, H., 212n
Sizer, Theodore R., 16
Skinner, B. F., 298, 301
Slow learners, teaching, 158
Social science, *see* Social studies
Social studies, 133-134, 260, 262
Spanish, 135-136 *see also* Foreign language
Special needs students, 9-10, 156, 204
Stetson, E. G., 213n
Stimulus variation, use of, 147, 203
Stout, A., 219n
Structuring, 178
Student conduct, 287
Student rights, 287
Students, drop-out prone, 17
Students, exceptional, 8
Students, special needs, 9-10, 156, 204
Student teaching, *see* Practice teaching
Student variables, 51
Style, teaching, 51, 57
Supervision, clinical, 60
Supervisor, 52, 60, 65-66, 77-78, 391, 394
Suspension, student, 288

Teacher and academic freedom, 92
Teacher behaviors, 11, 43, 177, 296, 375-376
Teacher, characteristics of, 11
Teacher comments, written, 214
Teacher competencies, 59-60, 370-372, 415-417
Teacher contract, 289
Teacher liability, 289
Teacher observation forms, 377-379
Teacher responsibilities, 10, 35-37
Teacher rights, 287
Teacher salary, 32
Teacher schedule, 7, 39
Teacher shortage, 16
Teacher sign in, 8
Teacher's manual, 89
Teacher style, 43, 57
Teacher's voice, 203, 273
Teacher tasks, 39
Teaching, delivery, 51, 61
Teaching, discovery, 204
Teaching, inquiry, 204
Teaching, textbook, 212-213
Teaching unit, 91
Teaching variables, 51, 61
Tenure, teacher, 289
Test construction, 331
Testing, 347
Test items, types of, 332-347
Textbook, 74, 87, 89
Textbook adoption, 87, 212
Textbook, examination of, 89
Textbook questions, 193
Textbook, use of, 212-213
Traditional education, 44, 52, 202

Transition, use of, 280, 298
Transparencies, sources of, 241
True-false test item, use of, 344-345
Turner, R. L., 12n
Typing, sample unit and lesson plan for, 124

Unit, contract, 137-138
Unit plan, 112-114
Unit, resource, 91
Unit, teaching, 91

Validity in testing, 323, 331
Vicarious experiences, 235

Visual modality, 52
Visitation, school, 23, 25, 27, 53
Vockell, Edward L., 236
Voice, teacher's, 203, 273

Wadsworth, Barry J., 44n, 45n
With-itness, 298, 301
Wolfgang, C., 296n
Wong, Janice, 139n

Zenhausern, Robert, 52n
Zevin, Jack, 206n